International Money Laundering Through Real Estate and Agribusiness

Fausto Martin De Sanctis

International Money Laundering Through Real Estate and Agribusiness

A Criminal Justice Perspective from the "Panama Papers"

Springer

Fausto Martin De Sanctis
Tribunal Regional Federal 3rd Region
São Paulo
Brazil

ISBN 978-3-319-52068-1 ISBN 978-3-319-52069-8 (eBook)
DOI 10.1007/978-3-319-52069-8

Library of Congress Control Number: 2016963740

Printed on acid-free paper

This Springer imprint is published by Springer Nature
The registered company is Springer International Publishing AG
The registered company address is: Gewerbestrasse 11, 6330 Cham, Switzerland

Acknowledgements

I acknowledge, with gratitude, the help that I have received from my friends and all of the civil servants in my chambers at the Federal Appellate Court in São Paulo, especially Noemia Maria Ferreira Fonseca, José Antonio Monteiro, and Tatyanne Costa.

I am particularly grateful to my sons Thomaz and Theodoro for their patience and understanding during my writing and their constant motivation and support.

Finally, I would like to express my respect for people who choose to live ethical lives by valuing social justice and resisting the temptation to launder the proceeds of criminal activity.

Contents

About the Author

Fausto Martin De Sanctis holds a Doctorate in Criminal Law from the University of São Paulo's School of Law (USP) and an advanced degree in Civil Procedure from the Federal University of Brasilia (UnB) in Brazil. He was a Public Defender in São Paulo from 1989–1990, and a State Court Judge, also in São Paulo, from 1990–1991, until he was appointed to the Federal Courts.

He is currently Appellate Judge in Brazil's Federal Court for the Third Region, with jurisdiction over the states of São Paulo and Mato Grosso do Sul. He is also the Deputy Director of the Federal Judicial School and a member of the Portuguese Language Law Jurists Community (CJLP).

In 2012, Judge De Sanctis was a fellow at Federal Judicial Center in Washington, DC. Since 2013, he has been Advisory Council Member for the Brazil-U.S. Legal and Judicial Studies Program at American University Washington College of Law.

Judge De Sanctis was selected to handle a specialized federal court created in Brazil to exclusively hear complex cases involving financial crimes and money laundering offenses. He is a world-known expert on this topic and has been invited to participate in programs and conferences both in Brazil as well as internationally.

His publications include, among others:

Books

Churches, Temples, and Financial Crimes: A Judicial Perspective of the Abuse of Faith. Cham, Heidelberg, New York, Dordrecht, London: Springer, 2015.

Football, Gambling, and Money Laundering: A Global Criminal Justice Perspective. Cham, Heidelberg, New York, Dordrecht, London: Springer, 2014.

Economic and Financial Delinquency (Delinquência Econômica e Financeira). Rio de Janeiro: Forense, 2015.

Criminal Law—General Rules (Direito Penal—Parte Geral). São Paulo, Método, Rio de Janeiro: Forense, 2014.

Money Laundering Through Art: A Criminal Justice Perspective. Cham, Heidelberg, New York, Dordrecht, London: Springer, 2013.

Money Laundering Through Gambling and Soccer: Analysis and Proposals (*Lavagem de Dinheiro. Jogos de Azar e Futebol. Análise e Proposições*). Curitiba: Editora Juruá, 2010.

Criminal Liability of Corporations and Modern Criminal Methods (*Responsabilidade Penal das Corporações e Criminalidade Moderna*). São Paulo: Saraiva, 2009.

Organized Crime and the Disposal of Seized Assets: Money Laundering, Plea Bargains, and Social Responsibility (*Crime Organizado e Destinação de Bens Apreendidos. Lavagem de Dinheiro, Delação Premiada e Responsabilidade Social*). São Paulo: Saraiva, 2009.

The Fight Against Money Laundering: Theory and Practice (*Combate à Lavagem de Dinheiro, Teoria e Prática*). Campinas: Millennium, 2008.

Criminal Tax Law: Highlights (*Direito Penal Tributário: Aspectos Relevantes*). Campinas: Bookseller, 2006.

Criminality in the National Financial System: Criminal Law and Protection of Brazil's National Financial System (*Punibilidade no Sistema Financeiro Nacional: Tipos Penais que Tutelam o Sistema Financeiro Nacional*). Campinas: Millennium, 2003.

Criminal Liability of Corporations (*Responsabilidade Penal da Pessoa Jurídica*), São Paulo: Saraiva, 1999.

Articles and Book Chapters

"Football: A Call for Transparency to Curb Corruption". Sociology and Criminology 4:133, OMICS International, 2016.

"Voice and Accountability: Improving the Delivery of Anticorruption and Anti-Money Laundering Strategies in Brazil". Washington, DC: The World Bank Legal Review, Vol. 6, 2015.

"Requirements for the 2014 FIFA World Cup in Brazil and Requirements of Governmental Bodies to Deter Financial Crimes in the Football Sector". California: Southwestern Journal of International Law, Vol. 21(1), 2014.

"Criminal Liability of Corporations" ("Responsabilidade Penal das Corporações"). In *A Book in Honor of Miguel Reale Junior* (*Livro Homenagem a Miguel Reale Junior*). Rio de Janeiro: GZ, 2014.

"Popular Action. Using Habeas Corpus in the Context of Financial Crimes" ("Ação Popular: A Utilização do Habeas Corpus na Dinâmica dos Crimes Financeiros"). In *Popular Action* (*Ação Popular*). São Paulo: Saraiva, 2013.

"Coherent and Functional Criminal Law" ("Direito Penal Coerente e Funcional"). São Paulo: Revista dos Tribunais, Vol. 919, 2012.

"Telephone Tapping and Fundamental Rights" ("Interceptações Telefônicas e Direitos Fundamentais"). In *A Tribute to Afrânio Silva Jardim: Writings and Studies* (*Tributo a Afrânio Silva Jardim: Escritos e Estudos*). Rio de Janeiro: Lúmen Júris, 2011.

"The Constitution and Freedoms" ("Constituição e Regime das Liberdades"). São Paulo: Revista dos Tribunais, 2009.

"Human Trafficking: The Crime and Victim Consent" ("Tráfico Internacional de Pessoas: Tipo Penal e o Consentimento do Ofendido"). In *Women and Criminal Law* (*Mulher e Direito Penal*). Rio de Janeiro: Forense, 2007.

"Crimes Against the National Financial System: A Precursor to Money Laundering" ("Crimes Contra o Sistema Financerio Nacional como Antecedentes de Lavagem de Valores"). In *Money Laundering—Commentary on the Law by Judges at Specialized Courts, In Honor of Gilson Dipp* (*Lavagem de Dinheiro—Comentários à Lei pelos Juízes das Varas Especializadas. Homenagem ao Ministro Gilson Dipp*). Porto Alegre: Livraria do Advogado, 2007.

Judge De Sanctis has also written a number of articles published in newspapers and magazines specializing in law and economics.

Introduction

Properties like real estate and agribusiness have been discovered by criminals as an effective and clandestine way to launder money nationally and internationally. Ownership of properties is obscured through shell companies, fake documentation, and variations on family names listed on deeds. Legal mechanisms available to hold property without disclosing the actual owner's name make tracing money difficult. Wealthy people, including foreigners, are buying property in the United States at a brisk pace with few questions asked, even as border security is tightened against poor immigrants trying to cross into the country. Figuring out whose money is behind these properties and shell companies proves difficult.

According to Peter Alldridge, mass media depicts money laundering as bad, interesting, and daring, but never explains exactly what it is, why it is done, or why it is so damaging.[1] This book explores the novel and known ways money is being laundered in the world. The book reveals how new financial techniques used by criminals are going ignored and undetected. Indeed, money laundering is an international crime challenging the very sovereignty of nations.

The core discussion of this book is money laundering involving real estate and agribusiness. The Panama Papers revealed that these sectors are replete with legal loopholes that easily permit the laundering of millions of dollars. Properties constitute an attractive line of business for the practice of money laundering given the large monetary transactions involved and the general confidentiality surrounding property transactions. The real estate and agribusiness sectors are susceptible to use by money launderers, who also use nonprofit organizations, foundations, remittance companies, offshore accounts, and clandestine wire transfers to launder ill-gotten gains.

The purpose of this book is to inquire into the scale of the problem and look into legislative and institutional loopholes that lend power and mobility to organized crime, thereby making it a more deeply entrenched source of unprecedented illicit

[1]Alldridge, Peter (2008, Dec). Money laundering and globalization. Journal of Law & Society, 35(4), 437–463.

wealth. The carefree attitude which has characterized law enforcement in this area must be confronted with a realistic understanding of the problem and must go beyond the adoption of measures taken in isolation or in an uncoordinated manner. I hope that this book will serve as a useful guide for law enforcement officials, prosecutors, judges, and others involved in efforts to curb money laundering and terrorism financing. I also hope that this book prompts specialists to speak up to prevent real estate and agribusiness from being used and manipulated for illegal purposes.

This book is divided into six chapters along with this Introduction. Chapter 1 addresses money laundering through real estate. This chapter first looks at two U.S. forfeiture actions against a government officer of Equatorial Guinea, revealing the difficult task of restraining financial criminals. It then discusses the influx of global cash fueling New York City's high-end real estate boom. The New York Times investigation pierced the secrecy of more than 200 shell companies that have owned condominiums at a single complex. Chapter 2 untangles the complex situation when criminals launder ill-gotten gains through agribusinesses. Chapter 3 analyzes various money laundering typologies that were revealed by the "Panama Papers". Chapter 4 discusses efforts to combat money laundering, including property confiscation, international legal cooperation, and asset repatriation. Chapter 5 offers conclusions. Chapter 6 covers national and international proposals for improving the industry so as to prevent money laundering and terrorism financing. These proposals call for a broader institutional and regulatory improvement, extending beyond mere regulation of the market.

Although this book may, at a glance, appear to have covered the subject, this is far from the case. The book aims at a logical and practical completeness in describing an unexplored and virtually unknown world in which real estate and agribusinesses are used in the commission of serious crimes.

Chapter 1
Money Laundering Through Real Estate

1.1 The Nguema Obiang Cases

In 2011, the United States government filed civil forfeiture complaints against approximately $70.8 million in real and personal property, which the government alleged were the proceeds of foreign corruption offences and were laundered in the United States.[1] According to the complaints, Teodoro Nguema Obiang Mangue (Nguema) used his position and influence as a government minister for Equatorial Guinea to acquire criminal proceeds through corruption and money laundering, in violation of both Equatoguinean and U.S. law. Nguema is the son of Teodoro Nguema Obiang Mbasogo (Obiang), the president of Equatorial Guinea.

The complaints alleged that on a modest government salary Minister Nguema amassed wealth of over $100 million. Former Assistant Attorney General Lanny A. Breuer stated as follows: "[W]hile [Nguem's] people struggled, he lived the high life—purchasing a Gulfstream jet, a Malibu mansion and nearly $2 million in Michael Jackson memorabilia. Alleging that these extravagant items are the proceeds of foreign official corruption, the Department of Justice is seeking to seize them through coordinated forfeiture actions. Through our Kleptocracy Initiative, we are sending the message loud and clear: the United States will not be a hiding place for the ill-gotten riches of the world's corrupt leaders."[2]

The investigation was initiated by the U.S. Immigration and Customs Enforcement (ICE) Homeland Security Investigations (HSI) in an effort to identify Nguema's assets in the United States after he was suspected of obtaining his wealth

---

[1]The property includes (1) a White Crystal Covered Bad Tour Glove and Other Michael Jackson Memorabilia, (2) a Gulfstream G-V Jet Airplane Displaying Tail Number VPCES, (3) Real Property Located on Sweetwater Mesa Road In Malibu California, (4) a 2007 Bentley Azure, (5) a 2008 Bugatti Veyron, (6) a 2008 Lamborghini Murcielago, (7) a 2008 Rolls Royce Drophead Coupe, (8) a 2009 Rolls Royce Drophead Coupe, (9) a 2009 Rolls Royce Phantom Coupe, and (10) a Ferrari 599 GTO. Messick (2014).
[2]U.S. Department of Justice (2011).

F.M. De Sanctis, *International Money Laundering Through Real Estate and Agribusiness*, DOI 10.1007/978-3-319-52069-8_1

from illicit activities, such as the misappropriation of public funds, theft, extortion, and embezzlement of the nation's natural resources.[3]

According to the complaints, despite an official government salary of less than $100,000 per year, Nguema amassed more than $100 million during a period in which he an inner circle of individuals who held critical positions of political and economic power in Equatorial Guinea and who were the near-exclusive beneficiaries of the extraction and sale of that country's natural resources. Under Equatoguinean law, the natural resources belong to the people of Equatorial Guinea. The complaints alleged that Nguema used intermediaries and corporate entities to acquire numerous assets in the United States, including more than $1.8 million worth of Michael Jackson memorabilia, a $38.5 million Gulfstream G-V jet, a $30 million house in Malibu, California, and a 2011 Ferrari automobile valued at more than $530,000. In court papers in 2012, prosecutors also alleged that Nguema had committed bank fraud by "concealing his association" with bank accounts opened on his behalf in the United States. Nguema then funneled his ill-gotten funds into those accounts and subsequently used the funds to pay for the "upkeep and maintenance" of his Malibu mansion and other assets.[4]

The forfeiture against Nguema's assets was announced with much fanfare in 2011. The U.S. Department of Justice (DOJ) accused Nguema of plundering billions of dollars of his country's resource wealth. Nguema was placed in charge of the country's forest industry in 1998. His father, President Teodoro Obiang Nguema Mbasogo, came to power of the oil-rich Middle African country in a 1979 coup.

Initially, Nguema won motions to dismiss both actions because there was no presentation of additional circumstantial evidence that the defendant assets were purchased with illicit funds. However, each court gave the DOJ the right to file an amended complaint, moving them forward with forfeiture on certain assets on the ground that Nguema committed bank fraud, and leaving the door open for prosecutors to re-apply for forfeiture on the foreign offence grounds with additional evidence.[5] U.S. District Judge George Wu ruled that prosecutors lacked probable

---

[3]"HSI established the FCIG in 2003 to conduct investigations into the laundering of proceeds emanating from foreign public corruption, bribery and embezzlement. The cases are worked jointly with representatives of the victimized foreign governments. The FCIG's goal is to prevent foreign-derived, ill-gotten gains from entering the U.S. financial infrastructure; to seize assets identified in the U.S.; and to repatriate these funds to the victimized governments. Since the initiative's launch, HSI has affected 220 seizures involving more than $146 million worth of property and assets until 2014." U.S. Department of Justice (2014).

[4]Matthews (2013).

[5]The United States District Court for the District of Columbia stated, in part, as follows:

> A recurring theme in the government's complaint is the allegation that Nguema's outlandish wealth raises suspicions about the lawfulness of his income. *Id.* 34 ("Nguema's level of spending is inconsistent with his salary as a Minister. His official salary today is approximately $6,799 per month, or less than $100,000 per year, according to official E.G. sources."). When viewed in tandem with other details suggesting illegal behavior, wealth might allow an inference of illegal activity—but standing alone, it does not. *See Mondragon*, 313 F.3d at 864 ("The presence of that much cash [half a million dollars],

cause to pursue forfeiture of the assets on the grounds that Nguema obtained them through extortion, misappropriation of public funds, or bribery of a public official. "Even assuming the government could show that [Nguema] generated revenue through the identified foreign offences, there is no evidence that the defendant assets were purchased with those funds," Judge Wu wrote in an eight-page decision. Judge Wu did allow the forfeiture to proceed on the bank fraud grounds.[6]

The DOJ sought in the complaints to seize the ten items listed as defendants and return them to their rightful owners, the citizens of Equatorial Guinea. What makes the Nguema Obiang cases different from previous actions, and thus precedent setting, is that they were the first time the DOJ won, or at least favorably resolved, an asset seizure case where a sitting ruling family appeared and contested the claim. The United States won both cases through a settlement agreement.[7]

Details of the judicial decision regarding the case:

UNITED STATES DISTRICT COURT FOR THE DISTRICT OF COLUMBIA, UNITED STATES: Plaintiff, : Civil Action No.: 11-1874 (RC) Re Document No.: 12: ONE GULFSTREAM G-V JET AIRCRAFT, Displaying tail number VPCES, its tools and Appurtenances: Defendant.: MEMORANDUM OPINION GRANTING THE CLAIMANTS'MOTION TO DISMISS WITHOUT PREJUDICE;GRANTING LEAVE TO

(Footnote 5 continued)

oddly packaged, could raise a suspicion that someone was up to no good, but without more it does not suggest a connection to drug trafficking."); *cf. United States v. $22,173.00 in U.S. Currency*, 2010 WL 1328953, at *2 (S.D.N.Y. Apr. 5, 2010) (deeming certain allegations "troubling" and noting that "a great deal more" would be necessary to survive summary judgment, but concluding that unusually large sums of cash could give rise to an inference of illegal activity when viewed in conjunction with other specific allegations "suggesting a pattern of drug trafficking"). The government itself has alleged that Ngema owns or controls a number of companies. Yet nothing is known about what income Nguema derives from them. Thus, without knowing what Nguema's means are, the court is hard-pressed to infer that he lives beyond them. Absent other details, the court cannot infer how Nguema's wealth may have been derived, nor from what sources, nor the legality of those sources. Although the government alleges that Nguema lives far beyond his means, the court cannot leap to the conclusion that his largesse is evidence of criminal activity. Faced with this complaint, the claimants would find it difficult to know where to begin their investigation, what individuals to interview, or what documents to review. *Cf. Mondragon*, 313 F.3d at 864. To be sure, the government paints a troubling picture of endemic corruption in Equatorial Guinea. But the government has done so with brushstrokes that are much too broad. The government cannot proceed by casting general allegations of lawlessness in the country in which the relevant transactions took place.

Absent some specific indication that the Jet is derived from or traceable to illicit activity, the complaint must be dismissed. *Id.* The court has little doubt that the government could cure these deficiencies by filing an amended complaint that alleges additional facts. Thus, the court will dismiss the complaint without prejudice and grant leave to amend the complaint.

United States v. One Gulfstream G-V Jet Aircraft, Displaying tail number VPCES, its tools and Appurtenances. Civil Case No. 11-1874 (1874).

[6]Matthews (2013).

[7]U.S. Department of Justice (2014).

AMEND I. INTRODUCTION The United States brings this forfeiture action against a $38.5 million dollar jet purchased by Teodoro Nguema Obiang Mangue ("Nguema"), Equatorial Guinea's Minister of Forestry and Agriculture1 and the son of Equatorial Guinea's president. The government alleges that Nguema purchased the jet with funds derived from extortion, misappropriation, theft, and embezzlement. Although the government describes a disconcerting pattern of corruption in Equatorial Guinea, the complaint does not link the jet to any specific illicit acts. Accordingly, the court grants the claimants' motion to dismiss. 1 Since this litigation commenced, Nguema appears to have been promoted to Equatorial Guinea's Vice President in charge of National Defense and State Security. See Equatorial Guinea Leader Promotes Son in Reshuffle, REUTERS (May 22, 2012), available at http://www.reuters.com/article/2012/05/22/us-guinea-equatorial-idUSBRE84L0ZC20120522. *Case 1:11-cv-01874-RC Document 22 Filed 04/19/13 Page 1 of 23. II. LEGAL & FACTUAL BACKGROUND. A. Legal Framework. Forfeiture is an ancient penalty; its origins can be traced to biblical times. See Calero-Toledo v. Pearson Yacht Leasing Co., 416 U.S. 663, 681 n.17 (1974) (citing Exodus 21:28) ("If an ox gore a man or a woman, and they die, he shall be stoned and his flesh shall not be eaten"). Based on the legal fiction that "the thing is primarily considered the offender," Goldsmith-Grant Co. v. United States, 254 U.S. 505, 511 (1921), forfeiture law allows suit to be brought against an inanimate object rather than a person. See, e.g., Various Items of Personal Property v. United States, 282 U.S. 577, 581 (1931) ("[I]t is the property which is proceeded against, and, by resort to a legal fiction, held guilty and condemned as though it were conscious instead of inanimate and insentient."). Commentators and judicial decisions have primarily understood the rationale for this peculiar concept to be a means of punishment for a wrongdoer. See, e.g., Austin v. United States, 509 U.S. 602, 611–14 (1993); Calero-Toledo, 416 U.S. at 681. The Civil Asset Forfeiture Reform Act of 2000 ("CAFRA"), 18 U.S.C. §§ 981 et seq., establishes several procedural and substantive rules governing forfeiture actions. The government may initiate a suit in rem2 by filing a complaint within sixty days of the item's seizure. Id. § 983(a)(1)(A)(i). Any person claiming an interest in the seized property—referred to as a "claimant"—may intervene after the seizure is effected. Id. § 983(a)(2)(A). The claimant may then contest the government's action. United States v. $515,060.42, 152 F.3d 491, 497 (6th Cir. 1998). Here, the government brings suit under two of CAFRA's substantive provisions: 18 U.S.C. § 981(a)(1)(A) and § 981(a)(1)(C). Under 18 U.S.C. § 981(a)(1)(C), "[a]ny property, real 2 Latin for "against a thing." Case 1:11-cv-01874-RC Document 22 Filed 04/19/13 Page 2 of 23 or personal, which constitutes or is derived from proceeds traceable to any offense constituting 'specified unlawful activity'" is subject to forfeiture to the United States. "Specified unlawful activity" may include offenses against a foreign nation involving "extortion," or the "misappropriation, theft, or embezzlement of public funds by or for the benefit of a public official." 18 U.S.C. § 1956(c)(7)(B)(ii), (iv). Under 18 U.S.C. § 981(a)(1)(A), "[a]ny property, real or personal, involved in a transaction or attempted transaction in violation of [18 U.S.C. § 1957], or any property traceable to such property," is subject to forfeiture to the United States. 18 U.S.C. § 1957 imposes a criminal penalty on any person who "knowingly engages or attempts to engage in a monetary transaction in criminally derived property of a value greater than $10,000 and is derived from specified unlawful activity." The term "specified unlawful activity" is again defined to include offenses against a foreign nation involving "extortion," or the "misappropriation, theft, or embezzlement of public funds by or for the benefit of a public official." 18 U.S.C. § 1956(c)(7)(B)(ii), (iv). To summarize both counts: the government alleges that the Gulfstream Jet is subject to forfeiture because it is either derived from or traceable to extortion, misappropriation, theft, or embezzlement of public funds by a public official. B. Factual Allegations and Procedural History Teodoro Nguema Obiang Mangue is the son of Equatorial Guinea's President. Id. 14. At the time the government filed suit, he was Equatorial Guinea's Minister of Forestry and Agriculture. Id. Despite his modest government salary, id. 34, Nguema has managed to* *acquire many of life's luxuries. Some of his recent purchases include a $6.5 million Bel Air mansion, id. 33, nearly $10 million in luxury cars (including eight Ferraris, seven Rolls Royces, five Bentleys, two Lamborghinis, and other top-notch acquisitions), id. 37, $3.2 million worth of Michael Jackson memorabilia, id. 42, a $30 million dollar Malibu mansion, Case 1:11-cv-01874-RC Document 22 Filed 04/19/13 Page 3 of 23 id. 40, and the aircraft at the heart of this case—a $38.5 million Gulfstream Jet. Id. The government claims these lavish purchases were made possible by a number of illicit and lucrative schemes. Id. 48. The government alleges that Nguema is a member of Equatorial Guinea's "Inner Circle," a coterie of powerful individuals who have ties to Equatorial Guinea's ruling family. The government alleges that members of the Inner Circle demand extortionate payments from oil companies seeking to do business in the country. Id. 49 ("For example, Nguema, as Minister of Forestry, is responsible for approving the export of timber logged in E.G., and refuses to sign such approvals until the exporter first pays a 'tax' for Nguema's personal benefit."). The government also alleges that members of the Inner Circle misappropriate government funds into a slush fund created for their personal use. Id. 58–62 ("Riggs Bank records show that money paid by oil companies to the government of E.G. was misappropriated by E.G. government officials and their family members."). Members of the Inner Circle allegedly steer government contracts to companies in which they have a financial interest. Id. 66 ("Because government contracts are awarded to companies owned by or associated with members of the Inner Circle without true competition, those companies are able to charge the E.G. Government fees that bear little, if any, rational relationship to the actual economic value of the services or products tendered to the E.G. Government. The bids from such companies include built-in mark-ups of from 50 percent to 400 percent or more, so that members of the Inner Circle can obtain the difference."). Finally, members of the Inner Circle have allegedly misappropriated valuable state-owned land. Id. 68–69 ("[I]n the early 1990 s, members of the Inner Circle began to transfer and register large amounts of state-owned land into their own names.... At the same time, the foreign oil and gas companies that were becoming active in E.G. in the 1990s needed to Case 1:11-cv-01874-RC Document 22 Filed 04/19/13 Page 4 of 23 lease land for their operations. Because the lands formerly owned by the state now were owned in the name of members of the Inner Circle, the oil companies' lease payments went to benefit the Inner Circle rather than the state."). The government alleges that these schemes provided the funds with which Nguema bought the Gulfstream Jet. After some initial difficulties, Nguema purchased the jet from a private party* via *a nominal buyer known as Ebony Shine International, Ltd., a British Virgin Islands company. Id. ¶ 77. After the government initiated this case, Nguema and Ebony Shine International, Ltd., filed claims to the defendant jet, and they subsequently filed a motion to dismiss. The court will now grant their motion without prejudice to the government's ability to file an amended complaint. III. ANALYSIS. A. The Court Denies the Claimants' Motion to Dismiss for Lack of Jurisdiction. 1. Legal Standard for a Motion to Dismiss for Lack of Jurisdiction3 Federal courts are courts of limited jurisdiction and the law presumes that "a cause lies outside this limited jurisdiction." Kokkonen v. Guardian Life Ins. Co. of Am., 511 U.S. 375, 377 (1994). Accordingly, a federal court should first determine that it has jurisdiction over a case before ruling on the merits. Al-Zahrani v. Rodriguez, 669 F.3d 315, 317–18 (D.C. Cir. 2012). On a motion to dismiss for lack of jurisdiction under Rule 12(b)(1), the plaintiff bears the burden of establishing jurisdiction by a preponderance of the evidence. Lujan v. Defenders of Wildlife, 504 U.S. 555, 561 (1992). When considering a motion under Rule 12 (b)(1), the court may look 3 The question of standing implicates the court's subject-matter jurisdiction, and the court will therefore construe the claimants' standing argument as if it had been brought under Rule 12(b)(1)and Supplemental Rule G(8)(b)(i). Case 1:11-cv-01874-RC Document 22 Filed 04/19/13 Page 5 of 23 beyond the allegations set forth in the complaint and "may consider materials outside the pleadings." Jerome Stevens Pharm., Inc. v. FDA, 402 F.3d 1249, 1253 (D.C. Cir. 2005). 2. The Court Has Jurisdiction*

Notwithstanding the Equatoguinean Government's Avowed. Refusal to Comply With This Court's Orders. The claimants argue that the government lacks Article III standing because its alleged injury cannot be redressed. Claimants' Mot. at 15. The claimants note that the jet is currently located in Equatorial Guinea, and the Equatoguinean government has emphatically stated that it will not comply with a forfeiture order issued by this court. Opp'n at 16. Due to Equatorial Guinea's intransigence, the claimants conclude that the government's claim cannot be redressed. Id.4 The government maintains that the claimants put the cart before the horse, arguing that the Equatoguinean government's decision to comply does not impair the court's jurisdiction to issue the order in the first place. Govt.'s Opp'n at 8–11. The language of 28 U.S.C. § 1355(b)(2) makes clear: "Wherever property subject to forfeiture under the laws of the United States is located in a foreign country … an action or proceeding for forfeiture may be brought in ... the United States District Court for the District of Columbia." Courts interpreting this provision have concluded that "Congress intended the District Court for the District of Columbia … to have jurisdiction to order the forfeiture of property located in foreign countries." United States v. All Funds in Account in Banco Espanol de Credito, 295 F.3d 23, 27 (D.C. Cir. 2002). Whether or not a foreign government will 4 The claimants also argue that absent Article III standing, any opinion rendered by this court would be "advisory." Of course, this merely restates the premise, as these closely related doctrines are simply two sides of the same coin. See Rainbow/PUSH Coalition v. FCC, 396 F.3d 1235, 1247 (D.C. Cir. 2005) ("[T]he standing requirement simply ensures that the petitioner has a defined and personal stake in the outcome of the litigation and that the court does not render an advisory opinion.") (citation and internal quotation omitted). Because the claimants' "advisory opinion" argument is merely a different way of arguing that the government lacks standing, the court's analysis is unaffected. Case 1:11-cv-01874-RC Document 22 Filed 04/19/13 Page 6 of 23 ultimately choose to comply with a judicial forfeiture order "determines only the effectiveness of the forfeiture order of the district courts, not their jurisdiction to issue those orders." Id. at 26 (emphasis added);5 see also United States v. Approximately $1.67 Million (US) in Cash, 513 F.3d 991, 998 (9th Cir. 2008) ("The plain language and legislative history of [28 U.S. C. § 1355] makes clear that Congress intended § 1355 to lodge jurisdiction in the district courts without reference to constructive or actual control of the res."); Contents of Account Number 03001288 v. United States, 344 F.3d 399, 405 (3d Cir. 2003) (noting that the foreign country's "compliance and cooperation with this forfeiture determines only the effectiveness of the District Court's order, not its jurisdiction to issue that order").6 Thus, the court has jurisdiction to issue a forfeiture order, regardless of whether the Equatoguinean government sees fit to comply. United States v. All Assets Held at Bank Julius Baer & Co., Ltd., 772 F. Supp. 2d 205, 211 (D.D.C. 2011) (rejecting the claimant's notion that a foreign government's potential refusal to obey a court-issued forfeiture order diminishes the government's Article III standing).7 5 The claimants concede that this court is bound by the Circuit's ruling in Banco Espanol, but submit that the Circuit has adopted faulty reasoning and should not be followed in the present case. Of course, judicial review is a one-way street, and this court has no power to reverse the Circuit. 6 In support of their contrary argument, the claimants cite to the Second Circuit's decision in United States v. All Funds On Deposit in Any Accounts Maintained in the Names of Meza, 63 F.3d 148, 152–53 (2d Cir.1995). But Meza's reasoning was squarely rejected by this Circuit in Banco Espanol. See 295 F.3d at 26–27. 7 The government also alleges that a number of treaty obligations make it likely that the Equatoguinean government will feel bound to comply with an order issued by this court. Whether or not this is true, Banco Espanol implicitly rejected this as a factor affecting the court's jurisdiction. There, the district court concluded that Spain was bound by a number of treaties and that there was a substantial likelihood that it would comply with its order. United States v. All Funds in Account Nos. 747.034/278, 141 F. Supp. 2d 548, 551–52 (D.D.C. 2001). The Circuit affirmed but applied a different standard, concluding that jurisdiction existed regardless of Spain's likelihood of *compliance. See 295 F.3d at 27. Case 1:11-cv-01874-RC Document 22 Filed 04/19/13 Page 7 of 23. B. The Court Grants the Claimants' Motion to Dismiss, But Grants the Government Leave to File an Amended Complaint. 1. International Comity. The claimants argue that the complaint should be dismissed on the basis of international comity. Claimants' Mot. at 19. Because adjudicating this case might require the court to pass judgment over Equatorial Guinea's application of its own laws, the claimants maintain that the court should decline to hear this case. Id. The government counters that the doctrine of international comity counsels U.S. courts to defer only to final judgments rendered by impartial foreign tribunals. Here, no such decision exists. Govt.'s Opp'n at 12–13. In addition, the government maintains that the doctrine of comity cannot be used to trump the United States' prerogative to enforce its own anti-money laundering statutes. Id. at 14. International comity is a doctrine of deference based on respect for the decisions of foreign sovereigns. United States v. Kashamu, 656 F.3d 679, 683 (7th Cir. 2011) (Posner, J.); see Hilton v. Guyot, 159 U.S. 113, 164 (1895) (noting that comity is "the recognition which one nation allows within its territory to the legislative, executive or judicial acts of another nation"). This doctrine provides that a U.S. court should give full effect to a foreign judgment that has been rendered with impartiality and due process. Hilton v. Guyot, 159 U. S. at 163, 202–03; Doe v. Exxon Mobil Corp., 654 F.3d 11, 64 (D.C. Cir. 2011). The purpose underlying the rule is to foster international cooperation and encourage reciprocal recognition of U.S. judgments in foreign courts. Oetjen v. Central Leather Co., 246 U.S. 297, 304 (1918) ("To permit the validity of the acts of one sovereign state to be reexamined and perhaps condemned by the courts of another would very certainly imperil the amicable relations between governments and vex the peace of nations."); Laker Airways, Ltd. v. Sabena, Belgian World Airlines, 731 F.2d 909, 937 (D.C. Cir. 1984) (stating that "the decisions of foreign tribunals should be given effect in Case 1:11-cv-01874-RC Document 22 Filed 04/19/13 Page 8 of 23 domestic courts, since recognition fosters international cooperation and encourages reciprocity, thereby promoting predictability and stability through satisfaction of mutual expectations."). Thus, the doctrine is accurately described as a "golden rule among nations—that each must give the respect to the laws, policies and interests of others that it would have others give to its own in the same or similar circumstances." Mich. Community Servs., Inc. v. NLRB, 309 F.3d 348, 567 (6th Cir. 2002).8 The doctrine of comity has no single definition, as the doctrine "summarizes in a brief word a complex and elusive concept." Laker Airways, 731 F.2d at 937; see also United States v. Nippon Paper Indus., 109 F.3d 1, 8 (1st Cir. 1997) ("Comity is more an aspiration than a fixed rule, more a matter of grace than a matter of obligation."). 9 A timeless characterization of the doctrine urges U.S. courts to recognize a foreign judgment if: there has been opportunity for a full and fair trial abroad before a court of competent jurisdiction, conducting the trial upon regular proceedings, after due citation or voluntary appearance of the defendant, and under a system of jurisprudence likely to secure an impartial administration of justice between the citizens of its own country and those of other countries, and there is nothing to show either prejudice in the court, or in the system of laws under which it was sitting, or fraud in procuring the judgment. 8 See also JP Morgan Chase Bank v. Altos Hornos de Mexico, S.A. de C.V., 412 F.3d 418, 423 (2d Cir. 2005) ("Whatever its precise contours, international comity is clearly concerned with maintaining amicable working relationships between nations, a 'shorthand for good neighbourliness, common courtesy and mutual respect between those who labour in adjoining judicial vineyards.'") (quoting British Airways Bd. v. Laker Airways Ltd., [1984] E.C.C. 36, 41 (Eng. C.A.)). 9 One scholar has described the doctrine as "an amorphous never-never land whose borders are marked by fuzzy lines of politics, courtesy, and good faith." Harold G. Maier, Extraterritorial Jurisdiction at a Crossroads: An Intersection Between Public and Private International Law, 76 AM. J. INT'L L. 280, 281 (1982). Case 1:11-cv-01874-RC Document 22 Filed 04/19/13 Page 9 of 23. Hilton v. Guyot, 159 U.S. 113, 202 (1895). If anything is clear, however, it is that the doctrine of international comity* *will not impede a judicial proceeding when no foreign judgment exists. A defendant invoking the doctrine of comity must either point to a valid legal proceeding to which the court must defer; or at the very least, the defendant must demonstrate that some alternate forum would be adequate. E.g., Doe v. Exxon Mobil Corp., 654 F.3d at 65 ("In order to invoke this doctrine, Exxon must either point to a legal proceeding in Indonesia involving these particular plaintiffs to which the court must defer or at least the availability of effective and nonfutile local remedies."); cf. Turner Entertainment Co. v. Degeto Film GmbH, 25 F.3d 1512, 1518–21 (11th Cir. 1994) (deferring to German litigation where a German court had reached judgment on merits of same issue). A foreign state's statutory remedies may also warrant deference, provided that they provide plaintiffs with an adequate remedy. Compare Ungaro-Benages v. Dresdner Bank AG, 379 F.3d 1227, 1239 (11th Cir. 2004) (indicating that Germany had provided an adequate forum to compensate plaintiffs for Nazi-era crimes) and Bi v. Union Carbide Chems. & Plastics Co., 984 F.2d 582, 586 (2d Cir. 1993) (determining that India had provided an adequate and comprehensive statutory remedy to victims of the Union Carbide disaster) with Cruz v. United States, 387 F. Supp. 2d 1057, 1070 (N.D. Cal. 2005) (determining that the Mexican Congress's creation of a special commission to investigate the plaintiffs' claims did not provide a sufficient basis for this Court to dismiss on comity grounds because the Mexican commission did not provide an adequate remedy). In addition, courts rarely abstain on the basis of comity if the court is not assured that foreign courts would accomplish the aim of the litigation. United States v. Lazarenko, 504 F. Supp. 2d 791, 802 (N.D. Cal. 2007) ("The Court also finds it inappropriate to disturb the criminal forfeiture based on comity principles. This Court has few assurances that Case 1:11-cv-01874-RC Document 22 Filed 04/19/13 Page 10 of 23 proceedings in Antiguan courts would accomplish the aims of criminal forfeiture—punishment of Lazarenko by seizure of his assets associated with the criminal activity for which he was convicted."). Here, the claimants have not identified any foreign proceeding to which this court should lend its deference. Instead, the claimants note that Nguema "is a sitting public official in good standing and has not been investigated or prosecuted for any wrongdoing, much less convicted of such." Claimants' Mot. at 21–22. But invoking the doctrine of international comity would be inappropriate under these circumstances, as there is no foreign adjudication of rights to which this court might defer. See Bodner v. Banque Paribas, 114 F. Supp. 2d 117, 130 (E.D.N.Y. 2000) (choosing not to abstain on comity grounds in part because "[t]here is no pending litigation in France, nor is the Court aware of any current law or policy of the French government which could either supplant or fully redress plaintiffs' claims"). In addition, the claimants have not put forth evidence to suggest that Equatorial Guinea would be an adequate forum for the U.S. government to pursue its interests. See Lazarenko, 504 F. Supp. 2d at 802. Two additional factors counsel against invoking the doctrine of comity here. First, the claimants believe that courts should decline to exercise its jurisdiction whenever a case touches upon the realm of foreign affairs. But it would be erroneous "to suppose that every case or controversy which touches foreign relations lies beyond judicial cognizance." Baker v. Carr, 369 U.S. 186, 211 (1962). Thus, few cases view international comity as a doctrine of preemption that would require courts to decline jurisdiction merely because foreign affairs are at play. United States v. Portrait of Wally, A Painting By Egon Schiele, 2002 WL 553532, at *10 (S.D.N.Y. 2002) (noting that "the principle of comity does not operate as a pre-emption doctrine, Case 1:11-cv-01874-RC Document 22 Filed 04/19/13 Page 11 of 23 barring this court from hearing a valid forfeiture action merely because there are foreign laws that might also apply"). Second, dismissal would not be appropriate when doing so "would be contrary to the policies or prejudicial to the interests of the United States." Pravin Banker Assocs., Ltd. v. Banco Popular Del Peru, 109 F.3d 850, 854 (2d Cir. 1997); see Allied Bank Int'l v. Banco Credito Agricola de Cartago, 757 F.2d 516, 522 (2d Cir. 1985); Laker Airways, 731 F.2d at 937 ("No nation is under unremitting obligation to enforce foreign interests which are fundamentally prejudicial to those of the domestic* *forum."). Thus, if the government viewed dismissal as necessary to protect its relationships with foreign countries, the doctrine would apply with greater force. Whiteman v. Dorotheum GmbH & Co. KG, 431 F.3d 57, 69–74 (2d Cir. 2005); Ungaro-Benages v. Dresdner Bank AG, 379 F.3d 1227, 1237 (11th Cir. 2004). But here, the government brings suit to enforce its anti-money laundering laws and to prevent the United States from being a haven for the proceeds of illegal activity committed abroad. United States v. All Assets Held At Julius Baer & Co., 571 F. Supp. 2d 1, 12 (D.D.C. 2008); United States v. Portrait of Wally, 2002 WL 553532, at *6 (noting that the United states "has a strong interest in enforcing its own laws as applied to conduct on its own soil. United States courts will not yield in the name of comity if doing so conflicts with the law or policy of the United States"). Thus, the Executive Branch's decision to bring this case could be viewed as evidence of its judgment that the delicate balance of foreign affairs would not be disturbed by the lawsuit. United States v. Baker Hughes Inc., 731 F. Supp. 3, 6 n.5 (D.D.C. 1990) (noting that it is "not the Court's role to second-guess the executive branch's judgment as to the proper role of comity concerns" when "the United States has decided to go ahead with the case"). Because the executive "has already done the balancing in deciding to bring the case in the first place," United Case 1:11-cv-01874-RC Document 22 Filed 04/19/13 Page 12 of 23 States v. Brodie, 174 F. Supp. 2d 294, 306 (E.D. Pa. 2001), the doctrine of international comity does not bar this lawsuit. 2. The Act of State Doctrine. The claimants also argue that the complaint should be dismissed due to the "act of state" doctrine. Claimants' Mot. at 19. They maintain that the doctrine is "based on notions of sovereign respect and intergovernmental comity," and that the court should be "reluctan [t] to complicate foreign affairs by validating or invalidating the actions of foreign sovereigns." Id. (citations and quotations omitted). The government counters that "Nguema's reliance on the Act of State Doctrine is unavailing," as the complaint does not impugn any official acts. Govt.'s Opp'n at 16. Instead, the government maintains that all relevant acts were perpetrated for Nguema's personal benefit. Govt.'s Opp'n at 16. The act of state doctrine precludes domestic courts from inquiring into the validity of the public acts that a recognized foreign sovereign power committed within its own territory. McKesson Corp. v. Islamic Republic of Iran, 539 F.3d 485, 491 (D.C. Cir. 2008); see Underhill v. Hernandez, 168 U.S. 250, 252 (1897) ("Every sovereign state is bound to respect the independence of every other sovereign state, and the courts of one country will not sit in judgment on the acts of the government of another done within its territory."); see also RESTATEMENT (THIRD) OF THE FOREIGN RELATIONS LAW OF THE UNITED STATES § 443 (1987). The doctrine applies when the relief sought or the defense interposed would require a court in the United States to declare invalid the official act of a foreign sovereign performed within its boundaries. W.S. Kirkpatrick & Co. v. Envtl. Tectonics Corp., 493 U.S. 400, 405 (1990). The policies underlying the doctrine include international comity, respect for the sovereignty of foreign nations on their own territory, and the avoidance of embarrassment to the Executive. Case 1:11-cv-01874-RC Document 22 Filed 04/19/13 Page 13 of 23. Branch in its conduct of foreign relations. World Wide Minerals, Ltd. v. Republic of Kazakhstan, 296 F.3d 1154, 1165 (D.C. Cir. 2002). The doctrine is not a principle of abstention, however—that is to say, a defendant may not raise the act of state doctrine as a complete bar to suit whenever the case touches upon the realm of foreign affairs. W.S. Kirkpatrick, 493 U.S. at 409 (noting that "[t]he Act of State doctrine does not establish an exception for cases and controversies that may embarrass foreign governments"). Rather, it serves as "a rule of decision for the courts of this country," id. at 405 (quoting Ricaud v. Am. Metal Co., 246 U.S. 304, 310 (1918)), which requires that "the acts of foreign sovereigns taken within their own jurisdictions shall be deemed valid," id. Application of the doctrine requires a fact-sensitive "balance of the relevant considerations," Banco Nacional de Cuba v. Sabbatino, 376 U.S. 398, 428 (1964), and this analysis "must always be tempered by common sense," Allied Bank Intern. v. Banco Credito Agricola de Cartago, 757 F.2d 516, 521 (2d Cir. 1985); see also Sabbatino, 376 U.S.*

at 428 (declining to announce "an inflexible and allencompassing rule" to govern the doctrine). There are two reasons why the doctrine does not bar this lawsuit. First: the applicability of this doctrine is weakened when the Executive Branch of the United States is the party that brings suit. One of the major concerns underlying the act of state doctrine is "the strong sense of the judicial branch that its engagement in the task of passing on the validity of foreign acts of a state may hinder rather than further this country's pursuit of goals both for itself and for the community of nations as a whole in the international sphere." Sabbatino, 376 U.S. at 423; cf. United States v. Curtiss-Wright Export Corp., 299 U.S. 304, 320 (1936) ("The Executive Branch is "the sole organ of the federal government in the field of international relations."). When the Executive Brank brings suit, therefore, the doctrine's rationale no longer applies. United States. Case 1:11-cv-01874-RC Document 22 Filed 04/19/13 Page 14 of 23 v. One Etched Ivory Tusk of African Elephant, 2012 WL 1802026 (E.D.N.Y. May 17, 2012) ("where the United States Government has brought suit, clearly the court need not worry that it will intrude into an area that the executive branch does not want it, or that the court's action will hinder its administration of its foreign affairs power"); United States v. Lazarenko, 504 F. Supp. 2d at 802 (concluding that the act of state did not apply where the government brought suit, as a judicial consideration of the matter would not "embarrass or hinder the executive in the realm of foreign relations" (citing Bigio v. Coca-Cola Co., 239 F.3d 440, 452 (2d Cir. 2000))); United States v. Giffen, 326 F. Supp. 2d 497, 502 (S.D.N.Y. 2004) ("The major underpinning of the act of state doctrine is the policy of foreclosing court adjudications involving the legality of acts of foreign states on their own soil that might embarrass the Executive Branch of our Government in the conduct of our foreign relations. Where the Executive Branch files an action, however, courts are reluctant to invoke the act of state doctrine on this rationale."). Second: even if the doctrine applied, its invocation would be premature at this stage because several factual disputes exist. In particular, the party invoking the doctrine must establish that the act was an exercise of its sovereign power. See Alfred Dunhill of London, Inc. v. Republic of Cuba, 425 U.S. 682, 695 (1976); Republic of the Philippines v. Marcos, 862 F.2d 1355, 1369 (9th Cir. 1988) (for the doctrine to apply, "the acts in question must have involved public acts of the sovereign"); Callejo v. Bancomer, S.A., 764 F.2d 1101, 1115 n.15 (5th Cir. 1985) (the doctrine only applies when the acts were "invested with the sovereign authority of the state."). Aside from vague allegations that this lawsuit would "interfere with Equatorial Guinea's right to administer its domestic laws within its borders," the claimants do not identify what acts, if any, were taken on behalf of the sovereign. Claimants' Mot. at 21. In fact, the claimants argue that Nguema purchased the jet with private funds obtained independently of his. Case 1:11-cv-01874-RC Document 22 Filed 04/19/13 Page 15 of 23 office. Thus, it is not clear whether any relevant acts were taken with the imprimatur of the Equatoguinean government. See Alfred Dunhill, 425 U.S. at 695 (requiring the party invoking the act of state doctrine to produce some "statute, decree, order, or resolution" to show that the government's act was vested with sovereign authority). Accordingly, the act of state doctrine poses no bar to this suit. 3. Equitable Estoppel. The claimants argue that the government should be equitably estopped from filing this suit because the claimants relied on a 2005 letter from the Department of Justice stating that it had no basis for believing that the purchase would violate the federal anti-money laundering laws. Claimants' Mot. at 22. The government responds that the doctrine of equitable estoppel only applies in sparing circumstances and is not warranted here. Govt.'s Opp'n at 16. Estoppel is an equitable doctrine invoked to avoid injustice by precluding a litigant from asserting an otherwise available claim or defense against a party who has detrimentally relied on that litigant's conduct. See Heckler v. Cmty. Health Servs. of Crawford Cnty., Inc., 467 U.S. 51, 59 (1984). "To apply equitable estoppel against the government, a party must show that (1) there was a definite representation to the party claiming estoppel, (2) the party relied on its adversary's conduct in such a manner as to change his position for the worse, (3) the party's reliance was reasonable, and (4) the *government 'engaged in affirmative misconduct.'" Morris Commc'ns, Inc. v. FCC, 566 F. 3d 184, 191 (D.C. Cir. 2009). The doctrine applies only if the government's conduct can be characterized as "misrepresentation or concealment" such that it will cause an "egregiously unfair result." GAO v. Gen. Accounting Office Pers. Appeals Bd., 698 F.2d 516, 526 (D.C. Cir. 1983); Heckler, 467 U.S. at 60 (noting that "the Government may not be estopped on the same terms as any other litigant"). For if the government "is unable to enforce the law. Case 1:11-cv-01874-RC Document 22 Filed 04/19/13 Page 16 of 23 because the conduct of its agents has given rise to an estoppel, the interest of the citizenry as a whole in obedience to the rule of law is undermined." Id. Thus, the doctrine's application to government conduct "must be rigid and sparing," and the evidence in favor of its application must be "compelling." ATC Petroleum, Inc. v. Sanders, 860 F.2d 1104, 1111 (D.C. Cir. 1988); see Int'l Union v. Clark, 2006 WL 2598046, at *12 (D.D.C. 2006) ("There is a clear presumption in this Circuit against invoking the doctrine against government actors in any but the most extreme circumstances."). Although the court has its doubts as to whether the claimants can successfully invoke this doctrine, it is unnecessary to weigh in on the matter at this stage in time. For the reasons explained below, the court will dismiss the government's complaint for failure to allege sufficient facts in support of its claim. And if an amended complaint is filed and proceeds to discovery, the parties can fully explore the factual underpinnings for an estoppel argument, which can be raised again in a summary judgment motion. 4. The Court Grants the Claimants' Motion to Dismiss for Failure to State a Claim a. Legal Standard for Failure to State a Forfeiture Claim. The pleading requirements in a civil forfeiture action are simultaneously governed by the Federal Rules of Civil Procedure and the Supplemental Rules for Admiralty or Maritime Claims and Asset Forfeiture Actions. 18 U.S.C. § 983(a)(3)(A). Although the Supplemental Rules govern, the normal set of rules may help to clarify any ambiguity. See SUPP. R. A; Unitd States v. $22,173.00 in U.S. Currency, 2010 WL 1328953, at *2 (S.D.N.Y. Apr. 5, 2010); United States v. $8,221,877.16 in U.S. Currency, 330 F.3d 141, 149 (3d Cir. 2003) ("Parties to civil forfeiture proceedings are the servants of two procedural masters: the Supplemental Rules specially devised for admiralty and in rem proceedings, and the generally applicable Federal Rules of Case 1:11-cv-01874-RC Document 22 Filed 04/19/13 Page 17 of 23 Civil Procedure. The balance between the two is struck in favor of the Supplemental Rules."). Supplemental Rule E(2)(a) requires that the government set forth its claims "with such particularity that the defendant will be able, without moving for a more definite statement, to commence an investigation of the facts and to frame a responsive pleading." Supplemental Rule G(2)(f) requires that the government "state sufficiently detailed facts to support a reasonable belief that the government will be able to meet its burden of proof at trial." Read in conjunction, these rules require the government to allege enough facts such that the court may infer that the property is subject to forfeiture. United States v. $22,173.00 in U.S. Currency, 2010 WL 1328953, at *2 (S.D.N.Y. Apr. 5, 2010); see SUPP. RULE G, Advisory Committee Notes, (noting that the "reasonable belief" standard in Rule G(2)(f) mirrors the sufficiency standard that was previously codified in Rule E(2)). The standards set forth in Supplemental Rules G and E impose a pleading that is somewhat more exacting than the liberal notice pleading standard contemplated by Rule 8(a)(2). See United States v. All Assets Held at Bank Julius Baer & Co., 571 F. Supp. 2d 1, 16–17 (D.D.C. 2008) ("Rule G (and its predecessor Rule E(2)) creates a heightened burden for pleading on the plaintiff."); cf. FED. R. CIV. P. 8(a)(2) (requiring only a short and plain statement of the claim in order to give the defendant fair notice of what the claim is and the grounds upon which it rests). This heightened particularity requirement is designed to guard against the improper use of seizure proceedings and to protect property owners against the threat of seizure upon conclusory allegations. See United States v. Mondragon, 313 F.3d 862, 865 (4th Cir. 2002); see also 12 WRIGHT &MILLER, FEDERAL PRACTICE AND PROCEDURE § 3242 (2d ed. 1997) (noting that the supplemental rules "require[] a more particularized complaint than is demanded in* *civil. Case 1:11-cv-01874-RC Document 22 Filed 04/19/13 Page 18 of 23 actions generally," and that "added specifics is thought appropriate because of the drastic nature of those remedies"). At the pleading stage, it suffices for the government to simply allege enough facts so that the claimant may understand the theory of forfeiture, file a responsive pleading, and undertake an adequate investigation. Mondragon, 313 F.3d at 864; United States v. $22,173.00 in U.S. Currency, 2010 WL 1328953, at *2 (S.D.N.Y. Apr. 5, 2010). And a court may not dismiss the complaint "on the ground that the government did not have adequate evidence at the time the complaint was filed to establish the forfeitability of the property." SUPP. R. 8(b)(ii); 18 U.S.C. § 983(a)(3)(D). A claimant in an in rem proceeding may move to dismiss in the same form provided by Rule 12(b). SUPP. R. G(8)(b)(i). As is the case under Rule 12(b), the plaintiff's factual allegations must be presumed true and should be liberally construed in his or her favor. United States v. Seventy-Nine Thousand Three Hundred Twenty-One Dollars, 522 F. Supp. 2d 64, 68 (D.D.C. 2007). Likewise, the plaintiff must be afforded every favorable inference that may be drawn from the allegations of fact set forth in the complaint. Id; accord United States v. 829,422.42 in U.S. Currency Seized from Account No. 202252771 at Citibank, N.A., 2009 WL 1743753, at *5 (D. Conn. June 18, 2009) ("When evaluating a motion to dismiss an in rem forfeiture complaint pursuant to Rule 12(b)(6), the Court still must accept as true all factual allegations made in the complaint and draw all reasonable inferences in favor of the plaintiff. "). b. The Government Fails to Allege that the Jet Is Derived From or Traceable to Illicit Activity. The government alleges that the Gulfstream Jet was purchased with funds that can be traced to or derived from illegal activity. The claimants counter that the complaint "merely states in a conclusory fashion that Minister Nguema and other members of the Equatoguinean. Case 1:11-cv-01874-RC Document 22 Filed 04/19/13 Page 19 of 23 government have amassed extraordinary wealth through 'corrupt schemes' and that because Minster Nguema's 'level of spending is inconsistent with his salary as a Minister,' the Aircraft must be derived from unlawful activity." Claimants' Mot. at 31. The government alleges that a group of Equatoguinean individuals—dubbed the Inner Circle—has amassed great wealth by siphoning funds from the public fisc. See Compl. 27. The government alleges that the Inner Circle committed a number of violations of Equatoguinean law, including "extortion and misappropriation, theft, and embezzlement of public funds." Id. The complaint describes a general process by which the Inner Circle took advantage of Equatorial Guinea's natural resources—yet careful scrutiny of the complaint reveals that Nguema is often implicated by association only. See id. 32 ("[Nguema] used ownership of Sofona and Somagui Forestal and his status as Minister of Forestry (and President Obiang's son) to enrich himself through corrupt schemes in the timber industry, as described below."); id. 35 ("In the 2000s, the rapid growth of the oil and gas sector in E.G. led to a boom in construction and other infrastructure-related activities in that country. This provided another opportunity for the Inner Circle, including Nguema, to obtain money corruptly, as the government began awarding large construction contracts to companies owned by the Inner Circle.") (emphasis added). To illustrate: under the heading "Illegal Corrupt Schemes Used by Nguema and the Inner Circle to Enrich Themselves," the government alleges that "members of the Inner Circle, such as Nguema, demand[ed] payments from companies doing business in E.G., in exchange for the performance of official acts." Id. 49. But the government does not allege what companies were victim to this scheme, or when this occurred, or which members of the Inner Circle were behind the acts. In the same vein, the government claims that "in order to engage in logging in Case 1:11-cv-01874-RC Document 22 Filed 04/19/13 Page 20 of 23 E.G.'s National Forests, timber companies must first receive a logging concession from Nguema. Nguema demands that timber companies seeking to obtain such concessions first pay him a personal fee." Id. 50. Again, the government does not provide enough detail for the court to infer the contours of the illicit scheme. Many of the complaint's allegations do not even give rise to an inference of illegal activity. See, e.g., id. 51 ("For instance, a major international civil* *engineering firm in E.G., which had obtained several substantial infrastructure contracts from the Government of E.G., built a mansion for Nguema in Malabo, E.G., at his request and direction. Upon completion of that project, however, Nguema refused to pay this firm for its work."); see also id. 63 ("Some of the money obtained by other members of the Inner Circle has made its way to Nguema; for example, on October 21, 2002, $200,000 was transferred from a personal account at Riggs Bank belonging to a member of the Inner Circle to Nguema's personal bank account."). Other allegations make no mention of Nguema whatsoever. See id. 54 ("In another extortion scheme, a businessman in E.G. who owned a construction company was forced to share 50 percent of his profits with a senior E.G. public official, and to provide the official with 50 percent of the equity in the company, in order to continue to secure government contracts in E.G. Ultimately, the businessman was forced to leave E.G. against his will, and the senior public official took over 100 percent of his company."). A recurring theme in the government's complaint is the allegation that Nguema's outlandish wealth raises suspicions about the lawfulness of his income. Id. 34 ("Nguema's level of spending is inconsistent with his salary as a Minister. His official salary today is approximately $6,799 per month, or less than $100,000 per year, according to official E.G. sources."). When viewed in tandem with other details suggesting illegal behavior, Nguema's Case 1:11-cv-01874-RC Document 22 Filed 04/19/13 Page 21 of 23 wealth might allow an inference of illegal activity—but standing alone, it does not. See Mondragon, 313 F.3d at 864 ("The presence of that much cash [half a million dollars], oddly packaged, could raise a suspicion that someone was up to no good, but without more it does not suggest a connection to drug trafficking."); cf. United States v. $22,173.00 in U.S. Currency, 2010 WL 1328953, at *2 (S.D.N.Y. Apr. 5, 2010) (deeming certain allegations "troubling" and noting that "a great deal more" would be necessary to survive summary judgment, but concluding that unusually large sums of cash could give rise to an inference of illegal activity when viewed in conjunction with other specific allegations "suggesting a pattern of drug trafficking"). The government itself has alleged that Ngema owns or controls a number of companies. Yet nothing is known about what income Nguema derives from them. Thus, without knowing what Nguema's means are, the court is hard-pressed to infer that he lives beyond them. Absent other details, the court cannot infer how Nguema's wealth may have been derived, nor from what sources, nor the legality of those sources. Although the government alleges that Nguema lives far beyond his means, the court cannot leap to the conclusion that his largesse is evidence of criminal activity. Faced with this complaint, the claimants would find it difficult to know where to begin their investigation, what individuals to interview, or what documents to review. Cf. Mondragon, 313 F.3d at 864. To be sure, the government paints a troubling picture of endemic corruption in Equatorial Guinea. But the government has done so with brushstrokes that are much too broad. The government cannot proceed by casting general allegations of lawlessness in the country in which the relevant transactions took place. United States v. $1,399,313.74 in U.S. Currency, 592 F. Supp. 2d 495, 499 (S.D.N.Y. 2008) ("The principal new allegation in support of the narcotics-Case 1:11-cv-01874-RC Document 22 Filed 04/19/13 Page 22 of 23 trafficking theory is that many of the funds were sent from Latvia, which the Government asserts is a notorious money laundering haven. This does not raise the right to relief above a speculative level."). Absent some specific indication that the Jet is derived from or traceable to illicit activity, the complaint must be dismissed. Id. The court has little doubt that the government could cure these deficiencies by filing an amended complaint that alleges additional facts. Thus, the court will dismiss the complaint without prejudice and grant leave to amend the complaint. IV. CONCLUSION. For the foregoing reasons, the court grants the claimants' motion to dismiss. But the government is granted leave to amend the complaint. An order consistent with this memorandum opinion is separately and contemporaneously issued this 19th day of April, 2013. RUDOLPH CONTRERAS. United States District Judge.*

The cases originated as part of the DOJ's Kleptocracy Asset Recovery Initiative, which targets and recovers the proceeds of foreign official corruption that have been laundered into or through the United States. As part of the initiative, the DOJ seeks to forfeit and recover stolen funds for the benefit of the people of the country from which it was taken.

Citing Mary Evans Webster, Donna R. Cline states that "in a kleptocracy, the kleptocrat controls both the economy and important government functions, like the judiciary and legislature. This control makes it impossible to stop corruption and hold offenders accountable, removing any check on the kleptocrat's use of power for self-enrichment. Grand corruption, and kleptocracy in particular, devastates a developing country by diverting funds from social programs to which impoverished citizens desperately need access, and from other development and infrastructure projects. It can also frustrate and discourage international aid efforts by siphoning off money and goods intended for the kleptocracy's citizens into the coffers of privileged rulers."[8]

In 2003, ICE HSI established the Foreign Corruption Investigations Group in Miami to target corrupt foreign officials around the world who attempt to utilize the U.S. financial institutions to launder illicit funds. The group conducts investigations into the laundering of proceeds emanating from foreign public corruption, bribery, and embezzlement. The objective is to prevent foreign-derived ill-gotten gains from entering the U.S. financial infrastructure, to seize identified assets in the United States, and to recover these funds on behalf of those affected by foreign official corruption.[9]

In October 10, 2014, the DOJ announced that Nguema agreed to relinquish more than $30 million of assets purchased with corruption proceeds. "Through relentless embezzlement and extortion, Vice President Nguema Obiang shamelessly looted his government and shook down businesses in his country to support his lavish lifestyle, while many of his fellow citizens lived in extreme poverty," said Assistant Attorney General Leslie R. Caldwell of the DOJ's Criminal Division and Acting Director Thomas S. Winkowski of U.S. Immigration and Customs and Enforcement. "After raking in millions in bribes and kickbacks, Nguema Obiang embarked on a corruption-fueled spending spree in the United States. This settlement forces Nguema Obiang to relinquish assets worth an estimated $30 million, and prevents Nguema Obiang from hiding other stolen money in the United States, fulfilling the goals of our Kleptocracy Asset Recovery Initiative: to deny safe haven to the proceeds of large-scale foreign official corruption and recover those funds for the people harmed by the abuse of office."[10] The settlement was signed and lodged with the U.S. District Court for the Central District of California.

---

[8]Cline (2015).

[9]"Individuals with information about possible proceeds of foreign corruption in the United States, or funds laundered through institutions in the United States, should contact ICE HSI at 866-DHS-2ICE, Eginfo1@ICE.DHS.GOV or 802-872-6199 if calling from outside the United States." U.S. Department of Justice (2011).

[10]U.S. Department of Justice (2014).

"While this settlement is certainly gratifying for the many investigators and prosecutors who worked tirelessly to bring it to fruition, it is undoubtedly even more rewarding for the people of Equatorial Guinea, knowing that at least some of the money plundered from their country's coffers is being returned to them," said Acting ICE Director Winkowski. "ICE remains steadfast in its resolve to combat foreign corruption when the spoils of these crimes come to our shores and we are committed to seeking justice and compensation for the often impoverished victims."[11]

Pursuant to the terms of the settlement, Nguema had to sell the $30 million Malibu mansion, a Ferrari automobile, and various items of Michael Jackson memorabilia purchased with the proceeds of corruption. Of those proceeds, $20 million had to be given to a charitable organization to be used for the benefit of the people of Equatorial Guinea. Another $10.3 million was forfeited to the United States and was used for the benefit of the people of Equatorial Guinea to the extent permitted by law.[12]

"Under the agreement, Nguema had also to disclose and remove other assets he owns in the United States. Nguema had also to make a $1 million payment to the United States, representing the value of Michael Jackson memorabilia already removed from the United States for disbursement to the charitable organization. The agreement also provided that if certain of Nguema's other assets, including a Gulfstream Jet, are ever brought into the United States, they are subject to seizure and forfeiture."[13]

As Kenneth Hurwitz, a senior legal officer on anticorruption with the Open Society Justice Initiative of the Open Society Foundations observed when the settlement was announced, "what is more important than how much was seized was the message sent: other kleptocrats will now know that cultivating close ties to Washington, as Equatorial Guinea's have, will not protect their assets from seizure. These cases have a meaning way beyond the money. People who are untouchable in their own countries are not globally untouchable."[14]

What is clear is that criminals have been able to make these multimillion-dollar purchases with few questions asked because of international laws that foster the movement of largely untraceable money through shell companies. Vast sums are flowing unchecked around the world as never before—whether motivated by corruption, tax avoidance or investment strategy, and enabled by an ever-more-borderless economy and a proliferation of ways to move and hide assets.

---

[11]Id.

[12]Id.

[13]Id.

[14]Grimaldi (2014).

1.2 New York Real Estate

For more than a year, The New York Times examined the influx of global cash fueling New York City's high-end real estate boom. The investigation pierced the secrecy of more than 200 shell companies that have owned condominiums at one complex, the Time Warner Center, which remains the New York archetype of the global phenomenon that has been increasing sums of foreign money in high-end real estate and the growing use of shell companies. Spurred in part by a series of stories by The Times, Bill de Blasio (mayor of New York City since January 1, 2014) imposed new disclosure requirements on shell companies buying or selling property in New York City.

These series of articles published in 2015 by The Times discussed possible money laundering through expensive New York City real estate. The Times ran these articles on consecutive days, and investigations into high-end New York and Miami real estate have resulted.[15]

These photographs are of the Time Warner Center, at the center of The Times' investigation:

Source: Skyscrapercity: (http://www.skyscrapercity.com/showthread.php?t=63363&page=8)

[15]Saul and Story (2015a, b, c, d).

Source: Skyscrapercity: (http://www.skyscrapercity.com/showthread.php?t=776476&page=303)

What The Times found was very surprising. Nearly half of the most expensive residential properties in the United States are currently purchased anonymously through shell companies.

It took The Times more than a year to unravel the ownership of shell companies with condos in the Time Warner Center. Journalists searched business and court records from more than twenty countries, interviewing people, examining hundreds of property records, and connecting information from lawyers or relatives named on deeds to the actual buyers. The Times concluded that the "real estate industry does little examination of buyers' identities or backgrounds, and there is no legal requirement for it to do so."

The precise impact of wealthy foreigners on the city maybe more complex. The Times revealed that as nonresidents, they pay no city income taxes and often receive hefty property tax breaks. A program aimed at new condo development hands out about a half-billion dollars in tax breaks a year, according to New York City's independent budget office. These savings are passed on to owners in the form of lower property taxes. The Time Warner Center was not part of the most lucrative tax break program, but many other buildings around Central Park benefited.

Shell companies registered in the names of accountants, lawyers, and relatives, as well as groups of investors or family members in a tangled web, make it difficult to identify the origin of funds, especially when the shell companies are registered abroad.

The advantage of offshore accounts is that they enable the free movement of capital, which is only taxed in negotiations taking place in-country, with exemptions for transfers to other offshore or nonresident accounts, corporate income taxes, and income tax withholding on payments made to nonresidents. Usually, there are treaties to avoid double taxation, and which allow governments to establish unilateral measures domestically (such as, for instance, exemptions for fiscal credits at a reduced proportional rate, and deduction of taxes paid abroad from domestic taxable income), which is why they are referred to as tax havens. It is true that they facilitate the circulation of goods, services and capital, but they are also an effective instrument for evading taxes with considerable legitimacy. They lend themselves to legal uses, of arguable utility, but also to illegal practices. There are considerable advantages to be had by using them as conduits, especially by those interested in laundering ill-gotten money, on account of defective or nonexistent government control, but also because they make it easy to generate false trails, and also handle international wire transfers.

Offshore bank accounts make it possible to disguise their real controllers, since ownership is—according to the legislation in the countries in which they are located—evidenced by bearer paper, and partners or officers are simply proxies, often proxies for hundreds of companies of the same pattern. It is easy to shift shell companies' ownership. All of this amounts to creating a veil for the actual owners to hide behind. Their paper cannot be traded on the domestic market nor cashed in without considerable expense and questions about possible complicity in money laundering directed at anyone who converts it. It is argued that these accounts are advantageous in that owning one does not involve liability to taxes, unless one were to actually invest in the country.

Loan agreements are often written so as to lay hold of funds from offshore accounts without exposing them to tax liability. There are transparency requirements for beneficiaries of companies, with countries required to obtain reliable real-time information (Financial Action Task Force (FATF) Recommendation No. 24), including information on trusts, settlors and trustees or beneficiaries (Recommendation No. 25), which would preclude anonymous accounts. This is why the customer and actual beneficiary must be identified (i.e. know-your-customer duties, often called Customer Due Diligence) along with a requirement to collect enough information about the institution to which service is rendered, so that the trustee, who administers the assets, is accountable for turning in suspicious transaction reports. Observe that the FATF takes a clear stand against the invocation of banking secrecy or professional privilege as a means of obstructing its recommendations (Recommendation No. 9).

As it is impossible to establish with certainty the source of money behind shell companies, the articles from The New York Times confirm what many people were already suspecting surrounding wealthy properties. What many people do not imagine is that in developing countries, as well as developed ones, laundering with real estate is sometimes not addressed by the legal and institutional systems.

Officials are clamoring for the foreign wealthy, offering tax breaks for condominium development owners looking for a second, or third, residence. Mayor

Michael R. Bloomberg said on his weekly radio program in 2013, shortly before leaving office: "If we could get every billionaire around the world to move here, it would be a godsend."[16]

The Times found that a growing proportion of real-estate owners in New York City are foreigners. It identified six foreign owners who had been the subject of government inquiries around the world, either personally or as heads of companies. The cases range from housing and environmental violations to financial fraud. Four owners have been arrested, and another four have been the subject of fines or penalties for illegal activities. The foreign owners include government officials and close associates of officials from Russia, Colombia, Malaysia, China, Kazakhstan, and Mexico.

According to the FATF's Money Laundering and Terrorist Financing Through the Real Estate Sector Report, "Corporate vehicles—that is, legal persons of all types and various legal arrangements (trusts, for example)—have often been found to be misused in order to hide the ownership, purpose, activities, and financing related to criminal activity. Indeed that practice is so common that it almost appears to be ubiquitous in money laundering cases. The misuse of these entities seem to be most acute in tax havens, free-trade areas and jurisdictions with a strong reputation for banking secrecy; however, it may occur wherever the opacity of corporate vehicles can be exploited. Apart from obscuring the identities of the beneficial owners of an asset or the origin and destination of funds, these corporate vehicles are also sometimes used in criminal schemes as a source of legal income. In addition to shell companies, there are other specialized companies that carry out perfectly legitimate business relating to real estate, which have sometimes been misused for money laundering purposes. This aspect is illustrated by the use, for example, of property management or construction companies. The use of corporate vehicles is further facilitated if the company is entirely controlled or owned by criminals."[17]

Legal persons formed and incorporated in one jurisdiction, but actually used by persons in another jurisdiction without control or administration of a natural or legal resident and not subject to supervision, can easily be misused in money laundering transactions. The possibilities for identifying the beneficial owner or the origin and destination of the money are at times limited. In these scenarios, actors with wrongful intentions have the distinct advantage of extra protection in the form of bank secrecy.

The Times articles, as well as that FATF Report, highlight successive sales and purchases, in which the property is sold in a series of subsequent transactions, oftentimes at a higher price. The sale was therefore fictitious, and the parties involved belong to the same criminal organization or are nonfinancial professionals in the real-estate sector who implicitly know the true purpose of the transactions or unusual activity.

---

[16]Gay (2013).

[17]FATF (2007).

In other words, placing obstacles to discovering the true owners of the property and the real origin of the funds is a very efficient tool used in the transactions in order to avoid the disclosure of buyer's or seller's identity.

The writers of the mentioned Times articles concluded that in many ways, the government has allowed the real estate industry to turn a blind eye to the source of money used to buy luxury properties.

Based on the Web site PropertyShark, The Times reveals that about $8 billion is spent each year for New York City residences that cost more than $5 million each, more than triple the amount of a decade ago, and just over half of those sales in 2014 were to shell companies. The Times' examination shows the workings of an opaque economy for this global wealth. Lacking incentive or legal obligation to identify the sources of money, an entire chain of people involved in high-end real estate sales—lawyers, accountants, title brokers, escrow agents, real estate agents, condo boards, and building workers—often operate with blinders on. As Rudy Tauscher, a former manager of the condos at Time Warner, said: "The building doesn't know where the money is coming from. We're not interested."

Being less and less transparent, regulatory efforts have failed to require more openness from these companies. For instance, The Times revealed that in 2003, one-third of the units sold in Time Warner were purchased by shell companies. By 2014, the figure was over 80 percent. Across the United States in recent years, nearly half the residential purchases of over $5 million were made by shell companies rather than named people, according to data from First American Data Tree analyzed by The Times.

As per the articles, Susan Pace Hamill, a University of Alabama professor who worked on limited liability company (LLC) policy while at the Internal Revenue Service in the 1990s, deems that nothing in the genesis of LLCs suggested they would be used to purchase personal real estate. However, LLCs are now commonly used in real estate for privacy, wealth transfer, and shared ownership. On many deeds, the line for the buyer's signature is left blank, is illegible, or is signed by a lawyer or other representative. Phone numbers are registered under lawyers' names. The owner's line on renovation permits is signed by Time Warner staff members. Tax statements are addressed to the LLCs.

And because most of the sales are in cash, there are few mortgage statements, another public document that might identify an owner or trigger scrutiny.

Based on these facts it is possible to highlight a number of common characteristics that, when detected individually or in combination, might indicate potential misuse of the real estate sector for money laundering purposes. These conclusions or red flag indicators can assist the sector in conducting customer due diligence for new and existing clients. They also may help in performing necessary risk-analysis in the more general sense for the sector.

The Times also revealed that "the shift to secrecy also reflects a fundamental change in the ownership structure of luxury real estate in New York. Many of Manhattan's finest addresses were traditionally organized as co-ops in which residents were joint owners of the building. Co-op boards generally prefer full-time residents and often subject would-be buyers to excruciating scrutiny. 'Those co-ops would n-ot accept billionaires, especially foreigners' said Raphael De Niro a broker at Douglas Elliman."

That is why an adequate customer due diligence, record-keeping, and reporting requirements for the real estate sector is an important step to prevent money laundering. To ensure effective compliance with these requirements, it is essential that authorities inform the sector of its obligations and share sector-specific indicators with the industry.

As key figures within the real estate sector and its transactions, designated non-financial businesses and professions (DNFBPs) need to be encouraged by organizations and legislators to implement effective anti-money laundering measures.

An important decision was made by the U.S. Treasury (a FinCEN order) on July 27, 2016, which expanded its hunt for international criminals who launder money through real-estate deals by ordering title insurance companies to report all-cash buyers' identities in parts of California, Texas, New York, and Florida. The program to unmask individuals behind shell companies that buy high-end houses with cash will cover New York City's Manhattan.[18]

Foreigners who buy real estate often have an easier time keeping it out of the reach of investigators. Related companies do not usually share details about buyers with board members and did not inform them of the sale.

Although the real estate and legal professions argue that background checks are impractical and would hurt the economy, professionals such as lawyers, accountants, real estate agents, financial advisers, and trust and company service providers are known as "gatekeepers" because, either wittingly or unknowingly, they can provide an entry point for those seeking to misuse legitimate financial and corporate systems for money laundering.

Services provided by professionals may assist criminals to launder money through real estate by establishing and maintaining domestic or offshore legal entity structures, facilitating or conducting transactions on behalf of the criminal, receiving, and transferring large amounts of cash, establishing complex loans and other credit arrangements, introducing criminals to financial institutions, and facilitating the transfer of ownership of property to nominees or third parties.

Businesses insist that tainted money is not likely to flow into real estate because anonymity and liquidity, two characteristics important to money launderers, typically do not exist in real estate transactions. However, the industry's assertions cannot ignore the increasing use of shell companies and how often wealthy foreigners seek out high-end estates as a safe deposit box.

According to The Times, registering shell companies has become profitable for states like Delaware and Nevada, which also have lobbied against transparency. "I don't see some kind of global effort to stop all this because the money's too good," said David M. Crane, a Syracuse University law professor who oversaw the United Nations' effort to recover money from Charles Taylor, the former Liberian president who was convicted of war crimes and thought to have plundered his

[18]Lambert et al. (2016).

country. A number of states do not require people forming companies to reveal the names of the owners or show any identification. This opacity presents challenges for law enforcement officials, who say billions of dollars in suspicious money move through shell companies each year. "It can be very, very difficult to penetrate who is the beneficial owner of these shell companies," said Leslie R. Caldwell, chief of the U.S. Department Justice Department's Criminal Division.

Supervision of the property market is totally inadequate, and poor enforcement has laid out a welcome mat for launderers and organized criminals.

The Times concludes that proliferation of shell companies incorporated in the United States has hurt Washington's attempt to get other countries to crack down on Americans who move money offshore to avoid taxes. "We are in a totally inconsistent position," said Carl Levin, a Michigan Democrat who pushed for transparency in shell companies when he served in the Senate. "We're way behind in terms of keeping up with what the international standard is, and it weakens our argument when we go to try to crack down the use of these offshore tax havens." In 2014, after the Group of eight industrialized nations issued goals requiring identification of shell company owners, a British representative met with Justice Department officials to complain about the United States' failure to comply. According to two people at the meeting, the British representative, Dominic Martin, delivered a stern message: The lax American laws were being used by other countries as an excuse for inaction.

Bibliography

Cline, D. (2015). Seizing Equatorial Guinea's future: Punishing foreign kleptocracy with civil asset forfeiture. *California International Law Journal, 23*(1), 34–38.

FATF. (2007, June). Money laundering and terrorist financing through the real estate sector. http://www.fatf-gafi.org/media/fatf/documents/reports/ML%20and%20TF%20through%20the%20Real%20Estate%20Sector.pdf. Accessed October 3, 2016. Força-tarefa aponta "patrimônio oculto" do ex-presidente (2016, March 4). UOL. http://noticias.uol.com.br/ultimas-noticias/agencia-estado/2016/03/04/forca-tarefa-aponta-para-patrimonio-oculto-do-ex–presidente.htm. Accessed March 22, 2016.

Gay, M. (2013, September 20). Mayor Bloomberg: Stark differences between the city's rich and poor are largely because so many billionaires want to live in New York. New York Daily News. http://www.nydailynews.com/news/politics/bloomberg-billionaires-godsend-article-1.1462346. Accessed April 4, 2016.

Grimaldi, J. (2014, October 10). When U.S. targets foreign leaders for corruption, recovering loot is a challenge. The Wall Street Journal. http://www.wsj.com/articles/u-s-reaches-34-million-corruption-settlement-with-equatorial-guinea-official-1412948259. Accessed September 23, 2016.

Lambert, L., Barlyn, S., & Dilts, E. (2016, July 27). U.S. Treasury expands hunt for money laundering in real estate. Reuters. http://www.reuters.com/article/us-usa-corruption-realestate-idUSKCN1072HU. Accessed on 3 October, 2016.

Matthews, C. (2013, August 23). Judge partially tosses Obiang forfeiture. The Wall Street Journal. http://blogs.wsj.com/riskandcompliance/2013/08/23/judge-partially-tosses-obiang-forfeiture/. Accessed 20 February, 2016.

Messick, R. (2014, October 15). U.S. Department of Justice/civil society—1; Kleptocrats—0. The Global Anticorruption Blog. http://globalanticorruptionblog.com/2014/10/15/u-s-department-of-justicecivil-society-1-kleptocrats-0/. Accessed February 20, 2016.

Saul, S., & Story, L. (2015, February 7). A summary: The hidden money buying condos at the Time Warner Center. The New York Times. http://www.nytimes.com/2015/02/08/nyregion/the-hidden-money-buying-up-new-york-real-estate.html?ribbon-ad-idx=6&&module=Ribbon&version=context&region=Header&action=click&contentCollection=Time%20Warner&pgtype=article. Accessed March 2, 2016.

Saul, S., & Story, L. (2015, February 8). Jho Low, well connected in Malaysia, has an appetite for New York. The New York Times. http://www.nytimes.com/2015/02/09/nyregion/jho-low-young-malaysian-has-an-appetite-for-new-york.html?ribbon-ad-idx=6&&module=Ribbon&version=context&region=Header&action=click&contentCollection=Time%20Warner&pgtype=article. Accessed March 2, 2016.

Saul, S., & Story, L. (2015, February 9). Amid complaints in India, a real estate deal in Manhattan. The New York Times. http://www.nytimes.com/2015/02/10/nyregion/kabul-chawla-bptp-india-real-estate-manhattan.html?ribbon-ad-idx=6&&module=Ribbon&version=context&region=Header&action=click&contentCollection=Time%20Warner&pgtype=article. Accessed March 2, 2016.

Saul, S., & Story, L. (2015, February 11). At the Time Warner Center, an enclave of powerful Russians. The New York Times. http://www.nytimes.com/2015/02/12/nyregion/russia-time-warner-center-andrey-vavilov.html?ribbon-ad-idx=9&&module=Ribbon&version=context&region=Header&action=click&contentCollection=Time%20Warner&pgtype=article. Accessed March 2, 2016.

United States v. One Gulfstream G-V Jet Aircraft, Displaying tail number VPCES, its tools and Appurtenances. Civil Case No. 11-1874 (D.D.C. April 19, 2013). https://www.gpo.gov/fdsys/pkg/USCOURTS-dcd-1_11-cv-01874/pdf/USCOURTS-dcd-1_11-cv-01874-0.pdf.

U.S. Department of Justice (2014, October 10). Second vice president of Equatorial Guinea agrees to relinquish more than $30 million of assets purchased with corruption proceeds. http://www.justice.gov/opa/pr/second-vice-president-equatorial-guinea-agrees-relinquish-more-30-million-assets-purchased. Accessed February 20, 2016.

U.S. Department of Justice (2011, October 25). Department of Justice seeks to recover more than $70.8 million in proceeds of corruption from government minister of Equatorial Guinea. http://www.justice.gov/opa/pr/department-justice-seeks-recover-more-708-million-proceeds-corruption-government-minister. Accessed January 31, 2016.

Chapter 2
Money Laundering Through Agribusiness

In a 2007 report, the FATF addressed money laundering and terrorist financing through the real estate sector and identified various methods, techniques, mechanisms, and instruments used.[1] Criminal organizations use real estate to introduce illegal funds into the system. They use nonfinancial professionals, corporate vehicles, and complex loans to preserve anonymity and confidentiality. Agribusiness, like real estate, is being misused in money laundering schemes. Agribusiness is barely covered by anti-money laundering obligations because prices in the sector vary across districts and jurisdictions. Huge sums of money are being invested in agribusiness not only by law-abiding citizens, but also by those who misuse the sector for criminal purposes.

Manipulation of the appraisal or valuation of cattle is one money laundering method in the agribusiness sector. It involves the overvaluing or undervaluing of a property followed by a succession of sales and purchases. A property's value may be difficult to estimate, notably when you consider a great number of cattle and varying levels of quality. Furthermore, money launderers can even use nonexistent cattle to launder their criminal proceeds. This area is particularly vulnerable because of the lack of government oversight and supervision.

Brazilian Federal Judge Odilon de Oliveira presides over a specialized court for organized crime in Campo Grande, Mato Grosso do Sul, and is considered a leader in the fight against money laundering. Drawing from his experience as a judge, he stated that financial criminals frequently use rural property to launder money from illicit origins and that it is "very easy" to launder money using cattle and farms.

According to Judge De Oliveira, criminals falsify property documents through misrepresentation. For example, farm owners misrepresent that they have livestock or other agricultural products and register them with the appropriate agency. They then create invoices, purchase vaccines, simulate sales, and pay taxes, thereby

---

[1]FATF (2007).

F.M. De Sanctis, *International Money Laundering Through Real Estate and Agribusiness*, DOI 10.1007/978-3-319-52069-8_2

laundering ill-gotten gains. This method is called “paper cow” and “soy paper” and is possible in part because government regulation of the agricultural sector is very difficult.[2]

There is little structure in place to monitor taxpayers who derive income from rural activity. Documentation is considered essential for transactions within the law because it ensures compliance with sanitary requirements as well as beef access at a stable price in the formal market. With records of cattle origin, invoices, receipts, and vouchers of health requirements in hand, experts say, it is possible to obtain the Guide to Animal Transport (GAT) in Brazil. GATs and Statements of Vaccination Against Foot-and-Mouth Disease related to property investigated are being used to show the occurrence of fraud in these livestock records.[3]

In a case of an international Colombian drug dealer who was convicted in Brazil of money laundering, sentenced to more than thirty years in prison, and extradited to the United States, his assets were confiscated, including farms, cattle, swine, sheep, horses, and fish. The judge (the author of this book) determined that the administration of these assets should be handed over to the Federal Police until their final sale.[4]

In another interesting case, also decided by this author, 27 farms were seized, as well as all of the farms’ assets, including more than 450,000 cattle. The facts of the case suggested that the defendant’s purpose in acquiring the cattle was to camouflage the illegal origin of funds and to distance the owners or beneficiaries from the funds’ origins. To inventory the goods seized, the court subpoenaed the state agricultural department to report the number of cattle recorded by farm, the registered owners, the number of vaccines used for the cattle, and the number of vaccines needed by the cattle. The state agricultural department was also required to provide information from the Traceability Service of the Supply Chain for Cattle and Buffalo from the National Agricultural Department (*Serviço de Rastreabilidade da Cadeia Produtiva de Bovinos e Bubalinos*—SISBOV). Another judge authorized the partial sale of the cattle because it was considered a fungible good.[5]

In the United States, the Animal and Plant Health Inspection Service[6] and the Farm Service Agency,[7] both part of the U.S. Department of Agriculture, provide information on farms, livestock, and livestock vaccines.

Jessie Bullock reveals that, in Mexico, drug cartels make millions of dollars annually on the black market and are considered the best in the world at laundering money. To launder their illegal gains, they invest in different activities, including

[2]Lavagem de dinheiro com gado é “facílimo”, diz juiz (2007).

[3]Lavagem de dinheiro com gado é “facílimo”, diz juiz (2007).

[4]See case nos. 2007.61.81.011245-7 and 2007.61.81.008076-6 from the 6th Federal Judicial District, specialized in Money Laundering and Financial Crimes in São Paulo, Brazil.

[5]See case no. 2009.61.81.005401-6 from the 6th Federal Judicial District, specialized in Money Laundering and Financial Crimes in São Paulo, Brazil.

[6]U.S. Department of Agriculture (2016a).

[7]U.S. Department of Agriculture (2016b).

agribusiness. In 2013, the Zetas, one of Mexico's most dangerous and violent cartels, were busted by U.S. law enforcement officials for a large-scale money laundering scheme of buying and selling quarter horses. The Zetas and their family members were caught laundering money through a cattle ranch in Mexico. The ranch was set up by the brother of a Zetas kingpin. According to Bullock, the brother laundering money through his wife and her father, who operated the ranch. He also received help from his wife's mother and her two uncles.[8]

In 2005, the U.S. Treasury Department announced that two Mexican cattle companies were fronts for drug cartels. The announcement was made in an attempt to block an elaborate money laundering scheme. The cattle sold by the companies to Texas ranchers was subject to seizure by the federal government. The two Mexican drug cartels named in the Treasury Department's statement were the Arriola Marquez organization (linked to Mexican drug kingpin Joaquin "El Chapo" Guzman) and the Arellano Felix cartel based in Tijuana. The Arriola Marquez group bought large herds of cattle in Mexico to launder its drug money. The Treasury Department also named the two Mexican cattle companies as well as a U.S. company that was a "mirror" entity—an organization that exists on paper to give a foreign company a U.S. outlet.[9]

Saul Elbein reveals how drug traffickers in Guatemala laundered cash over the years by clearing forests for commodity production and investing in land. "While clearing forest for cattle or palm in government forests is technically illegal, in practice, these ranchers operate and bring their goods to market just like their legal cousins outside the forest—and there is always the possibility of acquiring a valid title down the road through fraud, bribery, or the intervention of sympathetic officials." "Buying and clearing land 'allows dollars to be untraceably converted into private assets while simultaneously legitimizing a [trafficker's] presence at the frontier (e.g., as a ranching operation).'" Furthermore, drug traffickers strategically benefitted from big cattle estates by claiming territory from rivals.[10]

In Colombia, there are more examples of the misuse of cattle to launder money. Contraband smuggled into Colombia is part of multi-billion-dollar money laundering operations after decades of political and drugs violence. In complicated schemes, Colombian traffickers receive drug money from overseas dealers in the form of goods, often shipped along with legitimate merchandise. They pay above value for cattle farms, which in turn increase prices for neighboring property. Then they liquidate assets (the cattle) to receive quick cash, cutting the price of livestock in the area.[11]

---

[8]Bullock (2013).

[9]Hedges (2005).

[10]Elbein (2016).

[11]Murphy and Bocanegra (2013).

The 2012 Financial Action Task Force (FATF) Recommendations do not mention rural activity as a "Designated Non-Financial Business and Profession."[12] The Brazilian law on money laundering, however, was amended on July 9, 2012, to include "natural or legal persons trading or trade brokering in rural or animal goods of high value" on the list of entities required to keep detailed records of their clients' identities and of their financial transactions.[13] A shortcoming of this law is that the Brazilian Financial Intelligence Unit (*Conselho de Controle de Atividades Financeiras*—COAF) has not enacted a bylaw to regulate it.

When money launderers use cattle, they typically acquire it in what is known as the integration or final phase of money laundering. Because it is an extraordinary opportunity to make an investment while giving the appearance of legality, acquiring and misusing cattle offers criminals a business activity. This kind of criminal behavior is the result of weaknesses and loopholes in the prevention of money laundering. Enforcement bodies must develop appropriate measures to protect the agricultural sector from criminal activities and to stop the flow of illegal money.

Bibliography

Bullock, J. (2013, August 20). 3 ways drug cartels launder their money, right in front of you. Policy.Mic. https://mic.com/articles/60233/3-ways-drug-cartels-launder-their-money-right-in-front-of-you#.wt5pIlLNo. Accessed October 4, 2016.

Elbein, S. (2016, July 8). From cocaine cowboys to narco-ranchers. Foreign Policy. http://foreignpolicy.com/2016/07/08/guatemala-cocaine-central-america-drug-forest-maya-biosphere-reserve-cattle-ranching/. Accessed October 5, 2016.

FATF. (2007, June). Money Laundering and Terrorist Financing Through the Real Estate Sector. http://www.fatf-gafi.org/media/fatf/documents/reports/ML%20and%20TF%20through%20the%20Real%20Estate%20Sector.pdf. Accessed October 3, 2016.

FATF. (2016, June). The FATF Recommendations. http://www.fatf-gafi.org/publications/fatfrecommendations/documents/fatf-recommendations.html. Accessed August 3, 2016.

Hedges, M. (2005, Aug 22). U.S. links Mexican cattle business to cartels. Houston Chronicle. http://www.chron.com/news/nation-world/article/U-S-links-Mexican-cattle-business-to-cartels-1674193.php. Accessed October 4, 2016.

Lavagem de dinheiro com gado é "facílimo", diz juiz (2007, June 24). G1.globo.com. http://g1.globo.com/Noticias/Politica/0,,AA1571851-5601,00-LAVAGEM+DE+DINHEIRO+COM+GADO+E+FACILIMO+DIZ+JUIZ.html. Accessed August 2, 2016.

Law No. 9.613 of March 3, 1998. http://www.planalto.gov.br/ccivil_03/leis/L9613.htm. Accessed August 3, 2016.

---

[12]FATF Recommendation No. 22 identifies the following as "Designated Non-Financial Business Professions": casinos, real estate agents, dealers in precious metals and stones, lawyers, notaries, other independent legal professionals and accountants, trust and company service providers. FATF (2016).

[13]See Article 9, Part XVII. Law No. 9.613 of March 3, 1998.

Murphy, H., & Bocanegra, N. (2013, May 28). Money laundering distorts Colombia's economic comeback. Reuters. http://www.reuters.com/article/us-colombia-moneylaundering-idUSBRE94R03E20130528. Accessed January 22, 2017.

U.S. Department of Agriculture. (2016a, September 21). Animal and Plant Health Inspection Service, National Animal Health Monitoring System. https://www.aphis.usda.gov/aphis/ourfocus/animalhealth/monitoring-and-surveillance/nahms/!ut/p/z1/04_iUlDg4tKPAFJABpSA0fpReYllmemJJZn5eYk5-hH6kVFm8X6Gzu4GFiaGPu6uLoYGjh6Wnt4e5mYGBr7m-l76UfgVFGQHKgIALYjxjA!!/. Accessed September 27, 2016.

U.S. Department of Agriculture. (2016b). Farm Service Agency. http://www.fsa.usda.gov/. Accessed August 2, 2016.

Chapter 3
Money Laundering Typologies Evidenced in the "Panama Papers"

There have been many initiatives in the war on organized crime. In Mexico for instance, the war on drugs has had a central focus, with strategies built on the involvement of civil and military agents and where records have been set for cash forfeitures, drugs apprehended, and extraditions. The war on drugs has also had a central focus in Colombia. On September 10, 2007, in the municipality of Zarzal in the northeastern part of the department of Valle, the Colombian army captured Diego Montoya, better known as Don Diego, one of the top ten most wanted criminals on the DEA, CIA, and FBI lists. According to Juan Carlos Garzón, this arrest was probably the most notable achievement in the war on drugs for that year, in which over 57,000 people were arrested, with over 100 extradited to the United States.[1]

Eric Olson reveals that there are many similarities between Italian mafia organizations and Mexican criminal gangs. In his view, "Mexican organized crime is more market focused, less stable, and less durable. Moreover, Mexican criminal organizations are much more willing to attack the state. Additionally, the violence they employ is more gruesome and has different goals, including intimidating their rivals and terrorizing the public. Finally, they seek to shape public perceptions about organized crime by targeting the media either through violence and intimidation or to control the stories that are published."[2]

With regard to Italian mafia organizations, Francesco Messineo observes that white-collar criminals "not only help the Mafia, but also commit crimes in their specific sector. This can be said of all crimes dealing with public bidding processes, even where the hand of the Mafia is not involved, although it generally is, or in such cases as corruption, collusion, and other well-known crimes against the public."[3]

Important initiatives in the war on transnational organized crime also occurred in Brazil. In 2007, Colombian drug Lord Juan Carlos Ramirez Abadia, also known as

---

[1]Garzón (2008).
[2]Olson (2012).
[3]Messineo (2010). See p. 301.

F.M. De Sanctis, *International Money Laundering Through Real Estate and Agribusiness*, DOI 10.1007/978-3-319-52069-8_3

Chupeta, was arrested in São Paulo and sentenced, with several others, to more than 30 years in prison. He was later extradited to the United States.[4] Other important actions were taken against the First Command of the Capital (PCC), a powerful criminal organization involved in miscellaneous crimes such as robbery, extortion, and drug trafficking in São Paulo. The police have also stepped up their actions in the shantytowns of Rio de Janeiro.

Despite these initiatives, organized crime is still active and adapting itself to enforcement efforts—whether by moving to new territory or spreading out its activities in the so-called baby cartels or micro organizations. It has kept up its strength through well-armed groups, assuring its control over extensive regions and the ability to respond to government enforcement efforts.

Organized crime has indeed defied government control, and not just in poor suburbs or rural areas. One Brazilian example occurred in May 2006, when over eighty people were killed, thirty buses set on fire, and a large number of private homes attacked because the government had announced the transfer of PCC leaders to maximum security prisons.

One of the most effective instruments for crime fighting is to cut off crime's financing, that is, to confiscate the proceeds of drug sales and to cut off, limit, and control the flow of money across borders. The movement of money between States through the transportation of large sums of cash must be stopped. Further, the illegal transportation of money through prepaid access cards, stored value instruments, and black market moneychangers must be stopped.

Money laundering can also occur through the mechanism of fraudulent payments. This involves fixing the price below market value, or simply leaving out part of the amount payable, and then paying the price in cash or some untraceable means and delivering it to the seller under the table. When prices are pegged at artificially high levels, the launderer may wish to have illicit financing of his acquisition and, to that end, will resort to bad appraisers and fake documentation. Any time such facts or possibilities are known to authorities, all of them mindful that such crime is well-financed, no crime should go unpunished because this will surely lead to increased perpetration by others and ultimately to the financing of terrorism.

There is much intelligence work to be done, more than that involved in simply controlling one's borders. Intelligence forces need to work together because if they are kept apart, each may, in isolation, feel that someone else is responsible for the problem.

Because money is fungible, prosecution has difficulties when money subject to forfeiture is mixed with money not connected to illegal activity. This is why some federal prosecutors in the United States have tried to seize and forfeit all of the money based on a facilitation theory. This theory is based on the possessor's intent would be a good policy. The intent test explains why a bank account involved in

---

[4]Record No. 2007.61.81.0011245-7/SP. Conviction in 2008 upheld by the Regional Federal Court for Region 3 (São Paulo and Mato Grosso do Sul). Criminal Appeal No. 0001234-26.2007. 04.03.6181/SP, heard on June 3, 2012 (Rapporteur, Federal High Court Justice Johonsom di Salvo).

routine transactions is not subject to forfeiture and why all funds in a transaction made by someone suspected of money laundering are forfeitable.[5]

We must therefore approach the problem from a technical angle, for in many countries, there is an atmosphere that fosters the adoption of solutions that are ineffective, scattered, poorly coordinated, and not cohesive, especially owing to considerable social inequality.

It is not at all uncommon for officeholders to announce before elections that they will establish strategies to take the money out of crime. After elections, little is actually done other than budget cuts to the detriment of public safety.

The perception that money laundering is a victimless crime must come to an end. Society, politicians, and journalists must give money laundering more attention.

3.1 Offshore Companies and Concealing the Beneficial Owner

We are facing today unusual methodologies to launder money. For instance, through artworks, football, churches or temples, and so on. What do these methods have in common? Certainly, offshores are been used in an extended way in order to make it possible for the owner of some properties to conceal them.

For instance, an interesting case was featured by the seizure of works of art, their forfeiture and cooperation between the governments of Brazil and the United States in repatriating several of them back to Brazil.

Defendant Edemar Cid Ferreira was found guilty in December 2006 and sentenced to 21 years in prison and payment of 73 days equivalent in fines (a total of 7980 minimum monthly wages, which is some R$5,187,000 or US$2,594,000), for racketeering, fraudulent management of a financial institution (Banco Santos S.A.), exchange quota violations and money laundering through artworks. His wife and

[5]Under this theory, clean money facilitates the laundering of dirty money by hiding it. In doing so, the clean money becomes involved in money laundering. Thus, the clean money is itself tainted and subject to forfeiture. The Racketeer Influenced and Corrupt Organizations Act (RICO) provides for forfeiture of the proceeds of racketeering and reaches tainted assets even in the hands of others, except for bona fide purchasers for value. To make RICO an even more powerful weapon against organized crime, the U.S. Congress set forth harsh penalties: treble damages, recovery of reasonable attorney's fees, and recovery of costs for the violation of acts prohibited under 18 U.S.C. § 1962(c). In *United States v. Certain Funds on Deposit in Account No. 01-0-71417* and *United States v. Certain Accounts*, for example, the court held that the entire balances were subject to forfeiture under the facilitation theory, adding that even if only part of the legitimate money facilitated the offense, the entire sum was subject to forfeiture. See Gordon (1995), Hamm (2004).

In *European Union v. RJR Nabisco*, the United States Supreme Court, on June 20, 2016, issued a major decision restricting the extraterritorial application of RICO. "The Court held that RICO's criminal provisions apply extraterritorially to a limited extent but that its civil cause of action applies only to domestic injuries suffered inside the United States." Jones Day Law Firm (June 2016). Supreme Court limits extraterritorial application of RICO. http://www.jonesday.com/supreme-court-limits-extraterritorial-application-of-rico-06-22-2016/. Accessed 24 Oct 2016.

others were also convicted and given harsh terms in the lower court. There is no final decision yet.

The complaint reveals the creation of the Bank of Europe (sometimes called simply "BoE" or "BofE"), based in Antigua, which was intended to operate, in an international version, transactions that were concluded at the national level with "frontage" companies. Offshore companies headquartered abroad and indirectly linked to the Bank in Brazil (Banco Santos) used the BoE to conclude operations considered illegal. BoE would present the same graphic structure of the meeting minutes of Banco Santos, in addition to the coincidence of the initials of the names of several of its permanent members, were considered suitable elements to delineate the narrow link that united it to Banco Santos. Formally, it was stated as the parent company BoE to Dome Securities Limited, named beneficial owner. Valence Enterprises Inc., the parent company of that holding company, was entitled "ultimate beneficial owner", as described in its Articles of Association. At the time of its institution, and because it had no physical existence, Beauford Financial Services Uruguay Sociedad Anônima was created, with the purpose of providing "technical support services and representation of foreign financial institutions and institutions", among others, aiming at the structure of the institution (BoE), as described in the Statute of Beauford. Some accused initially appeared as BoE prosecutors on a current account with the Swiss Bank Corporation of New York Branch.

The defendant Edemar stated that he and his family owned a bank abroad, the BoE, but that they could no longer be related to it (BoE). This would belong to the Trust called Friborg, which, in turn, was owned by Edemar's family. The name of the Trust, i.e. Friborg was changed to Eurotrust, with the support of lawyers. Just below this structure were the offshore companies Simington Investments Inc., based in the British Virgin Islands, Beauford Services, based in Friborg/Switzerland, and Beauford Bahamas, which controlled the BoE.

Their assets were confiscated (cash, computers, real estate, wine and works of art). The works of art were turned over to cultural entities (Museum of Archaeology and Ethnology at the University of São Paulo, the Paulista Museum or *Museu do Ipiranga*, the Museum of Contemporary Art at the University of São Paulo, Institute of Brazilian Studies Sacred Art Museum, the Latin America Memorial Foundation, the Navy Cultural Center in São Paulo, and the Secretariat of Culture for the State of São Paulo), to be permanently incorporated into their holdings—usually considered the beginning of the process of being declared a treasure by the São Paulo City Council for the Preservation of Historical, Cultural and Environmental Patrimony (CONPRESP).

The artworks consisted of framed art, photographs, archaeology, ethnography, sculptures, Brazilian regional literature and antiquities by renowned artists going back to the fourteen to ninth century B.C. (Togatus Romanus) and even contemporary pieces (Basquiat, Hirst, etc.), totaling over 12,000 pieces.

The decision was made to turn the defendant's home (Rua Gália 120, borough of Morumbi), furniture and all artworks within it over to the State Secretariat of Culture as they were deemed cultural goods subject to state protection.

Artworks that had been shipped abroad were also decreed a forfeiture, and INTERPOL was formally notified, which made possible the repatriation of some of the works through diligent efforts by U.S. authorities.

Regarding the final destination of artworks, there was an interesting debate in the Courts.[6]

---

[6]The understanding set forth in the sentence uttered by the author of this study is that a work of art, be it a sculpture, painting, photographs, etc., ought not to belong to any person or even to a given location, for here one is dealing with an asset of all humankind. To properly deal with this issue rather than become embroiled in economic discussions we rely entirely upon the Convention Concerning the Protection of the World Cultural and Natural Heritage passed by the General Conference of the UN Educational, Scientific and Cultural Organization (UNESCO) held 11/16/1972, stating that both works by men and notable places are considered cultural patrimony, and therefore protected by the Convention (Article 1), and that it is the duty of States to protect, preserve and present them for future generations (Article 4) and give them a function in the life of the community (Article 5). This was incorporated into Article 23, Subsections III and IV of Brazil's Federal Constitution, which charges the various branches of government with the protection of historic, artistic and cultural goods, so as to prevent their deterioration, and is also written into legislation under the Constitution (e.g., Legislative Decree No. 25 of 11/30/1937 in its Articles 1 and 24). No such treatment would apply to any other goods apprehended, seized or libeled in criminal prosecution, other than works of art. In the decision rendered, mindful of the valuation of culture and its diffusion to poorer boroughs surrounding big city centers, in confidential records of Cooperative Debriefing, the Sixth Federal Criminal Court for São Paulo decided to turn over 1/15 of the amount as voluntary payment to culture, thus: *Pursuant to the decision uttered in these records, on this date, I FIND: This court has earmarked sums obtained as voluntary indemnity in Plea Bargaining directly to charitable entities, duly listed with the court, and required to render accounts. This has been the established rule to preclude diversion of resources while obtaining a prompt, effective and useful result from Criminal Law, provided, of course, that the accused are in fact willing to disclose the facts and circumstances in all of their magnitude, and thereby fully comply with the requirements of law. It would be sad for a nation's government not to see in CULTURE a source of knowledge and meaning: INTELLECTUAL STIMULATION no less important. Our country possesses artists of capacity and renown, among them, Vik Muniz, Gustavo Rosa, Takashi Fukushima, Romero Brito, Tarsila do Amaral, Aldhemir Martins, Cândido Portinari, Galileo Emendabili, and Alfredo Volpi, more on account of their determination to make use of innate talent than of any government incentive. Yet it is not uncommon to receive reports of artists who lack the necessary resources to meet the costs of producing a work of art which, albeit important, is not duly recognized. Artistic activity ought not be burdened by lack of sponsorship, the more so if it is a valuable piece of work, oftentimes recognized only abroad. Society's concern for CULTURE, so evidently in short supply, makes this decision more than a mere gesture of institutional support. To support and believe in humanity, and full expression, is recognition indispensable to the benefits CULTURE has to offer: it evokes a sentiment in people, notably a feeling of reflection and pleasure, or sometimes one of conciliation and generosity. One could not, on this historic date, fail to mention the UN Universal Declaration of Human Rights of 1948, which declares the following:* Article XXVI: 1. Everyone has the right to education. Education shall be free, at least in the elementary and fundamental stages. Elementary education shall be compulsory. Technical and professional education shall be made generally available and higher education shall be equally accessible to all on the basis of merit. 2. Education shall be directed to the full development of the human personality and to the strengthening of respect for human rights and fundamental freedoms. It shall promote understanding, tolerance and friendship among all nations and racial or religious groups, and shall further the activities of the United Nations for the maintenance of peace. (…) Article XXVII. 1. Everyone has the right freely to participate in the cultural life of the community, to enjoy the arts and to share in scientific advancement and its benefits. (…) *Furthermore, Brazil, as a signatory to the 11/16/1972 UNESCO Convention Concerning the*

(Footnote 6 continued)

Protection of the World Cultural and Natural Heritage (promulgated by Ministerial Decree No. 80978 of 12/12/1977), is bound to "protect, preserve and present to future generations" cultural patrimony, including "works of man" (Articles 1 and 4). It should also give them, again, pursuant to the aforesaid Convention, "a function in the life of the community" (Article 5). It would therefore appear that this court, by the values it espouses, could take no other course than EXCEPTIONALLY find other than as it has and simply cannot let such an important opportunity pass. The presentation of an artwork that is exceptional in its magnitude and beauty, would allow all manner of persons to appreciate the beauty of it and to enjoy, albeit only fleetingly, a gratuitous moment of happiness. It would make no sense, especially given our overriding pedagogic and cultural function, to fail to recognize, even if symbolically, in this decision the manifest public interest, likewise expressed in legislation on the subject. The decision is therefore justified, even given the realization that this is no everyday event. Criminal Justice must exist for perpetuation of an essential Power: that of judging well, cautiously and prudently all of the questions placed before it. Nor could it shy away from making a decision, even if unprecedented. Our preoccupation ought not limit itself, pending better judgment, solely to the application of Criminal Law in its purest sense. It ought also to make of it, if possible, the best for society, without, clearly, straying from its original purpose. Article 23 of Brazil's Federal Constitution, in its Subsections III and IV sets forth the responsibility of all Branches of Republican Government to protect artistic goods, to the point of stopping their deterioration, which itself denotes understanding on the part of the constitutional legislator of the inescapable duty to protect and present works of art because they constitute an extremely important social value. Legislative Decree No. 25 of 11/30/1937, duly received by the Constitution, provides in its Article 1 the duty of Government to provide opportunities for access to and dissemination of CULTURE. It is incumbent upon the State Secretariat of Culture—with the assistance of the City of São Paulo, the district enfolding the criminal liability—to make such allocation as best serves the spirit of this decision which is, I repeat, an attempt to lend weight and substance to essential constitutional values. By way of example, we have as one of the fundamental purposes of the Federative Republic of Brazil, that of "ensuring national development" (Article 3, Subsection II, Federal Constitution), which encompasses all knowledge had by people in all fields: awareness of their own existence. This is to say, knowledge acquired directly, with no intermediaries, bringing about a pure reaction or interpretation from each and every one (collective right to public access, yet also individual, both subjective, to freely appreciate and express). One may not favor this or that artist, or reward some laudable stance. This is about reaffirming a value very dear to humanity and to our society, yet so distant from the ordinary citizen. In view of the foregoing, and pursuant to the Universal Declaration of Human Rights, to the Federal Constitution, to the aforesaid UNESCO Convention, and to that body of laws determining that all of humanity, from its humblest member, shall have substantive access to CULTURE, I find as follows: (a) Allocation of one hundred thousand reals (R$100,000.00), that is, 1/15 of the total received or receivable, to the Government of the State of São Paulo, which shall contact the City of São Paulo, the district enfolding the criminal liability, for its use to benefit CULTURE, notably its true purpose: to recover artworks or hold cultural expositions or provide direct access to same to needy populations, said use being AT ITS DISCRETION targeted to that end and NEVER to intermediate activities. If understood to be necessary it may, LIKEWISE at its discretion, suggest earmarking such funds or part of such funds to one or more nongovernment organizations of an exclusively cultural nature, whose purpose is to put on programs for the cultural development of low-income populations, it being incumbent upon them to use the funding for the purpose set forth above. The Secretariat shall notify the court in advance of the decision; (b) I also order, however, that after the decision by the State body, in cooperation with the municipality, to be given within 60 days, that a RENDERING OF ACCOUNTS be placed before this court within 30 days of all resources received by the State Secretariat of Culture; (c) One of the defendants shall set up a specific

The managers of *Banco Santos S.A.* took pains to give the necessary appearance of legitimacy to their criminal acts, even though, in compliance with the rules of the Central Bank, they did organize a department for the prevention of money laundering, which was itself unable to detect suspicious transactions by the directors of that very institution.

It was found that money from the financial management of *Banco Santos S.A.*, sometimes from operations in Brazil, other times from operations abroad, returning afterward to Brazil, was used to benefit managers and directors (who received large bonuses from affiliated companies *Alpha* and *Maremar*), when not from their own customers, and primarily from defendant Edemar Cid Ferreira and his family members, sometimes through persons from outside of his family environment. The diverted money was used for several different purposes: maintenance of cash flow for *Banco Santos S.A.* and its nonfinancial companies listed on its organizational chart, payment of bonuses to directors and employees, and investment in real estate and works of art. Finally, sums obtained through the commission of antecedent crimes were brought back into the formal economy with no connection to their shady origins.

Brazilian companies, whose partners are offshore companies, were provided with large sums brought into Brazil, in part through exchange contracts recorded at the Central Bank under the heading of foreign investments by partners, clothing them with legitimacy which, however, gave way before the discovery that these companies were credited abroad with money deriving from crimes committed in Brazil.

There was considerable resistance to the obtaining of vital information from tax havens, and the issue was resolved with the valuable cooperation of U.S. authorities who sent Brazil a considerable amount of important banking information that made it possible to access and check the names of those responsible for offshore companies operating bank accounts in the United States.

(Footnote 6 continued)

checking account, provided with the amounts established, and provide documentary proof of the fact in court within 24 *h; (d) Defendants may not interfere in the decision-making by the State Government, and must comply in full once they are informed of the purpose of the funding, and must make all necessary bank transfers. It is hereby ordered: That notice of this decision shall be served on the State Secretariat of Culture and on the Municipal Secretariat of CULTURE for the city of São Paulo. Serve notice to the Office of the Federal Prosecutor Serve all parties notice of this finding, which shall be part of today's decision. São Paulo, December 10, 2008. (60th anniversary of the Universal Declaration), FAUSTO MARTIN DE SANCTIS, Federal Judge.* The Second Section of the Appellate Court in Conflicts of Jurisdiction Nos. 76740/SP (record No. 2006/0280806-2, Questioner being the Office of the Public Prosecutor for the State of São Paulo) and 76861/SP (2006/0279583-9, Questioner being the No. 2 Court of Bankruptcy and Recovery for São Paulo), where the jurisdiction is, in both cases, the Sixth Federal Criminal Court, held on 05/13/2009, through Minister and Rapporteur Massami Uyeda, that the No. 2 Court of Bankruptcy and Recovery of the County of São Paulo ought to see to the recovery of the apprehended artworks, but only after the sentence handed down by the Federal Court becomes final, at which time forfeiture would be completed and it would fall to the bankruptcy judge to decide who are good faith third parties (see also De Sanctis 2013).

The unlawful acts could only be carried out, in theory, thanks to the efficient and comfortably large holdings of its controller who, oddly enough, owned practically nothing in his own name (no vehicles, no artworks, just two lots and an apartment in Pompéia in São Paulo).

For this there was good reason. The evidence produced showed that the holdings of Edemar Cid Ferreira and his wife, Márcia de Maria Costa Cid Ferreira, had no legal foundation. The property owned by the couple was always involved in events related to the diversion of money from *Banco Santos S.A.*

Indeed, as of their entering into the bonds of matrimony, in anticipation of events, they decided to harden their assets—actual preparation for the crimes they had decided to commit.

Márcia revealed that her husband had decided to keep his property separate in order to protect her from the ups and downs of his business activities, and also because, should bankruptcy occur, the couple's children could keep money having to do with the Bank. When questioned as to whether the cash spent in constructing the home at Rua Gália 120 might have come from her husband's activities at *Banco Santos S.A.*, she was emphatic: "Of course. On account of the profits he had at the bank, right? All of it, I believe."

She asserted that she was included among management personnel at several companies at the request of her husband, who saw to that in order to protect her. This strategy, in the words of the accused, was certainly in his interest while seeking to engage in the laundering of money. With the couple's every new acquisition, Edemar signed the property over to her, with the exception of the bank and the brokerage house.

Dissimulation as to the origin and ownership of sums used for the purposes named and the deception of Brazilian authorities became discernible on account of systematically repeated organization of companies and amendment of articles of association, most notably in tax havens.

On its organizational chart, *Banco Santos S.A.* was subdivided into several committees, each managing a given area. The credit area was called upon to approve Proposed Credit Operations (POCs) for the officers—the account managers working on the business platforms. In addition to this committee there was an informal committee consisting of Edemar Cid Ferreira, Mário Arcangelo Martinelli, Álvaro Zucheli Cabral, Ricardo Ferreira de Souza e Silva and Rodrigo Rodrigues de Cid Ferreira.

Acting as planned then, toward a common purpose, they dissimulated the origin and ownership of the proceeds of crimes committed against the National Financial System by the criminal organization using, among other mechanisms, conversion of part of the money into legal assets.

It became clear that the controller, with the avid cooperation of others, acquired assets thanks to the commission of financial felonies by a criminal organization which garnered him a large sum of money, real estate—especially the house at 120 Rua Gália—a veritable work of art,[7] in addition to thousands of other works of art

[7]The house cost approximately R$143,000,000 (US$72 million) to build in August 2004.

comprising one of the largest, if not *the* largest collection in Brazil, which sadly, was the result of unlawful activity.

The use of football as a way to money laundering can be summarized in the following typologies, well portrayed in the discussions by the Financial Action Task Force—FATF: acquisition and investments in football clubs; the international market for transfer of players; their “acquisition”; handling game tickets for unlawful purposes; bets; misuse of the image rights; sponsorship and advertising.[8]

Regarding investment in clubs, it can be said that many cases were reported by the FATF and ill-gotten money were laundered with the appearance of regular application in the economic system. In fact, football investments have not been clear enough. The darkness is a rule and causes too much trouble to verify the origin of funds because presents hard evidence of the entrance of dirty money. Investments have been made from amateur clubs to the most graduated ones, but it is curious that they often find themselves in precarious financial situation, requiring more and more resources, although some are the most prestigious clubs and objects of large commercial contracts.

There were reports of drug traffickers also invested in football. A case reported by Mexico showed that a humble person from the countryside moved to the coast and subsequently brought a vast amount of money and set up several companies. There was the acquisition of a soccer team in the third division, which had no reason to attract such investments. Salaries and infrastructure paid for with the new administration were high and the team finished climbing the second division. It gave some legitimacy to the investor, but after it was found that the investment had origin from drug trafficking, specifically from the network headed by him.

It is known the “emotional launder,” i.e., the possibility of investment in clubs without giving due importance to the origin of the funds invested. Investments in football can give rise to one secured favorable status.

Investments in the acquisition of clubs can be reversed through fictitious loans or transactions that actually would mean an effort to allow ill-gotten gains. The investor, through an agent, located in an offshore tax haven, buys players and the seller company pays fees through this agent. Such fees are passed on to another offshore controlled by original investor. The value of the fees is similar to the investments. To avoid such methods of money laundering, it is important to obtain appropriate documentation and further information in order to identify the people, the transactions involved and the source of funds for each club or player. It is also relevant to recognize the real beneficiary (beneficial owner) and the real controllers of the club.[9]

---

[8]Money laundering through the football sector. Disponível: www.fatf-gafi.org (http://www.fatf-gafi.org/media/fatf/documents/reports/ML%20through%20the%20Football%20Sector.pdf), accessed on Nov. 3rd, 2016.

[9]See De Sanctis (2014).

Regarding to the use of churches and temples as means for money laundering purposes, given the suspicion with new religious movements which are often regarded whether the faith as a whole is fraudulent, or whether particular instances of conduct are fraudulent.[10]

It is a well-known fact that some religious institution acts in a very controversial way when it comes to collecting financial resources through donations from church members—especially protestant churches of neo-charismatic orientation, which are commonly referred in Brazil as "evangelicals." On some occasions, there has already been reports and investigation from the press and governmental bodies based on evidence of criminal activity related to financial collection and administration. Some leaders of those organizations are, sometimes, target of charges regarding crimes such as money laundering, participating in organized crime, larceny by fraud, among others.

A high-profile case, one of the first scandals of this kind in Brazil, came out after the arrest of the Universal Church of the Kingdom of God's leader (IURD's leader), bishop Edir Macedo Bezerra, on charges of larceny, "false-healing" and quackery. After 15 days, the pastor was released, but, since then, the church was involved in many charges regarding various criminal activities. That is what happened in 2007, when some charges, made by state congressman Afanásio Jazadji, led to an investigation by Federal Police of Edir Macedo to verify the occurrence of crimes of misrepresentation against public faith, money laundering and tax evasion.

Acting under the command of Bishop Macedo, the money raised in the services was supposedly transferred to companies Cremo and Unimetro that, in turn, remitted it to other two companies based in tax havens: Cabeinvest and Investholding. The money would then return to Brazil in the form of loans simulated in contracts between the two companies located in tax havens and intermediaries, members of the group charged. The repatriated funds would then be used to buy media companies such as TV record.

According to the investigation by state prosecutors, adding atypical transfers and bank deposits made by people connected to the IURD, the financial volume of the temple from March 2001 to 2008 was nearly $4 billion. Such information was confirmed by the Council for Financial Activities Control—COAF (Brazilian Intelligence Unit).

Initially the case was filed in 2009 at the state court of São Paulo (Case No. 1121/2009) and the charges were upheld by a single judge, as following:

> *There are enough elements of materiality and indication of the participation of each and every one of the defendants in the infractions imputed to them for the criminal charges to be received.*
>
> *Indication of the commission, by the group, of the behaviors described by the criminal charges stand out from the case file, especially from: the Council for Financial Activities Control – COAF (Brazilian Intelligence Unit) report; from the successive atypical contracts (pages 115/285 and 978/995); from the financial operations that are incompatible*

[10] De Sanctis (2015).

with the economic and physical conditions of Cremo S.A. (pages 328/329), including interbank transactions (TED, transferência eletrônica disponível) with significant amounts received from the Universal Church of the Kingdom of God - IURD; from the information from the State Treasury Office and from the Brazilian Internal Revenue Service; from the statements of its ex-delegates and church followers (pages 422/426, 955/957, 968/970, 1246/1249); from bank statements; from other documents including those sustaining the preliminary injunction.

According to the result of initial investigations, there were many peculiar transfers of resources - that were allegedly collected through illegal means during religious services – to companies that were not really practicing activities consistent with its corporate purpose, but, instead, were passing them on to businesses interesting to the defendants. By effectively controlling legal persons or participating in simulated transactions, they increased private assets, without any exchanges, thus ultimately thwarting the goal of tax exemptions given to Churches. The dynamics of facts preconized by prosecution is consistent, theoretically, with the subsumption of the acts to the criminal offenses cited.

Thus, in face of a preliminary and perfunctory analysis of the aforementioned investigation data, the charges presented are reputed admissible, considering the presumption of innocence and the due process of law.

It is impracticable for the description of the facts to be more specific, for each defendant, than those presented in the diagrams contained in the prosecution's pleading, whereas the evidence of the adherence of each one of them to the undertakings is crucial for the establishment of the procedural relationship. Those undertakings are glimpsed, by the way, through: contracts signed – especially those supposedly simulated -, performance in positions within the companies involved, and personal references made by witnesses.

Considering the principles of the presumption of innocence and the due process of law, any profound evaluation of the inquest's evidence, any conclusion regarding the preceding behaviors, any final judgment about the simulations or any incursion in the subject of description and classification of the actions attributed to each defendant would be unnecessary and premature.

It is of interest the fact that the content of the indictment allows each one of those accused to defend and contemplates concrete cogent evidence, obtained during the inquisitorial phase, especially by virtue of investigations and documents' analysis. Under these conditions, the pleading cannot be considered vague or devoid of a just cause, thus authorizing criminal persecution under the scrutiny of an adversarial process.

Therefore, in light of the aforementioned reasons, I RECEIVE the current indictment. Let all necessary measures be taken in order to preserve the secrecy of the information referred to on page 120 of the appended records.

Let the defendants be summoned to present written responses to the charges within ten days, according to article 396 of the Brazilian Code of Criminal Procedure, altered by Act No. 11.719/2008.

In the summons document, let it be clear that those accused must present their responses through a lawyer and, in case they do not have financial conditions to appoint one, a Public Defender shall be appointed to represent them.

The court clerk charged with the summons shall collect forthwith the manifestation of the defendants regarding potential interest in appointing a Public Defender.

If the summon is done by letter rogatory, let the requested judge be asked to send us a copy of the court clerk's certificate by fax, not forgetting to send it by usual means.

Once expired the established time lapse, if there is no response, let the judicial staff certify the expiry of the deadline and appoint the Public Defender.

If there is response, let the case file return to me.

Let the criminal record be requisitioned, asking, first and foremost – independently from any other order, certificates from the Assignment Office, the Criminal Enforcement Judge of this jurisdiction and from the criminal procedures potentially notified in the first one, as well as the Criminal Enforcement Judge potentially indicated in the last, if it is the case. The documents shall be attached in their own appended records.

I grant the Public Prosecution's request in page 1274, item 3.

Let the orders be followed.

São Paulo, August 10, 2009.

Glaucio Roberto Brittes De Araújo

STATE JUDGE

The 9th Criminal Court of São Paulo—SP accepted the indictment against the bishop and nine other members of the church, arguing that there had been diversion of social purpose when resources from donations were employed on corporations that only sought to profit for church leaders. According to the indictment, part of the tax immune money collected by the church was transferred to fake shelf companies. Then, the funds were transferred to foreign companies on tax havens. In order to return the money to Brazil, these foreign companies used financial operations that involved money loans to natural persons on the Country linked to Edir Macedo, who allegedly used these funds to acquire companies, real estate property and other goods.

In October 19, 2010 (published on October 26, 2010), the case was dismissed by the State Appellate Court,[11] considering that when the charges involve international

[11]"2. From the analysis of the facts imputed to the defendants, a preliminary question arises from the case that must be faced before any procedural or substantial matter. It is indicated in the pleading that the money collected from Universal Church of the Kingdom of God's followers was transferred to publicly traded corporations CREMO and UNIMETRO, which, on their own turn, sent it to other two companies headquartered in tax havens, called "INVESTHOLDING LIMITED" and "CABLEINVEST LIMITED", located, respectively, on Cayman Islands (British territory in the Caribbean, south of Cuba) and Channel Islands (UK islands located near the French coast). According to the accusatory pleading, that capital sent to foreign countries would return to Brazil by means of simulated "loans" between "CABLEINVEST" and "INVESTHOLDING" and intermediaries owned by the criminal group. Then, repatriated money was, supposedly, used to acquire communication companies, such as it happened with TV Record. CREMO and UNIMETRO, led, in fact, by some of the defendants and formally directed by others, were, allegedly, according to the indictment, used to disguise and occult the nature, origin, location, disposition, movement and property of those expressive funds that came from larceny by fraud perpetrated against church followers and the religious entity itself. "CABLEINVEST" and "INVESTHOLDING", according to prosecution, constitute **"offshore companies"**, i.e. companies located on privileged investment zones abroad. They are located in territories known as "tax havens", where tax exemptions, reduced income taxes, as well as businesses secrecy attract companies and entrepreneurs searching for greater profitability and privacy. **"Offshores"** are subject of a differentiated legal regime, thus,

(Footnote 11 continued)

extraterritorial, when the residence of its owners and shareholders are taken into consideration. They exist, legally, because some countries adopted a radical policy of tax exemption aiming at attracting investments and foreign capital. Thus, the behaviors attributed to defendants involve, hypothetically, foreign territories, marking the alleged crimes of money laundering with a "transnational" character. Transnationality is a characteristic of a criminal behavior whose execution and fulfillment occurs on foreign territory, outside national borders. This theme is a subject of the United Nations Convention against Transnational Organized Crime, concluded on December 15, 2000, in Palermo, Italy, ratified by Legislative Decree No. 231/03 and promulgated by Presidential Decree No. 5.015/04. It is called "Palermo's Convention". In view of the insertion process of the Convention's text in national Law, it integrates our national legal order with a "federal act" status. This is the major position of national legal doctrine, which is aligned to the understanding of the Supreme Federal Court itself. A brief incursion in international norm is indispensable for full knowledge of the matter. Article 1 of the Palermo Convention states that "*The purpose of this Convention is to promote cooperation to prevent and combat transnational organized crime more effectively*". Its article 3, which disciplines its scope, is very explanatory regarding the meaning of transnationality. According to item 2 of article 3, " *an offence is transnational in nature if: (a) It is committed in more than one State; (b) It is committed in one State but a substantial part of its preparation, planning, direction or control takes place in another State; (c) It is committed in one State but involves an organized criminal group that engages in criminal activities in more than one State; or (d) It is committed in one State but has substantial effects in another State.*". In the present case, the money that was allegedly acquired by illegal means was supposedly sent to two "tax havens", integrated the property of two "offshore companies" and returned as simulated loans, which would characterize the internationalization of the offence hypothetically committed. With this evident transnationality, a matter arises regarding what court has jurisdiction to process criminal cases of money laundering and its related crimes. About jurisdiction, Act No. 9.613/98, in its article 2nd, item III, states that *"Federal Justice's jurisdiction includes: (a) those crimes practiced against the financial system and financial–economic order, or to the detriment of goods, services and interests of the Union, or its public companies and independent agencies; (b) those crimes whose preceding crimes are within Federal Justice's jurisdiction"*. Out of these expressly stated hypotheses, the jurisdiction would belong to State Justice. There are two situations (line "a") that can find their basis in the general rule of article 109, items IV and VI, of the Constitution, and a third (line "b") which arises from the connection rule recognized by Superior Court of Justice's Precedent No. 122, that states: *"Federal Justice has jurisdiction for processing and judging, in a unified manner, related crimes that normally belong to State jurisdiction, since article 78, II, a, of the Brazilian Criminal Procedures Code, is inapplicable"*. For part of national legal doctrine, Federal Justice always has jurisdiction for processing and judging money laundering offences, given the complexity of the legal subject treated, which certainly involves the national financial system. For Souza Nucci, as an example, "*when money is laundered, taxes are left uncollected and the national economy might get affected. In sum, in face of this, there is an interest of the Union and there must be an ascertainment within the federal sphere*". {*in* Leis Penais e Processuais Penais Comentadas 4ª ed., 2009, Ed. RT, PP. 834/835}. In spite of this venerable doctrinal understanding, I believe that jurisdiction must be verified in each case. It will be State Justice's if none of the hypotheses referred to in item III (article 2 of Act No. 9.613/98)—which, we must emphasize, is not a thorough list—is applicable. Apart from these cases, another determining factor for excluding State Justice's jurisdiction is precisely "transnationality", which makes it, in my view, imperative for Federal Justice's jurisdiction. I start from the premise that Federal Justice's jurisdiction is not limited by the three hypotheses of article 2, item III, of Act No. 9.613/98. On that non-thorough list, there must be the inclusion of "transnational money laundering", which is not present in Act No. 9.613/98, but is shaped and disciplined by Palermo's Convention, obviously, not as a different crime definition, but

(Footnote 11 continued)

as a subject of combat measures that must be created and implemented by signatory countries. It brought, thus, its concept. The aforementioned Convention did not create an autonomous international money laundering definition—it could not do so. In light of the principle of the necessity of a legal definition for crimes, it is indispensable that legislation—in the strict sense—must be enacted, according to ordinary legislative procedure and as manifestation of the will of the Parliament, for a criminal offence to be created. The Convention established, in fact, general prevention and combat measures against money laundering and corruption in general. It uses instruments such as confiscation and seizure of goods, special investigation techniques and international cooperation programs, for protection of witnesses and victims and, at last, regulating extradition. It also specified requirements for laundering to acquire transnationality outlines and, from that, the jurisdiction for processing and judging in Brazil must observe currently enacted norms, interpreting them systematically. Therefore, money laundering partially or totally fulfilled abroad constitutes, per se, a crime that induces Federal Justice's jurisdiction. In other words, transnationality constitutes another criterion, other than those given by article 2, III, of Act No. 9.613/98, for the laundering offence to be subject of judgment and processing by Federal Justice. Even if preceding offences are within State Justice's jurisdiction, transnationality is a determining element for establishing federal jurisdiction. That is what happens in the current case, in which the pleading mentions, as preceding offences, larceny by fraud practiced within religious organizations (article 1, item VII, of Act No. 9.613/98). Such conclusion arises from article 109 of the Federal Constitution, which, in its item V, determines that federal judges have jurisdiction for processing and judging "crimes predicted in international treaties or conventions, if, once initiated the execution in the Country, the result has or should have happened abroad, or vice versa". Now, transnational money laundering, as noted, encounters its definition in Palermo's Convention, ratified by Legislative Decree 231/03 and promulgated by Presidential Decree 5.015/04, inserting itself, in that manner, in our national legal order. Without doubt, it is an offence defined—yet not legally defined, or typified—in an international convention and, whose execution, initiated in Brazil, touched the territory of another country. It is present, then, another hypothesis that defines federal jurisdiction: if, once initiated the *iter criminis* of money laundering, any of the offence's phase (assets collection, occultation or disguise and integration) happens in Brazilian territory and abroad, then, based on article 109, V, of the Constitution, the jurisdiction of Federal Justice is set. Therefore, if the pleading attributes to the defendants the participation in capital laundering in which "offshore" companies, located in the Cayman Islands and Channel Island—safe havens to which the money that came from larcenies by fraud practiced against church followers was sent and then returned to Brazil as simulated loans, so that they could be used to buy companies, were used, then transnationality is constituted. We are, thus, facing a constitutional commandment, an absolute jurisdiction rule, whose strictness does not admit any alteration or prorogation, under penalty of violating the principle of the natural judge (Constitution, article 5, LIII). In sum, notwithstanding the solution aimed by HC No. 990.09.289589-0 was different—the closure of the criminal procedure in face of defendant Veríssimo de Jesus -, by better analyzing the matter, I review, in this opportunity, the prior understanding set and, by the aforementioned arguments, I recognize that State Justice has no jurisdiction for processing and judging this criminal procedure, as well as this Court for judging the current *habeas corpus*. The scope of the current judgment is limited to the recognition of the lack of jurisdiction of this Court of Justice, so much so that any other deliberations are hampered, for which reason the effects of this decision, regarding ratification or not of procedural acts practiced until now for this criminal procedure, constitute subjects exclusive for Federal Justice's jurisdiction. 3. For these reasons, by my vote, *ex officio*, I recognize the State Justice's jurisdiction does not cover processing and judging the proposed criminal procedure against the defendants, as well as judgment on the merits of the current *habeas corpus*, by which reason I annul the procedure since the pleading was received—including the pleading itself—and I determine the case file and the criminal procedure (Proc. No. 1121/09—

money laundering. It was granted habeas corpus annulling the criminal procedure, determining that it should be judged by Federal Justice.[12]

The charges in the 2nd Federal Trial Court were partly upheld by the federal judge Marcelo Costenaro Cavali on Sept. 16, 2011, as demonstrated by the following decision[13]:

> *Finally, the prosecution describes those mechanisms by which the money collected from IURD's followers was supposedly transferred in a clandestine and reiterated way, according to statements given by Waldir Abraão.*
>
> *One of these mechanisms for transferring unreported currency from Brazil allegedly counted with the participation of partners and operators, initially from IC Câmbio e Turismo Ltda., and, between 1993 and 2005, from Diskline Câmbio e Turismo Ltda. – based in São Paulo, with a branch office in Rio de Janeiro.*
>
> *Luiz Augusto Cunha Ribeiro and Cristina Marini Rodrigues da Cunha Brito, defendants in a criminal procedure ascertaining illegal transfers to foreign countries (pages 17/19 of the Police Investigation No. 2550-78.2010.403.6181, and pages 13/16 of the Police Investigation No. 2550-78.2010.403.6181, respectively), were partners at Diskline and described in detail the operations with IURD, which were summarized by Public Prosecution:*
>
> *'Between 1991 – IC Câmbio e Turismo Ltda.'s creation year – and 1993, when they became partners at Diskline Câmbio e Turismo Ltda., along with Sílvio Roberto Anspach, aka 'Fifo', a notorious money changer from this capital, the operations for sending values to foreign countries happened exclusively in Rio de Janeiro. Since then, IURD started to operate with Diskline in Rio de Janeiro and São Paulo.*
>
> *The aforementioned money changers' statements demonstrate the enormous amount of bills brought to currency exchange houses using vehicles and armed security guards from IURD. Marcelo says that the bills came in bags and many of them were 'crumpled, torn, glued with Durex, sweaty and scribbled', which made it difficult for the money to be counted by the machines at the currency exchange house. Higher value bills – fifty and one hundred reais – came from the so-called 'businessmen masses', with greater contributing capability. The values received were counted and checked, always in presence of a IURD*

(Footnote 11 continued)

control number) to be sent to Federal Justice, which has jurisdiction over the case." (*Habeas Corpus* n.º 990.10.247420-8, 16th Criminal Panel, Judge Almeida Toledo, in São Paulo State Appellate Court site, in http://esaj.tjsp.jus.br/cjsg/getArquivo.do?cdAcordao=4776713&cdForo=0, accessed on Oct. 12, 2014; Justiça comum não pode julgar caso da Universal, in Consultor Jurídico, http://www.conjur.com.br/2010-out-20/justica-comum-nao-competencia-julgar-universal-tj-sp, on Oct. 20, 2010, accessed on Nov. 03, 2016).

[12]FERREIRA, F. Justiça de SP anula processo contra bispos da Universal. *Folha.com:* São Paulo, out. 2010. In http://www1.folha.uol.com.br/poder/817422-justica-de-sp-anula-processo-contra-bispos-da-universal.shtml, accessed Nov. 3, 2016. The decision will be analyzed by the Brazilian Supreme Court (Recurso Extraordinário com Agravo, ARE n.º 737566, Justice Teori Zavascki, in http://www.stf.jus.br/portal/processo/verProcessoAndamento.asp?incidente=4375014, accessed on Nov. 3, 2016).

[13]*Habeas Corpus* n.º 0038794-85.2011.4.03.0000/SP, 5th Panel, Federal Appellate Judge Luiz Stefanini, (in Tribunal Regional Federal da 3ª Região site, published on Sept. 11, 2012, http://web.trf3.jus.br/acordaos/Acordao/BuscarDocumentoGedpro/2279490, accessed on Nov. 3, 2016). There is no a final decision yet.

pastor. Cristina stated that, because of the security needed to handle such a great amount of money in cash, she and IURD rented adjacent vaults in financial institutions and transferred the cash between vaults on such institutions. In other occasions, the cash transfer was made by putting the money in the trunks of some vehicles in the IURD temples' parking lots. Luiz Augusto, which left Diskline around the time of 1997, stated that, because of these operations for transferring money, he had intense contact with IURD members, mainly Mauro Macedo – Edir Macedo's cousin – and Paulo Roberto Gomes da Conceição. Luiz Augusto also gathered with Edir Macedo in New York. By that time, Edir asked him to study other ways to fulfill the operation structured to send values to foreign countries, so that these operations 'sounded legitimate'. On that occasion, Edir also mentioned to Luiz the possibility of IURD creating a bank in foreign countries[...]"

"[...] from the aforementioned reports, the accusation concludes that, directed by EDIR MACEDO, mentor of IURD's criminal policy, and JOÃO BATISTA, national president of the Church, ALBA MARIA and PAULO ROBERTO determined and oriented the illegal money transfers to the following foreign bank accounts, which received, according to documents adduced as evidence, millions of reais from IURD's believers between 1999 and 2005:

(i) *Chase Manhattan Bank – NY: (a) account No. 3100 6678 0465, owned by Genesis Holding Group; (b) account No. 140 094 221, of Lehman Brother Inc. subaccount No. 74326634-1-2-115; (c) other three accounts owned by the Universal Church of the Kingdom of God (IURD).*
(ii) *Republic Nacional Bank – NY: account No. 310 407 915 owned by I.F.P.C. Inc.*
(iii) *HSBC – NY: account No. 610 114 948, owned by T.I.F.P.C. Inc;*
(iv) *Northern Trust International Banking Corp – NY: account No. 238 522 of Merryl Lynch, as a beneficiary: (a) subaccount 163-07Q32, of Harman Holdings; (b) subaccount 163-07158, by Steele Resources or Steele Internacional Ltda.;*
(v) *JP Morgan – NY: account owned by Universal Church of the Kingdom of God (IURD).*

Based on these facts, the accusation imputes to EDIR MACEDO, as an organizer of criminal activities, according to article 62 of the Brazilian Penal Code, to JOÃO BATISTA, president of the IURD in Brazil and partner of Cremo, to ALBA MARIA, representative of offshore companies in Brazil, operator of Cremo, signed by her, along with PAULO ROBERTO, director of Banco de Crédito Metropolitano, succeeded by Credinvest Facility, the following criminal offenses [...]

[...] As to the crime of transferring unreported currency to foreign countries (Act No. 7.492/1986, article 22, single paragraph), I understand the indictment must be received.

The accusing pleading narrates the means by which the values were sent clandestinely to foreign companies had already been shown, in an incipient way, by the notarized statement of Waldir Abrão. However, more recently, with the statements given by money changers responsible for the transactions, the modus operandi was really made clear.

Such money changers supposedly were operators of IC Câmbio e Turismo Ltda. companies and, between 1993 and 2005, of Diskline Câmbio e Turismo Ltda. Luiz Augusto Cunha Ribeiro, Cristina Marini Rodrigues Cunha Brito and Marcelo Bismarcker, defendants in a procedure ascertaining the occurrence of the remittance of unreported money to foreign countries, were partners at Diskline Câmbio e Turismo Ltda. and described in detail the operations supposedly made in favor of IURD (pages 13/16, 17/19 and 20/22).

An important amount of money that would be clandestinely – merely by accounting operation – sent, as it happens in underground banking systems, came, according to

Marcelo Bismarcker, in bags, with many crumpled, glued, torn and scribbled bills. The money was supposedly delivered by IURD security guards, armed with shotguns, pistols and revolvers (page 20).

Luiz Augusto Cunha Ribeiro affirmed that the intense contact between members of IURD was done mainly by defendant PAULO ROBERTO, as well as Mauro Macedo. EDIR MACEDO also allegedly gathered with him in New York, where he supposedly asked him to search for operations for money remittance that 'sounded legitimate' (pages 17/19).

Cristina Marini Rodrigues Cunha Brito affirmed that ALBA MARIA was responsible for giving orientations about the clandestine remittance of funds, also stating that IURD was Diskline's main client (page 15).

Many documents were gathered that are able provide sustainable evidence to such statements, demonstrating, thus, the clandestine remittances (pages 23/77 and 91).

As national president of IURD, JOÃO BATISTA, along with EDIR MACEDO, was supposedly the one responsible for controlling the facts, orienting the way the funds should be sent abroad by illicit means. PAULO ROBERTO and ALBA MARIA, on their own turn, were, allegedly, the operational branch for these transactions, the members of IURD responsible for ordering money changers to send money abroad by clandestine ways.

The requisition for bank secrecy for the accounts that supposedly received money in this way was granted. The bank account statements and/or documents linked to accounts No. 365-1-024410, No. 365-1-018248, No. 365-1-007852 – kept at MORGAN CHASE – No. 365-5-00081565, No. 365-5-0010265 – kept at THE CHASE MANHATTAN BANK -, No. 610114956 and No. 610114948 – kept at HSBC BANK USA – all obtained by the international cooperation request completed by the USA, are contained in the CD appended to page 98.

Appended to the case file, there is also the notarized statement of Waldir Abrão, specifying this supposedly illegal mechanism (pages 153/175).

The underground banking operations correspond, in my view, to article 22, caput. The operation occurs with a structure for withdrawing currency at distance: an amount of a determined currency is deposited in the account of the seller in Brazil, which delivers a corresponding amount of money abroad [...]"

"[...] Only during the examining phase of the procedure it will be possible to compare all documents gathered with the pleading and the statements given by money changers, as well as other evidence, to ascertain if there was, in fact, remittance of unreported money in a clandestine way to foreign countries from Brazilian territory.

Thus, the pleading must be received, in order for the facts to be verified with due deepness, in light of the adversarial system and full defense rights.

In regard of the attribution of conspiracy (Brazilian Penal Code, article 288), the definition of the crime demands the association of more than three persons in a gang, aiming to commit crimes.

At first, the facts narrated fulfill the minimum requirements for the pleading to be received. In fact, it can be extracted from the pleading that the defendants EDIR MACEDO, ALBA MARIA, JOÃO BATISTA and PAULO ROBERTO allegedly associated, in a stable, longstanding, pre-adjusted way and with unity of desires for committing the crimes of larceny, misrepresentation and unreported remittance of funds to other countries.

Departing from the offenses of larceny and misrepresentation, as previously demonstrated, the money-laundering and unreported remittance of funds to other countries still remain.

One concludes, from the imputation, that the defendants acted in a concerted manner to enable the delivery of national currency in Brazil in exchange of the equivalent in foreign currency abroad by means of a clandestine mechanism– i.e., disregarding the Central Bank of Brazil control – known as underground banking. Also in a concerted way, these assets were sent abroad without any communication regarding its existence to authorities in Brazil.

The pleading shows - even though in a generic manner, which is admitted in crimes practiced within legal persons – the participation of each and every one of the accused in contacting money changers, attributing to EDIR MACEDO the role of leader of this kind of actions.

Supposedly, the defendants also acted in an associated manner in constituting and administrating shelf companies – Cremo Empreendimentos S.A. and Unimetro Empreendimentos S.A. – with the aim of occulting its true owner, which, in theory, can characterize the misrepresentation offense.

JOÃO BATISTA e PAULO ROBERTO allegedly were directors of Cremo Empreendimentos S. A. and ALDA MARIA director of Unimetro Empreendimentos S. A. EDIR MACEDO, on his own turn, as leader of the group composed by entities connected to the IURD, was supposedly the greatest beneficiary and mentor of these deceits.

All those accused were key figures in structuring the actions of IURD, which consisted in using shelf companies, simulated legal businesses and clandestine remittances of assets to other countries, always intending to hide, from its followers and competent authorities, the true owners of the high financial movement verified.

At the moment the pleading was received, the coherent narrative of the supposedly illegal facts is enough, at least, to give the defendants the opportunity to express themselves about the imputations, without disconsidering its reanalysis after written responses to the accusations were presented.

Lastly, regarding the crime of money laundering, the pleading attributes its commission to the accused, identifying larceny and criminal organization as precedent crimes (page 135).

According to the typical structure of money laundering offenses adopted by Brazilian criminal legislation, these infractions can only be characterized if a precedent crime – included in article 1st's list at Act No. 9.613/1998 - can be pointed out.

That is to say that capital laundering is a crime dependant on a preceding crime. If the illegal character of the supposed larceny offenses is removed, as demonstrated earlier, as a logical result, the imputation of money laundering cannot be sustained.

However, Federal Public Prosecution also attributed to the defendants the crimes of sending unreported currency to foreign countries, a crime against the national financial system, which is equally a preceding crime for money laundering, as stated by article 1st, item VI, at Act No. 9.613/1998.

In order to hide those assets that resulted from sending unreported funds to other countries, the defendants allegedly included straw-men as partners in their companies, even though these were not real owners.

Some legal businesses were also simulated – real estate sales in Niterói/RJ, aircraft sales of a Cessna, money lending – between Cremo Empreendimento S. A. and Record S. A. or IURD, which were able to demonstrate that these intermediaries were not the real owners of those companies.

At first, at least in this perfunctory analysis typical for receiving the pleading, if these facts are confirmed, then it is possible that some funds resulted from unreported currency remittance to other countries – which were covertly retransferred to Brazil, as described by prosecution - were occulted.

There are documents appended to the case file related to such businesses and alleged shelf companies (pages 140/152 and pages 115/285 from records No. 0001910-41.2011.403.6181), by which the Federal Public Prosecution intends to demonstrate that these offenses really happened.

The link between the facts, in my view, is complexly ascertained, in such a way it is not admissible to overcome the in dubio pro societatis principle that guides the judgment about receiving or not the pleading [...]"

"[...]In view of these arguments, I RECEIVE PARTIALLY THE PLEADING presented by Federal Public Prosecution in face of EDIR MACEDO BEZERRA (hereinafter called 'EDIR MACEDO'), Brazilian, married, religious entity administrator, born in February 18, 1945, bearer of RG: 26.995.020-SSP/SP and CPF No. 066.929.747-04, ALBA MARIA SILVA DA COSTA (hereinafter called 'ALBA MARIA'), Brazilian, married, economist, born in May 11, 1952, bearer of RG No. 26.995.020-SSP/SP and CPF No. 066.929.747-04, JOÃO BATISTA RAMOS DA SILVA (hereinafter 'JOÃO BATISTA'), Brazilian, married, economist, born in February 24, 1944, bearer of RG No. 1.984.491-IFP/SP and CPF No. 002.402.221.72, and PAULO ROBERTO GOMES DA CONCEIÇÃO (hereinafter called 'PAULO ROBERTO'), Brazilian, married, born in August 29, 1955, bearer of RG No. 336.540.777-49 IFP/SP and CPF No. 336.540.777-49, regarding the imputation of the crimes of conspiracy (Brazilian Penal Code, article 288, caput), unreported currency sending to other countries (Act No. 7.492/1986, article 22, single paragraph, first and second figures) and money laundering (Act No. 9.613/1998, article 1st, VI). I REJECT THE COMPLAINT, however, with regard to the allocation of commission of offenses of embezzlement (Penal Code, article 171, caput), based on article 395, I, Criminal Procedure Code, given its manifest ineptitude, and perjury (Penal Code, article 299, caput), based on article 395, item II, Criminal Procedure Code, given the occurrence of the statute of limitations claim. They include the accused to submit reply to the complaint within ten (10) days in which they could claim all that interests their defense and may give rise to their acquittal, provide documents and evidence, and specify the evidence sought, call witnesses, calling them and demonstrating the relevance of their hearing as well as their relation to the facts described in the complaint. I emphasize at the outset that, in the case of merely provides confidence witness, the witness must be submitted by written declaration, which will be given the same value. In that time, the defendant were aware that the expiry of the statutory period without manifestation, or in case it does not have a financial position to hire a lawyer, something which should be reported to the bailiff upon their communication, this Court appointed dative advocate to act on his defense, who should be aware, though, that he should follow this criminal action in all its terms and acts until the final judgment, in accordance with article 367 of the Criminal Procedure Code: "the process will continue without the presence of the defendant, who personally summoned or cited for any act, fails to appear without good reason, or in the case of change of residence, not to communicate the new address to the court." The defendant must be also aware that further subpoenas related to the case will be made in the persons of his lawyers made through published in the official press. Due to adversarial principle which must govern the Brazilian criminal proceedings for constitutional order, particularly in light of the recent reform of the Criminal Procedure Code, the initiative and subsequent evidential burden should be primarily in the hands of the parties and only complementarily in the

hands of that judicial body. Federal prosecutors are responsible to bring to the court criminal record/or other records about the defendants (article 8, II, III, V, VII and VIII of Complementary Law No. 75/93), because such papers relate to their institutional prerogatives (article 129, VIII, of the Constitution and article 236, III, Supplementary Law No. 75/93). Such information must be provided and attached to the file until the end of if, in accordance with article 231 of Criminal Procedure Code. In this sense, moreover, it has been oriented by jurisprudence (Habeas Corpus 200503000451893, Second Panel of the Federal Appellate Judge of the Third Region, Judge Rapporteur Cotrim Guimarães, published on Sept. 22, 2006; COR 2009.04.00.041563-0, Eighth Panel of the Federal Appellate Court of the Fourth Region, Judge Rapporteur Paulo Afonso Vaz Brum, published on Dec. 9, 2009; ...). The office must expedite up request for international cooperation for citation and summons of the defendant EDIR MACEDO in the U.S. The course of the limitations period is suspended until the fulfillment citing of defendant EDIR MACEDO, under article 368 of the Criminal Procedure Code. In addition, in view of the existence of documents in the record that are protected by confidentiality, and in order to safeguard the interests of any persons involved, I determine the confidentiality of the documents under article 792, 1st paragraph, Criminal Procedure Code, and article 155 of the Civil Procedure Code, by analogy with article 3 of the Criminal Procedure Code, article 7, 1, item 2, of the Statute of the Brazilian Bar Association (Law no. 8906, April 7, 1994). They should have access only by authorities who officiate the case and the defendants, according to Binding Precedent n. 14, Feb. 2, 2009, from the Supreme Court, and Resolution n.° 58, May 25, 2009, of the Council of the Federal Judiciary (restricted advertising). However, except for these documents that are limited to tax and banking data, I highlight that the decisions and proceeding are public, according to article 93, section IX, of the Federal Constitution.

São Paulo, September 11, 2011.

Marcelo Costenaro Cavali

FEDERAL JUDGE

On an international level, aside from cases as those above, some of the most famous scandals involving religious entities—this time connected to the Catholic Church—concern the Institute for the Works of Religion (the so-called "Vatican Bank").

So far, the most known crisis involving the Catholic Church was the sexual abuse of minors by some members of the U.S. Catholic clergy. The aforementioned crisis led to two fundamental issues regarding to how individuals with disposition to prey sexually upon minors gained admission to the priesthood and managed to remain in that condition even after allegations and evidence of such abuse. Although it is not possible to pinpoint any cause of the problem, it could be said that dioceses and orders would not have screened candidates for the priesthood properly, and seminaries would not form candidates for the priesthood adequately.

The United States Conference of Catholic Bishops in June 2002 considered a collective response to the crisis. The Charter for the Protection of Children and Young People, chartered by the U.S. aforementioned Conference, set forth national standards for dealing with abuse cases involving minors. The Essential Norms, which include, among other things, a mandate that nay priest who has engaged in a single act of sexual abuse of a minor be removed permanently from ministry.[14] It is not recommended feeling more comfortable forgiving, forgetting and immunizing, rather than punishing or condemning conduct that violated both canon and civil law, even where condemnation was demanded by the nature of the offence. The Catholic Church, assuming that priests bring the "word of God" to the "People of God," and that this would be impossible without a strong spiritual life, consider that sexual abuse represents a failure in maintaining a daily prayer life.

The Institute for Works of Religion (IOR) is a privately held financial institution located inside Vatican City. Founded in 1942, the IOR's role is to safeguard and administer property intended for works of religion or charity. The bank accepts deposits only from top Church officials and entities, according to Italian legal scholar Settimio Caridi. It is run by a president but overseen by five cardinals who report directly to the Vatican and the Vatican's secretary of state. Because so little is known about the bank's daily operations and transactions, it has often been called "the most secret bank in the world." Hence, the IOR is a sort of central body of the Holy See (as the Church's government is called) whose profits are at the Pope's disposal. Its purpose is to provide for the protection and administration of moveable and immovable assets transferred or entrusted to the institute and destined for religious works or charity. Financial transparency and successful cooperation with Europe's anti-money laundering agency Moneyval should continue to remain a priority for the institution, especially in recent years.

The Vatican bank is not a true bank. There are no check books. It does not make loans. It is more a fund deposit and transfer institution than a bank. The IOR generates income by placing deposits in short-term government securities and in interest-bearing accounts at other banks.

On September 21, 2010, Italian police declared that it was investigating Gotti Tedeschi and another manager from the IOR under charges of money laundering. On that occasion, 23 million Euros were blocked after a Banco d'Italia's division alerted authorities about two suspicious transactions from an Italian bank to JP Morgan Chase and the Banca del Fucino bank. The original account, as well as the two destination accounts, was controlled by the IOR, which allegedly defied Italian law by not declaring the origin of the values.[15]

As an answer to those suspicions, the former pope, Benedict XVI, established on December 30, 2010, a Financial Information Authority to supervise all monetary and commercial activities from all institutions related to the Vatican. The organ had the function of ensuring that such operations met the requirements of international

[14]"When even a single act of sexual abuse by a priest or deacon is admitted or is established after an appropriate process in accord with canon law, the offending priest or deacon will be removed permanently from ecclesiastical ministry, not excluding dismissal from the clerical state, if the caso so warrants" (A Report on the Crisis in the Catholic Church in the United States, in http://old.usccb.org/nrb/nrbstudy/nrreport.htm, accessed on June 26, 2014, p. 22 and 25).

[15]Vatican Bank investigated over money laundering. *Bbc.co.uk.* [S.l.], set. 2010. In http://www.bbc.co.uk/news/world-europe-11380628, accessed on Nov. 3, 2016.

norms against money laundering and terrorism financing. Apparently, as an answer to the Vatican initiative, Rome's prosecutor liberated the previously blocked values. Besides, in June 2013, Pope Francis determined the creation of a Special Investigative Pontifical Commission to evaluate the Institute.[16]

Shortly after the creation of this commission, a new scandal hit the Holy See, when Monsignor Nunzio Scarano was arrested under charges of aiding an attempt of smuggling 20 million Euros from Switzerland to Italy. According to the investigation, the cleric was accused of money laundering for hiding a sum of 560 thousand Euros, attributing to them, as source, the donations of worshippers.

In 2012, Italian prosecutors have detained the former head of the Vatican's bank after searching his home and former office for suspected criminal behavior. The Vatican's bank appeared to be embroiled in yet another financial scandal. After a number of very embarrassing episodes in recent years, Pope Benedict XVI pledged to comply with international standards on illicit finance and clean up the bank's image. The European Union had an important role to play in helping the Vatican mitigate risks and come into full compliance; the Financial Action Task Force (FATF) , set up by the G-7 to combat money laundering and terrorist financing.

The bank's president, Ettore Gotti Tedeschi, a well-known and well-regarded figure throughout European banking and social circles, was effectively sacked when the board passed a unanimous "no-confidence" vote in May 2012. Hired in 2009 with the hope that he would clear the IOR's reputation, he was fired, according to the Vatican announcement, because he failed to fulfill the "primary functions of his office." Tedeschi echoed this when he told prosecutors that he came to the office only two days a week, spending the vast majority of his time as the head of Spain's Banco Santander office in Milan.

According to Forber, it appeared that the Vatican's promise to comply was nothing less than controversial in the Holy See's inner circle. A book published in 2012 by Italian journalist Gianluigi Nuzzi details intrigue, corruption, power struggles, bribes, money laundering, and a lack of desire to follow the dictates of the Financial Action Task Force/FATF (from the Organization for Economic Cooperation and Development/OECD)—and its European sister organization, MONEYVAL (the Committee of Experts on the Evaluation of Anti-Money Laundering Measures and the Financial of Terrorism)—to fight illicit finance. The "Vatileaks" scandal, as it has come to be known, is based on over 4000 internal Vatican documents. It has embarrassed the Vatican and cast a cloud over its effort to demonstrate financial transparency and shed its reputation as a tax haven.

In November 2011, MONEYVAL carried out an assessment to determine how well the Vatican has complied with best practices, and to what degree it has

[16]Papa nomeia comissão de inquérito para o Banco do Vaticano: Integrantes responderão diretamente a Francisco. *Globo.com*. Cidade do Vaticano, jun. 2013. In http://oglobo.globo.com/mundo/papa-nomeia-comissao-de-inquerito-para-banco-do-vaticano-8818007, accessed on August 26, 2014.

implemented controls to curtail abuse of the international financial sector—according to MONEYVAL insiders. The Vatican had made a request to be put on MONEYVAL's money laundering "white list," a coveted grade in the international financial market. Both Nuzzi's book and Tedeschi's removal as head of the bank casted doubt on the Vatican's ability to achieve this status.

As the international community reviews its options vis-à-vis the Vatican, both the FATF and the MONEYVAL are uniquely placed to pressure the IOR to reform. Both organizations have scores of trained staff members who can assist the Vatican to implement a robust anti-money-laundering regime that would satisfy both the EU and the international community.

It would also be beneficial if the Italian government were to step in, given its close ties with the Vatican. Traditionally, the Ministry of Economy and Finance has designed the policy aspects of Italian money laundering and terrorism finance efforts, while the financial intelligence compliance functions fall under the Ufficio Italiano dei Cambi (UIC), in collaboration with the Guardia di Finanza (GdF). Italy has received high marks from the international community for its part in ensuring the safety and soundness of the international financial sector. Italian government agencies would thus seem to be the ideal candidates to lead the Vatican back to the straight and narrow road.

In July 2013, however, there are reports that the charges against Tedeschi—who had been ousted from its functions were dropped.

In July 11, 2013, Pope Francis signed a Decree changing the criminal law of the Vatican to make crime the facts of sexual and financial abuse or misconduct and the leakage of sensitive information.

In January 14, 2014, Pope Francis changed four out of five members of the cardinals commission established to deliver the conclusions of its recent analysis of the Institute for Religious Works to the Pope.

Last year, Pope Francis charged the pontifical commission with drawing up an "exhaustive" report into the juridical standing and activities of the Vatican's financial institution.

The pontifical commission—issued via a chirograph with immediate effect on June 24—is chaired by Cardinal Raffaele Farina and is composed of five people.

Retired pontiff Benedict XVI renewed the cardinals commission on Feb. 16 of 2013. Because members of the commission serve for 5 years, the mandate of the IOR Cardinal Commission for Oversight will expire in 2017.

Benedict XVI nearly confirmed all the members of the IOR cardinals commission: the then Secretary of State Tarcisio Bertone, and cardinals Odilo Pedro Scherer, Telesphore Toppo, and Jean Louis Tauran.

Only Cardinal Attilio Nicora left the commission as he was also president of the Authority for Financial Information, which could have leaded to a conflict of interest.

The cardinals commission is by custom chaired by the Cardinal Secretary of State. As Cardinal Bertone is no longer in charge of the post, Archbishop Pietro Parolin, now Secretary of State, would be inserted in the ranks of the commission.

The cardinals commission convenes at least biannually and oversees the compliance of the IOR with its statutory norms.[17]

The Pope has stepped up the fight against corruption at the Vatican by strengthening supervision of financial transactions at its internal bank. Pope Francis issued in 2013 a decree designed to combat money laundering and prevent any financing of terrorism. It was the latest move to stamp out abuses at the Vatican bank, which handles funds for the Catholic Church.

In 2013, the Vatican froze the account of a senior cleric, Monsignor Nunzio Scarano, suspected of involvement in money laundering. He and two others were arrested by Italian police in June on suspicion of trying to move 20 m euros ($26 m; £17 m) illegally.

The Vatican bank handles the payroll for some 5000 Vatican employees. It also handles the funds for the central administration of the Catholic Church and holds the accounts of cardinals, bishops, priests, nuns and religious orders around the world. It does not lend money and has assets worth $8.3bn (£5.4bn; 6.2bn euros). It was found that the bank had not always exercised due diligence.

The Guardian revealed that few passing London tourists would ever guess that the premises of Bulgari, the upmarket jewellers in New Bond Street, had anything to do with the pope. Nor indeed the nearby headquarters of the wealthy investment bank Altium Capital, on the corner of St James's Square and Pall Mall. But these office blocks in one of London's most expensive districts are part of a surprising secret commercial property empire owned by the Vatican. Behind a disguised offshore company structure, the church's international portfolio has been built up over the years, using cash originally handed over by Mussolini in return for papal recognition of the Italian fascist regime in 1929. Since then the international value of Mussolini's nest egg has mounted until it now exceeds £500 m. In 2006, at the height of the recent property bubble, the Vatican spent £15 m of those funds to buy 30 St James's Square. Other UK properties are at 168 New Bond Street and in the city of Coventry. It also owns blocks of flats in Paris and Switzerland.

According to the mentioned newspaper, the surprising aspect for some will be the lengths to which the Vatican has gone to preserve secrecy about the Mussolini millions. The St James's Square office block was bought by a company called British Grolux Investments Ltd, which also holds the other UK properties. Published registers at Companies House do not disclose the company's true ownership, nor make any mention of the Vatican. Instead, they list two nominee shareholders, both prominent Catholic bankers: John Varley, recently chief executive of Barclays Bank, and Robin Herbert, formerly of the Leopold Joseph

[17]Cardinal commission for Vatican bank could undergo changes, in Patheos site, published on January 10, 2014, http://www.patheos.com/blogs/catholicnews/2014/01/cardinal-commission-for-vatican-bank-could-undergo-changes/, accessed on Nov. 3, 2016.

merchant bank. Letters were sent from the Guardian to each of them asking whom they act for. They went unanswered. British company law allows the true beneficial ownership of companies to be concealed behind nominees in this way.

The company secretary, John Jenkins, a Reading accountant, was equally uninformative. He told the Guardian journalists the firm was owned by a trust but refused to identify it on grounds of confidentiality. Research in old archives, however, revealed more of the truth. Companies House files disclose that British Grolux Investments inherited its entire property portfolio after a reorganisation in 1999 from two predecessor companies called British Grolux Ltd and Cheylesmore Estates. The shares of those firms were in turn held by a company based at the address of the JP Morgan bank in New York. Ultimate control is recorded as being exercised by a Swiss company, Profima SA.

British wartime records from the National Archives in Kew complete the picture. They confirmed Profima SA as the Vatican's own holding company, accused at the time of "engaging in activities contrary to Allied interests". Files from officials at Britain's Ministry of Economic Warfare at the end of the war criticized the pope's financier, Bernardino Nogara, who controlled the investment of more than £50 m cash from the Mussolini windfall.

Nogara's "shady activities" were detailed in intercepted 1945 cable traffic from the Vatican to a contact in Geneva, according to the British, who discussed whether to blacklist Profima as a result. "Nogara, a Roman lawyer, is the Vatican financial agent and Profima SA in Lausanne is the Swiss holding company for certain Vatican interests." They believed Nogara was trying to transfer shares of two Vatican-owned French property firms to the Swiss company, to prevent the French government blacklisting them as enemy assets.

Earlier in the war, in 1943, the British accused Nogara of similar "dirty work", by shifting Italian bank shares into Profima's hands in order to "whitewash" them and present the bank as being controlled by Swiss neutrals. This was described as "manipulation" of Vatican finances to serve "extraneous political ends."

For The Guardian, the Mussolini money was dramatically important to the Vatican's finances. John Pollard, a Cambridge historian, says in Money and the Rise of the Modern Papacy: "The papacy was now financially secure. It would never be poor again."[18]

From the outset, Nogara was innovative in investing the cash. In 1931, records show he founded an offshore company in Luxembourg to hold the continental European property assets he was buying. It was called Groupement Financier Luxembourgeois, hence Grolux. Luxembourg was one of the first countries to set up tax-haven company structures in 1929. The UK end, called British Grolux, was incorporated the following year.

---

[18]Leigh, David, Tand, Jean François and Benhamou, Jessica. How the Vatican built a secret property empire using Mussolini's millions. Papacy used offshore tax havens to create £500 m international portfolio, featuring real estate in UK, France and Switzerland. The Guardian published on January 21, 2013 (in http://www.theguardian.com/world/2013/jan/21/vatican-secret-property-empire-mussolini, accessed on Nov. 3, 2016).

When war broke out, with the prospect of a German invasion, the Luxembourg operation and ostensible control of the British Grolux operation were moved to the US and to neutral Switzerland.

The Mussolini investments in Britain are currently controlled, along with its other European holdings and a currency trading arm, by a papal official in Rome, Paolo Mennini, who is in effect the pope's merchant banker. Mennini heads a special unit inside the Vatican called the extraordinary division of APSA—Amministrazione del Patrimonio della Sede Apostolica—which handles the so-called "patrimony of the Holy See."

Car Wash Operation was a criminal investigation in Brazil that revealed how money launderers use offshore accounts and conceal beneficial owners. Specifically, Brazilian construction companies Norberto Odebrecht and Andrade Gutierrez used companies in Panama and Uruguay to control accounts that paid kickbacks to former directors and managers of Petrobrás, a Brazilian oil company with mixed capital and state participation. These paper companies were used to open secret accounts, particularly in Switzerland.[19]

Mossack and Fonseca firm, revealed by the so-called Panama Papers (the International Consortium of Investigative Journalists—ICIJ information publishing), was subject to a judicial search warrant in 2014 in Brazil. There is some evidence that this firm also has been used to launder money for people linked directly or indirectly to Petrobrás.

The so-called Panama Papers (through the International Consortium of Investigative Journalists) revealed that the Mossack Fonseca firm was subject to a judicial search warrant in 2014.

Three offshore companies are being investigated by the Operation Car Wash task force in search for more evidence of the alleged involvement of Odebrecht and Gutierrez in the cartel scheme involving corruption and money laundering with Petrobrás between 2004 and 2014. With the respect of Odebrecht, there are two opened offshore companies in Panama and Uruguay: Constructora Internacional Del Sur SA and Hayley SA, respectively. Opened by third parties, the companies were created on paper outside Brazil to move bribes in a sophisticated money laundering, according to evidence discovered so far by federal prosecutors and federal police.

An article by journalist Fausto Macedo mentions the following statement by District Attoeny Carlos Fernando Lima about the offshore companies: "[T]he relationships that have been reported are of a relatively simple scheme and very easy to prove, because it was built here in our country."

A central player in the use of Constructora Del Sur by Odebrecht is the currency broker Bernardo Freiburghaus, identified by informants as a corrupt payment operator who lives in Switzerland and is considered a fugitive.

"The finding that Constructora Internacional Del Sur made deposits in offshore accounts of at least three directors of Petrobrás, Paulo Roberto Costa (former supply

[19]Macedo (2015).

director), Pedro Barusco (former engineering manager), and Renato Duque (former services director), shows its connection with the criminal cartel scheme and kickbacks that affected Petrobrás," stated federal judge Sergio Moro, according to the article of Fausto Macedo, in a decision that ordered the arrests of executives.

Documents held by the Operation Car Wash task force indicate that Constructora Del Sur was the source of at least five deposits made in secret accounts of Petrobrás's former supply director. Freiburghaus was be the operator of those accounts.

As the first whistleblower, Costa admitted in September 2014 that the $23 million he had in a secret Swiss bank account, which he returned after a tipoff agreement, were bribes from Odebrecht. Costa identified accounts in the name of the offshore companies Sygnus Assets SA, PKB PrivateBank SA, Quinus Services SA, HSBC, Sagor Holding SA, and Julius Bae, all at Deutsche Bank, were controlled by Bernando Freiburghaus but owned by him. One of these accounts had a value of US$9 million in October 2012.

The currency broker Alberto Youssef, also a whistleblower in Operation Car Wash, said to the federal court that he operationalized payments of bribes to Odebrecht, having been in contact with the executives Márcio Faria and Cesar Rocha. In this case, the path taken by researchers led to another destination: Hong Kong. Accounts were owned by the offshore companies FRY and DGX, a holder at Standard Chartered, and HSBC banks in Hong Kong, all controlled by the money changer Leonardo Meirelles.

Constructora Del Sur is also being examined for transactions with Odebrecht and the alleged bribery in the Pretrobrás services area through the former director Renato Duque. His former right arm, then Engineering Manager Peter Barusco, another defendant who confessed, confirmed the use of Constructora Del Sur by Odebrecht and traced the money to his account in the name of the offshore company Pexo Corporation. The former manager reported that Odebrecht did not perform deposits from its accounts, but instead used a registered account in the name of the offshore company Constructora Del Sur.

Report 0777/2015 from the federal police identified from bank documents that Pexo Corporation deposited US$1,020,672.00 from an account of Constructora Del Sur, held at the Union des Banques Suisses AG (UBS AG). The same report identified two deposits from account Constructora Del Sur held in Credicorp Bank S.A for the offshore account Milzart Overseas Holdings Inc., in the Bank Julius Baer, located at the Principality of Monaco. Renato Duque is the sole beneficiary in this regard, according to the Operation Car Wash task force and based on documents submitted by the Monaco authorities.

Constructora Del Sur was dissolved on August 25, 2014, five months after being identified as a suspicious entity in Operation Car Wash.

Other offshore targets of the investigations were Odebrecht SA Hayley opened in Uruguay and Hayley of Brazil Empreendimentos e Participações opened by former Odebrecht former executive John Antonio Bernardi Filho. There was evidence of the use of Hayley in bribe payments according to the federal prosecutors. Hayley paid bribes totaling US$125,000 (in Brazilian Currency Reais, R$406,250[20]) to Renato Duque. Hayley, represented by Bernardi Filho, also sold to the company D3TM Consultoria e Participações, opened by Renato Duque after leaving Petrobrás, two commercial properties in Rio in November 2013. The recorded value of the transaction was US$192,500 (R$625,625). Hayley was investigated by the Operation Car Wash task force after the lobbyist Julio Gerin Camargo said he used it to pay part of the US$30 million fee to lobbyist Fernando Antonio Falcon Soares, Fernando Baiano, and Nestor Cervero. Camargo said that Hayley kept an account at the Banque de Commerce et Placement in Geneva, Switzerland, where two installments of approximately US$500,000 were deposited in September and October 2011 at the request of Fernando Soares.

Andrade Gutierrez, in the report provided to the IRS, said that it hired the company Technis Planejamento e Gestão em Negócios Ltda., owned by Fernando Baiano, his sister Claudia Soares Furlan, and his brother Armando Furlan Junior, for a supposed service totaling US$950,000 (R$3.1 million). A judicial order breaking bank secrecy confirmed the transfer of around US365,000 (R $1,187,975.82) in 2007 from Andrade Gutierrez to that company (Technis), leaving unclear the transfer mode for the remaining amount. According to the Operation Car Wash task force, the "use of Technis Planejamento e Gestão em Negócios Ltda. by Fernando Baiano for the laundering of funds from Andrade Gutierrez and Petrobrás is clear."

Publicist João Santana, responsible for the political campaigns of former President Luiz Inácio Lula da Silva (2006), known as Lula, and President Dilma Rousseff (2010 and 2014), was aware that the money deposited in their accounts abroad had illegal origin, according to the federal police. He was one of the targets of the 23th stage of Operation Car Wash, initiated on June 22, 2016. According to federal police chief Philip Hille Pace, Santana and his wife "knew it was not a mere evasion of taxes. […] They worked directly with a person who was a representative and bribery operator of Petrobrás."[21]

The Operation Car Wash investigators also received information from Citibank in New York, which provided data through legal cooperation with Brazilian authorities. "Citibank's statements make clear reference that these deposits were made on the basis of false contracts to justify shipment of money," said the federal police chief. Santana was arrested, and his apartment in an upscale neighborhood of Salvador and his house in Camaçari were raided.

In all, about three hundred federal police officers executed 51 warrants, including 38 searches, two arrests, six temporary detentions, and five mandatory attendances.

In investigation continues as new bribes from operators linked to Odebrecht were discovered. According to the federal prosecutor Carlos Fernando Lima,

---

[20]On July 20, 2016, US$1 = R$3.25.

[21]It was extracted from Marqueteiro de Dilma sabia que dinheiro era de origem ilegal, diz PF (2016, Feb 22). UOL. http://noticias.uol.com.br/politica/ultimas-noticias/2016/02/22/marqueteiro-de-dilma-sabia-que-dinheiro-era-de-origem-ilegal-diz-pf.htm. Accessed 20 Mar 2016.

evidence was discovered involving a group of employees linked to Odebrecht and controlled payments abroad. The company's former president, Marcelo Odebrecht, was arrested in June 2015.

There is evidence that former president Luiz Inacio Lula da Silva, target of the 24th stage of Operation Car Wash, and his institute, the Lula Institute, received US $9.23 million (R$30 million) between 2011 and 2014, from contractors investigated in the corruption scheme in Petrobrás.[22] According to prosecutors, the former president and his family also received undue advantages from contractors, including payments for renovations of properties in Guarujá and Atibaia. Prosecutors say that they believe that the former president owns the real estate, but he denies being the owner. According to district attorney Carlos Fernando Lima, 60% of the donations to the Lula Institute and 47% of the amounts paid to LILS Lectures, Events and Publications (a company that has the former president as partner) came from major contractors involved in Operation Car Wash. Resources benefited people linked to the Labor Party (PT) and close relatives of Lula. Odebrecht, OAS, Camargo Correa, Queiroz Galvao, Andrade Gutierrez, and UTC are considered the central cartel that squandered the assets of Petrobrás, according to the prosecutor. According to the Prosecutor's Office were made "sizeable payments" of contractors involved in Petrobrás scheme in favor of the entity and lectures company.[23]

In sum, the details of Operation Car Wash in Brazil revealed the illegal use of accounts in the name of offshore companies, which makes it possible to hide the real beneficiary of the accounts, the beneficial owners.

On June 18, 2009, the U.S. Senate Homeland Security Committee considered a bill introduced by Senators Levin, Grassley, and McCaskill titled the "Incorporation Transparency and Law Enforcement Assistance Act" (the "Levin Bill"). The Levin Bill requires that states maintain an accurate and updated list of all beneficial owners of corporations and limited liability companies created in the state and make that list available to law enforcement and others by subpoena. "The [Levin] Bill's uncertainty over the definition of 'beneficial ownership' makes honest compliance difficult, and the risks the [Levin] Bill introduces of public knowledge about proprietary business information could destroy business development projects. The general philosophy behind the Levin Bill is founded on an erroneous assumption of reliable self-reporting of ownership information from individuals who are simultaneously engaged in fraud."[24]

The justification of the bill is thus described as following[25]:

---

[22]Há evidências de que Lula recebeu R$ 30 mi desviados da Petrobrás, diz MPF (2016, Mar 4). UOL. http://noticias.uol.com.br/politica/ultimas-noticias/2016/03/04/lula-e-seu-instituto-receberam-valores-expressivos-de-empreiteiras.htm. Accessed 22 Mar 2016.

[23]Força-tarefa aponta "patrimônio oculto" do ex-presidente (2016, Mar 4). UOL. http://noticias.uol.com.br/ultimas-noticias/agencia-estado/2016/03/04/forca-tarefa-aponta-para-patrimonio-oculto-do-ex–presidente.htm. Accessed 22 Mar 2016.

[24]Verret (2010).

[25]The bill hasn't been passed yet. It continues to be introduced by representatives. See https://www.congress.gov/bill/114th-congress/house-bill/4450/text. Accessed 4 Nov 2016.

Congress finds the following:

(1) *Nearly 2,000,000 corporations and limited liability companies are being formed under the laws of the States each year.*
(2) *Very few States obtain meaningful information about the beneficial owners of the corporations and limited liability companies formed under their laws.*
(3) *A person forming a corporation or limited liability company within the United States typically provides less information to the State of incorporation than is needed to obtain a bank account or driver's license and typically does not name a single beneficial owner.*
(4) *Criminals have exploited the weaknesses in State formation procedures to conceal their identities when forming corporations or limited liability companies in the United States, and have then used the newly created entities to commit crimes affecting interstate and international commerce such as terrorism, drug trafficking, money laundering, tax evasion, securities fraud, financial fraud, and acts of foreign corruption.*
(5) *Law enforcement efforts to investigate corporations and limited liability companies suspected of committing crimes have been impeded by the lack of available beneficial ownership information, as documented in reports and testimony by officials from the Department of Justice, the Department of Homeland Security, the Financial Crimes Enforcement Network of the Department of the Treasury, the Internal Revenue Service, the Government Accountability Office, and others.*
(6) *In July 2006, a leading international anti-money laundering organization, the Financial Action Task Force on Money Laundering (in this section referred to as the "FATF"), of which the United States is a member, issued a report that criticizes the United States for failing to comply with a FATF standard on the need to collect beneficial ownership information and urged the United States to correct this deficiency by July 2008.*
(7) *In response to the FATF report, the United States has repeatedly urged the States to strengthen their incorporation practices by obtaining beneficial ownership information for the corporations and limited liability companies formed under the laws of such States.*
(8) *Many States have established automated procedures that allow a person to form a new corporation or limited liability company within the State within 24 h of filing an online application, without any prior review of the application by a State official. In exchange for a substantial fee, 2 States will form a corporation within 1 h of a request.*
(9) *Dozens of Internet Web sites highlight the anonymity of beneficial owners allowed under the incorporation practices of some States, point to those practices as a reason to incorporate in those States, and list those States together with offshore jurisdictions as preferred locations for the formation of new corporations, essentially providing an open invitation to criminals and other wrongdoers to form entities within the United States.*
(10) *In contrast to practices in the United States, all 28 countries in the European Union are required to have formation agents identify the beneficial owners of the corporations formed under the laws of the country.*
(11) *To reduce the vulnerability of the United States to wrongdoing by United States corporations and limited liability companies with hidden owners, to protect interstate and international commerce from criminals misusing United States corporations and limited liability companies, to strengthen law enforcement investigations of suspect corporations and limited liability companies, to set minimum standards for and level the playing field among State incorporation practices, and to bring the United States*

> *into compliance with its international anti-money laundering standards, Federal legislation is needed to require the States to obtain beneficial ownership information for the corporations and limited liability companies formed under the laws of such States.*

U.S. House Representatives Carolyn B. Maloney and Peter King reintroduced their legislation in the House of Representatives to require the disclosure of a corporation's beneficial owner on February 3, 2016.

According to Carolyn B. Maloney, the introduction of the Incorporation Transparency and Law Enforcement Assistance Act follows a groundbreaking investigation by Global Witness, which exposed the common practice of using U.S.-based shell corporations to launder money linked to criminal enterprises. She considers "this is unacceptable, and it has to stop. Our national security and our law enforcement priorities depend on it. And it is the right thing to do: our legal system should not protect the rights of bad people to do bad things in secret. The bill I am introducing this week would require the states to obtain information about the true ownership of the corporation when incorporation papers are filed with the state. And if the states don't collect this information, then the Treasury Department would. Our message is simple: tell us who the real owner is, or take your business elsewhere."

For his part, Peter King stated that "criminals are taking advantage of state laws by establishing firms—often without a physical presence or business activity—to access our banking system."

So the Incorporation Transparency and Law Enforcement Assistance Act would target this problem by requiring a company that has the characteristics of a shell corporation to disclose who benefits from the company's operations and makes that information available only to law enforcement.[26]

At the beginning of 2016, the Brazilian IRS set out to establish rules for defining "final beneficiary" or "beneficial owners" of legal entities and legal arrangements, such as trusts and asset managers, especially for those located outside the country. IRS Normative Instruction No. 1634, of May 6, 2016, defines the final beneficiary as the natural person who ultimately, directly or indirectly, has, controls, or significantly influences a particular entity. The Legal Companies National Registry's knowledge of this relationship is essential for tax and customs administration and for proper accountability and punishment of the behaviors outside the law (article 8). The Normative Instruction closed a gap in Brazil with regard to access to information by supervisory, prosecutorial, and enforcement bodies. Furthermore, opening procedures, modification, and closure of companies have become more simplified. The obligation to inform the final beneficiaries has a specific deadline,

[26]Reps. Maloney, King and Senator Whitehouse introduce bills to stop anonymous money laundering operations by requiring disclosure of shell corporation beneficial owners, Carolyn B. Maloney Press Release https://maloney.house.gov/media-center/press-releases/reps-maloney-king-and-senator-whitehouse-introduce-bills-to-stop. Published 3 Feb 2016, accessed 5 Nov 2016.

allowing the adaptation of the register of investors to Brazilian rules, up to the limit of December 31, 2018 (article 52).[27]

On the other hand, the Financial Crimes Enforcement Network (FinCEN), the U.S. financial intelligence unit, amended the existing Bank Secrecy Act regulations to clarify and strengthen customer due diligence (CDD) requirements for certain financial institutions. According to the FinCEN guidance, the "CDD Rule outlines explicit customer due diligence requirements and imposes a new requirement for these financial institutions to identify and verify the identity of beneficial owners of legal entity customers, subject to certains exclusions and exemptions. Within this construct, as stated in the preamble to the Rule, FinCEN intends that the legal entity customer identify its ultimate beneficial owner or owners and not 'nominees' or 'straw men.' The CDD Rule applies to covered financial institutions, i.e., federally regulated banks and federally insured credit unions, mutual funds, brokers or dealers in securities, futures commission merchants, and introducing brokers in commodities. The CDD Rule requires covered financial institutions to establish and maintain written procedures that are reasonably designed to identify and verify the beneficial owners of legal entity customers. These procedures must enable the institution to identify the beneficial owners of each customer at the time a new account is opened, unless the customer is otherwise excluded or the account is

---

[27]Article 8 reads as follows:

The registration information relating to the entities and entities referred to in sections V, XV, XVI and XVII of the caput of art. 4 shall cover the persons authorized to represent them, as well as the chain of ownership interest, to reach individuals characterized as final beneficiaries or any of the entities mentioned in § 3.

§ 1. For the purposes of the caput, it is considered final beneficiary:

I—the natural person who ultimately, directly or indirectly owns, controls or significantly influences the entity; or

II—the natural person on whose behalf a transaction is conducted.

§ 2. It is assumed significant influence, referred to in § 1, when the natural person:

I—has more than 25% (twenty five percent) of the capital of the entity, directly or indirectly; or

II—directly or indirectly holds or exercises the preponderance in corporate resolutions and the power to elect a majority of the entity's management, even without controlling it.

§ 3 Exempt from the provisions in the heading:

I—legal entities incorporated as a public company in Brazil or in countries that require public disclosure of all shareholders considered relevant and are not incorporated in jurisdictions with favorable tax or subject to preferential tax regime that in arts. 24 and 24-A of Law 9430 of December 27, 1996;

II—nonprofit entities that do not act as fiduciary managers and are not incorporated in jurisdictions with favorable tax or subject to preferential tax regime that in arts. 24 and 24-A of Law No. 9430, of 1996, provided that regulated and supervised by government authorities;

III—multilateral organizations, central banks, government agencies or linked to sovereign wealth funds;

IV—the pension funds, pension funds and similar institutions, if regulated and supervised by government authorities in the country or in their country of origin; and

V—national investment funds regulated by the Securities and Exchange Commission, provided it is informed to the RFB in e-Financial the Register of Individuals (CPF) or CNPJ of unit holders of each fund managed by it. Instrução Normativa RFB no. 1634 (2016, May 6). http://normas.receita.fazenda.gov.br/sijut2consulta/link.action?idAto=73658. Accessed 5 Aug 2016.

exempted. Also, the procedures must establish risk-based practices for verifying the identity of each beneficial owner identified to the covered financial institution, to the extent reasonable and practicable. The procedures must contain the elements required for verifying the identity of customers that are individuals under applicable customer identification program ("CIP") requirements. In short, covered financial institutions are now required to obtain, verify, and record the identities of the beneficial owners of legal entity customers. The CDD Rule amends the AML program requirements for each covered financial institution to explicitly require covered institutions to implement and maintain appropriate risk-based procedures for conducting ongoing customer due diligence, to include: understanding the nature and purpose of the customer relationships; and conducting ongoing monitoring to identify and report suspicious transactions and, on a risk basis, to maintain and update customer information."[28]

The CDD Rule requires title insurance companies to identify the real owners behind shell companies making all cash purchases for high-end real estate applying only where there is no mortgage issued, and at least some of the proceeds are paid in currency or bank checks, personal business checks, traveler's checks, or money orders.

Also, the expanded geographic targeting order, which came into effect Aug. 28, went beyond Manhattan and Miami to include all five boroughs of New York City, as well as two more counties in southern Florida, Los Angeles, the San Francisco area and the county that includes San Antonio, Texas.

The order requires title insurance companies to identify the real owners behind shell companies making all-cash purchases for high-end real estate in each of the markets. It applies only where there is no mortgage issued, and at least some of the proceeds are paid in currency or bank checks, personal business checks, traveler's checks or money orders.

Treasury's Financial Crimes Enforcement Network—FinCEN, stated that "a significant portion" of the purchases covered in the initial order "indicated possible criminal activity" associated with the individuals reported to be beneficial owners behind shell company purchasers in Miami and Manhattan. It "corroborates FinCEN's concerns" that the transactions covered by the order are vulnerable to money laundering, and state and local authorities told FinCEN that information generated by the initial order has generated leads and "provided greater insight" into potential assets held by people of investigative interest.

Under the expanded order, all-cash purchases of real estate in Brooklyn, Queens, the Bronx and Staten Island of more than $1.5 million would be covered. Purchases in cash of more than $2 million in San Diego, Los Angeles, San Francisco, San Mateo and Santa Clara counties would be covered. In Florida, cash purchases of more than $1 million in Broward and Palm Beach counties would require the disclosure. And in Bexar County, Texas, which includes San Antonio, cash

---

[28]U.S. Department of Treasury (2016).

purchases of more than $500,000 would be tracked. The requirements on Manhattan ($3 million) and Miami ($1 million) remain the same.[29]

By June 2016, the Panama Papers had already identified 214,000 shell companies with hundreds of thousands of people behind them, including impressive names from political figures and business moguls to celebrities. In the wake of all these discoveries, the importance of due diligence to identify beneficial owners and final beneficiaries and to monitor transactions and payments has become even more significant. Certainly, there is increasingly greater international and political interest around shell companies and their role in anti-money laundering and tax avoidance activity.

The Panama Papers has affected correspondent banking and third party entity identification, with possible transaction monitoring. The issue raises glaring gaps in anti-money regulations and possible implications for global banks.[30] As banks mitigate risk and keep in line with existing compliance requirements, forensic accountants will find themselves quite busy and recruited by financial institutions. There will be more stringent guidelines to follow and more stringent Know Your Customer procedures. Banks have to flag and or block transactions directly associated with Mossack Fonseca (a prolific generator of offshore shell companies and questionable accounting advisory services) to comply with Know Your Client and internal processes. Regulators will alter their expectations in relation to customers, who must be reclassified and subject to Know Your Customer (KYC), Customer Due Diligence (CDD), Politically Exposed Persons (PEPs), and Transaction Monitoring (TM) processes and evaluations. In the wake of the Panama Papers, significant revisions and updates will be necessary for any clients identified. The cost of declaring "innocent" will be expensive and individuals and firms may take a significant hit on their reputations.

The collective consciousness of how risky banking has become is clear. For example, on February 23, 2016, Bahraini authorities discussed with the U.S. Treasury the problem of international banks becoming reluctant to deal with banks in Bahrain and the Gulf because of tight U.S. regulations. Bahrain's central bank governor, Rasheed Mohammed al-Maraj, commented that "[m]any international banks have curtailed their correspondent services with regional and local banks. Some of the banks have refrained from dealing with exchange houses.... This has affected a wide sector of the population, especially the expatriates." The tight U.S. regulations include scrutiny for potential tax avoidance and anti-money laundering rules. These impose extra costs on U.S. banks, prompting many to reduce the number of foreign institutions with which they do business, and making international banks operating in the United States more wary of ties with the Gulf.

According to an article in Reuters, "Some banks in the Gulf have been under particularly close scrutiny by U.S. authorities because of a drive to curb financing of

---

[29]U.S. Department of Treasury (2016, July 19). FinCEN Expands Reach of Real Estate "Geographic Targeting Orders" Beyond Manhattan and Miami, Fincen site, https://www.fincen.gov/news/news-releases/fincen-expands-reach-real-estate-geographic-targeting-orders-beyond-manhattan. Accessed 4 Nov 2016.

[30]Grewal (2016).

Islamist militancy and flows of money to Iran. United Arab Emirates (UAE) central bank governor Mubarak Rashid al-Mansouri complained of the problem in December, saying it had become harder for UAE banks to obtain dollar clearance services—the processing of transactions in the U.S. currency. Maraj said Bahrain was engaging with U.S. authorities including the Federal Reserve and the Office of the Comptroller of the Currency, as well as with international banks, to convince them that the compliance standards of Bahraini and Gulf banks were in line with global practices."[31]

The questions here are: can the credibility of any action against money laundering imposed by international law greatly undermine the inclusion of measures aimed at limiting international tax competition? May favorable tax regimes coexist with actions against financial crime?

"Interests of the powerful have dominated discourse in a rapidly changing globalized world, and the shift of power from the people to the market and from state to the corporation under the rubric of globalization has resulted in imbalanced structures of international trade and investment, uneven distribution of new technologies and an unjust allocation of resources as well as employment practices that work against the interests of the poor."[32]

Deterring money laundering today requires the adoption of comprehensive transparency-enhancing measures, as well as the abandonment of various regulatory and corporate devices allowing for investor anonymity and the non-traceability of assets. Persistently noncooperative Offshore Financial Centers (OFCs) may and should be deemed to be violating their obligations under international law with respect to fighting crime. These OFCs, for sure, according to Antoine Cousin and Jean Albert, "contribute to the occurrence of a continuous damage that the OECD countries should consider remedying."[33] This has no opposition.

In addition to the Panama Papers, Bahamas Leaks has revealed owners of offshore accounts involving front companies that were used to conceal money.[34]

3.1.1 Remittance Companies and Black Market Moneychangers

According to Michael Levi and Peter Reuter, "by the early twenty-first century (and long before), there was a large and growing range of methods for moving money across international boundaries, yet another facet of globalization. Thus there has

[31]Al Sayegh and Torchia (2016).

[32]Mubangizi (2007) quoting Das L. "The spectre of poverty in the Commonwealth: A serious violation of human rights?" http://www.jha.ac/books/br025.htm (accessed 1 March 2006).

[33]Cousin and Albert (2002, p. 89).

[34]Vazamento revela ligação de políticos com offshores nas Bahamas (2016).

evolved a highly differentiated set of financial institutions to meet the needs of various population groups such as low-income migrant workers who repatriate earnings home to poorer countries, very rich investors seeking to find the most politically secure and profitable location for their capital, and a broad array of businesses, from jewelry shops and car dealers to financial services firms themselves."[35]

When people or companies seek to send or receive money from unlawful behavior across national borders, undetected by government institutions, they have come to rely more and more on transfers known as dollar wires or Euro wire, operated by agents known as dollar changers (*doleiros*) whose activities stretch the legal envelope.

Along these lines, Terry Goddard informs us that the Arizona Financial Crimes Task Force searches for financial anomalies, disproportionate events unconnected with economic reality. "They immediately saw that Arizona was a huge net importer of wired funds. At the top-ten Arizona wired-funds locations, over $100 were coming in for every dollar wired out. Wire transfers into Arizona from other states, in amounts over $500, totaled more than $500 million per year. Since there was no apparent business reason for this imbalance, the investigators took a closer look."[36]

To preclude the use of fake identities for structuring or fragmentation of operations by companies and individuals in order to keep below the regulatory daily limit of $10,000, which would justify reporting the operation to the authorities, the State of Arizona established Geographic Targeting Orders (GTOs) that require additional identification, such as fingerprints and signatures from all persons receiving wire transfers in excess of $500. Based on such information, 25 warrants were issued in 2001 through 2006 for the seizure of wire transfers supposedly made in payment for human smuggling or narcotics trafficking.[37]

The FATF recommends that participating nations obtain detailed information on all parties to wire transfers, both senders and beneficiaries, for monitoring purposes. This would enable the barring of transactions by certain people in accordance with UN Security Council Resolutions 1269/1999 and 1373/2001 on the prevention of terrorism and its financing (Recommendation No. 16).

The idea is eliminating the flow of funds through underground channels by making formal channels a better option for consumers.

Brazil's foreign exchange legislation spells out a number of issues that are often unheard of, even in the United States. Take, for instance, Law No. 4131 of October 19, 1962,[38] which requires contracts for currency exchange operations in its Sect. 7, included by Law No. 11371/2006:

---

[35]Levi and Reuter (2006, p. 293).

[36]Goddard (2012).

[37]Goddard (2012).

[38]In www.planalto.gov.br/ccivil_03_leis)L4131.htm. Accessed 16 July 2016.

Article 23. Operations on the free exchange rate market shall be conducted through establishments licensed to conduct foreign-exchange operations, with the intervention of an official broker whenever the law or regulations so provide, both of entities being required to know the client's identity, and how to correctly classify information provided by said client, pursuant to regulations established by Brazil's Currency and Credit Authority.

(…)

§ 2 False statements of identity on the form which, in number of copies and following the model established by the Brazilian Central Bank shall be required in each operation to be signed by the client and checked and initialed by the banking establishment and broker therein intervening, shall render the banking establishment subject to charges for infraction, which carry a penalty of a fine in the amount of fifty percent (50%) to three hundred percent (300%) of the amount of the operation assessed against each of the violators. (New language given by Law No. 9069 of 1995)

(…)

§ 7 Completion of the form referenced in § 2 of this article is not required for foreign currency purchase and sale operations of up to three thousand dollars (US$3000) or its equivalent in other currency. (Included by Law No. 11371 of 2006).[39]

Because of Brazil's currency exchange regulations, remittance companies are required to conduct all of their operations exclusively through financial institutions duly licensed by Brazil's Central Bank, and this also holds for international banking institutions. They must have agreements on file with accredited banks to engage in exchange operations in Brazil, under penalties provided by several regulations, in particular, Law No. 9069 of June 29, 1995 (the *Lei do Plano Real*),[40] which established the *real* as Brazil's legal tender. It is the currency used to settle all transactions in Brazil.

Its Article 65 provides:

The entry into and departure from Brazil of domestic and foreign currency must be processed exclusively through bank transfers, where banking establishments are required to fully establish the identity of the customer or beneficiary.

§ 1 Excepted from the provisions contained in the heading of this article is the transportation, in cash, of the following amounts:

I – When in Brazilian currency, up to ten thousand reals (R$10,000);

II – When in foreign currency, the equivalent of ten thousand reals (R$10,000);

III – When it can be shown to have entered or left Brazil in accordance with pertinent regulations.

---

[39]The fact that the Central Bank deals more simply with amounts of up to $3000, dispensing with the currency exchange agreement, in no way constitutes a waiver of the requirement that all debits and credits in customer accounts or through financial instruments be recorded so as to allow tracking of assets.

[40]See www.planalto.gov.br/ccivil_03/leis/L9069.htm. Accessed 16 July 2016.

§ 2 The National Monetary Council shall, according to the guidelines from the President of the Republic, regulate the provisions of this article and also provide limitations and conditions for entry into and exit from Brazil of national currency.

§ 3 Failure to comply with the provisions of this article shall, in addition to sanctions provided in specific legislation and following due legal process, entail forfeiture to the National Treasury of all amounts in excess of those set forth in § 1 of this article.

Legislative Decree No. 857 of September 11, 1969,[41] requires the use of national legal tender in all domestic operations, rendering null and void all operations stipulated in foreign currency or which would, in effect, restrict or refuse Brazilian currency as legal tender, but lists several exceptions to the ban.

In this regard, it provides:

Art. 1 – All contracts, securities and documents, and bonds callable in Brazil, which stipulate payment in gold, in foreign currency, or in any way serve to restrict or refuse the cruzeiro as legal tender, are null and void by law.

Art. 2 – The provisions of the preceding article do not apply to:

I – Contracts and paper relating to the importation and exportation of goods;

II – Contracts for financing or putting up bonds or guarantees relating to the exportation of nationally produced goods, sold abroad on credit;

III – Foreign-exchange purchase and sale agreements in general;

IV – Loans and any other obligations in which the creditor or debtor is a person residing and domiciled abroad, excepting only contracts for the lease or rental of real property within Brazilian territory;

V – Contracts for purposes of assignment, transfer, delegation, assumption or modification of obligations referenced in the preceding item, even if both parties to the agreement are residents of and domiciled in Brazil.

Sole Paragraph – Real property lease or rental agreements stipulating payment in foreign currency must, to be enforceable, and be registered in advance with the Brazilian Central Bank.

For its part, Decree No. 23,258 of October 19, 1933,[42] provides that the purchase and sale of foreign currency shall be made exclusively in institutions authorized by the Brazilian Central Bank to engage in currency exchange operations, and establishes that:

Art. 1 All foreign exchange operations conducted between banks, natural persons or legal persons domiciled or doing business in Brazil, with any entities abroad—whenever such operations are made other than through banks licensed to operate in foreign exchange through prior accreditation by examiners on behalf of the Brazilian Central Bank—are considered illegal exchange operations.

This set of codes (Law No. 4131/1962, Article 23; Law No. 9069/1995, Article 65, heading, and Legislative Decree No. 23258/1933, Article 1) makes foreign

---

[41]In www.planalto.gov.br/ccivil_03/Decreto-Lei/Del0857.htm. Accessed 17 July 2016.

[42]In www.planalto.gov.br/ccivil_03/decreto-1930-1949/D23258.htm. Accessed 17 July 2016.

exchange agreements mandatory (or, for operations of up to US$3000, more simplified forms), thereby establishing Brazilian currency (the *real*) as legal tender while requiring identification of customers and declaring illegal all foreign exchange operations not conducted through banks accredited by the Central Bank.[43]

Pursuant to the rules of Brazil's Financial Intelligence Unit (COAF), the item "Cash Transfers" covers remittances and applies only to the mail and Brazilian postal money orders, both domestic and international, since everything coming from abroad and involving currency exchange operations comes under Central Bank supervision.

There is an official market in the United States that often made use of gray market operators (currency brokers) to allow transfers of money belonging to uninformed foreigners residing in Brazil. To stock its operations, Brazilian currency (*reals*) usually in cash (from illegal conduct in Brazil) was deposited by the Currency Exchange into the accounts of beneficiaries of wire transfers coming from abroad, while the dollars or euros received from the senders (easy prey) are diverted to redeem and deposit money as part of this bartering in funds. This is the so-called wire operation.

One should bear in mind that whenever the number of immigrants in a given location increases, there is a proportional increase in the gray market transfer of money. Similarly, wherever there is an increase in illegal immigration,[44] it is easier to commit financial crimes.

Another topic of concern is the entry of several factoring companies, which pump money into the accounts of wire transfer beneficiaries in the receiving country, thereby contributing to the offsetting of amounts in furtherance of an illegal black market in unauthorized financial dealings. Quite apart from their main purpose, which is short-term business financing of creditors' claims for goods and services provided on credit, the factor, or invoicer, is only required to keep a record of sales and perform administrative work relating to accounts receivable, receiving no sums and guarding against debtor insolvency.

According to the 1988 Convention on International Factoring held in Ottawa, a factoring contract is a contract between two parties, the client (supplier) and the factor. The factoring company should perform at least two of the following functions: (1) provide financing for the supplier, including loans and advances on payments; (2) maintenance of accounts relating to the receivables; (3) collection of receivables; and (4) protect against default in payment by debtors.[45] Nothing is

[43]International Capital and Foreign Exchange Market Regulations (RMCCI). www.bcb.gov.br/?RMCCI. Accessed 29 Oct 2016. Resolution No. 3568 of May 29, 2008, is the primary regulation http://www.bcb.gov.br/pre/normativos/busca/normativo.asp?tipo=Res&ano=2008&numero=3568. Accessed 20 July 2016.

[44]For more on the influx of new immigrants who wire money back to their countries of origin, and their profiles, see Inter-American Dialogue (2012).

[45]International Institute for the Unification of Private Law (1988).

said, therefore, about assisting remittance companies or currency brokers so as to obtain financial compensation on their balances.

Something similar to what occurs in the Black Market Peso Exchange, which has long served international drug traffic, also applies to Brazil, with the establishment of the black market in *reals*.

According to COAF Resolution No. 13, factoring companies are required to report to COAF, even if not accredited as financial institutions by the Central Bank, which is why they do not apply for licenses or registration. The COAF code is intended, however, to make it possible to identify their owners and directors, perform due diligence on customers, and check whether internal controls are in place.

The Brazilian Federal Reserve (Central Bank Circular No. 3542 of March 12, 2012), establishes in its Article 1, XI, a requirement to notify the Financial Intelligence Unit if, for instance, the customer does not provide justification for the origin of the money, or where the amount is incompatible with the customer's financial strength (item f); upon the realization of *resources from abroad*, check for financial incompatibility or absence of proper grounds (item g); or should payments occur abroad after deposit of credit in reals into accounts held by persons named in the currency exchange operations, absent any business or financial links (item j). In the United States, FinCEN requires banks to perform due diligence on wire transfers to foreign agents or counterparties (31 CFR § 103).

This is why irregular deposits show up in the accounts of recipients of wire transfers with no identification of the depositor, cash transfers to a beneficiary account from a company not authorized by the Central Bank to operate in the currency exchange market, or cash transfers to beneficiary accounts from individuals, for only financial institutions are eligible to receive Central Bank authorization to operate in currency exchange markets.

An occasional such operation may be deemed acceptable if it has, in addition to an investigation as to the origin of funds, proof of deposit through a financial institution accredited by the Central Bank (such as a letter from the bank responsible for settling the operation).

Due diligence is not called for when the sending company has its home office in the United States (where that is the source of the dollars).

In the United States, money transmitters are regulated at both the federal and state level, but for different purposes. At the federal level, they are subject to regulation under the Bank Secrecy Act (BSA). The BSA was enacted in 1970 to prevent money laundering and focuses primarily on creating a paper trail of all large financial transactions. FinCEN is tasked with promulgating and enforcing BSA Rules. FinCEN regulates money transmitters with an eye toward preventing money laundering and terrorist financing. A wide range of potential money transmitters is subject to regulation because the scope of FinCEN's authority is drawn broadly. FinCEN regulates money services businesses "wherever located doing business, whether or not on a regular basis or as an organized or licensed business concern, wholly or in substantial part within the United States,...[operating in any of the listed categories]."[46] Money transmitters are one of those categories and encompass any "acceptance of currency, funds, or other value that substitutes for currency from one person and the transmission of currency, funds, or other value that substitutes for currency to another location or person by any means."[47] Effectively, any business or person that accepts value from one entity to transmit to another would count as a money transmitter.

Fortunately, FinCEN has spelled out several exemptions from this broad definition. In particular, the Rule exempts a person from money transmitter regulation in six circumstances: (1) providers of network infrastructure to money transmitters; (2) certain payment processors; (3) certain clearance and settlement systems; (4) physical transporters of currency; (5) providers of prepaid access; and (6) persons accepting and transmitting funds only integral to the sale of goods or services. These exemptions carve out businesses that pose lower money laundering risk, again reflecting the BSA's primary focus on preventing money laundering rather than enhancing consumer welfare. FinCEN's basic premise appears to be: if a business transmits funds between well-regulated entities and well-understood channels, it is less likely to require regulation as a money transmitter. Its administrative guidance on the various exemptions supports this view.[48]

Cases have been observed of payments for drugs through the use of remittances from the United States in a triangle involving Colombia, the United States, and Europe. Euros were brought in by mules (or smurfs) to Colombian currency exchanges, which shipped them to the United States, where they were bundled and sent to Europe, where the receiving company exchanged them for dollars which were then wired to the United States. These operations usually involve immigrants. With the arrival of greater numbers of immigrants in any country, the number of transfers from one person to another increases annually.

International banks are shutting remittance accounts in the Pacific islands in response to global financial regulation aimed at hampering money laundering. But

---

[46]Code of Federal Regulations—C.F.R. § 1010.100 (ff) (2016). https://www.gpo.gov/fdsys/granule/CFR-2011-title31-vol3/CFR-2011-title31-vol3-part1010. Accessed 10 Sept 2016. The Code of Federal Regulations (CFR) annual edition is the codification of the general and permanent rules published in the Federal Register by the departments and agencies of the federal government. It is divided into fifty titles that represent broad areas subject to federal regulation. The fifty subject matter titles contain one or more individual volumes, which are updated once each calendar year, on a staggered basis. The annual update cycle is as follows: titles 1–16 are revised as of January 1; titles 17–27 are revised as of April 1; titles 28–41 are revised as of July 1; and titles 42–50 are revised as of October 1. Each title is divided into chapters, which usually bear the name of the issuing agency. Each chapter is further subdivided into parts that cover specific regulatory areas. Large parts may be subdivided into subparts. All parts are organized in sections, and most citations to the CFR refer to material at the section level. See https://www.gpo.gov/help/about_code_of_federal_regulations.htm.

[47]Code of Federal Regulations—C.F.R. § 1010.100 (ff)(5)(i)(A) (2016). https://www.gpo.gov/fdsys/granule/CFR-2011-title31-vol3/CFR-2011-title31-vol3-part1010. Accessed 10 Sept 2016.

[48]See Lo (2016, pp. 113–114).

the closures are hitting companies and families that rely on international money transfers.

According to Michael Field, "Westpac Group, one of two Australian banks that until recently dominated banking in the Pacific, said in April [2016] that it would cut business ties with the government of Nauru, having ceased operations in five other Pacific island countries last year. Australia and New Zealand Banking Group, the other Australian bank with major operations in the region, is also thought to be considering reducing its exposure—a move that would mark a significant backward step for the islands."[49]

Mr. Field considers that "anti-money laundering laws have been tightened globally, in part to reduce the flow of funds to terrorist groups. As part of these efforts, banks have been reducing their exposure to potential risks—a procedure known as 'de-risking.' In the Pacific this has included closing the accounts of money transfer operators (MTOs), the financial groups or middlemen through which remittances are sent. For the islands, this is bad news. The World Bank has estimated that Pacific island countries receive annual remittances of around $470 million. The funds can be crucial—remittances account for up to 26% of gross domestic product in Tonga and 20% in Samoa, according to the bank. The Reserve Bank of New Zealand says that MTOs handle most of the transfers. If MTOs were to be unable to operate, families could end up having to pay hundreds of dollars in transaction fees for bank transfers. Mark Flaming, regional project manager for the Pacific Financial Inclusion Programme, a UN administered non-governmental organization based in Fiji, said it would cost Tongan families $950 a year in fees to receive remittances from banks. 'This is really bad for [financial inclusion],' he said."[50]

"Pacific MTOs, which range from global groups such as Western Union to small village and island-based suppliers, handle most of the remittances from Australia, New Zealand and the U.S. to families in the Pacific. Ranil Manohara Salgado, the International Monetary Fund's chief of Asia and Pacific regional studies, said the organization was working with international bodies to create an environment where banks would not have to withdraw their services. 'There are signs that some of the Western banks could withdraw, and that's raising concerns,' he told Nikkei Asian Review."[51]

In turn, Lauren Resnick, considers that "in the environment of increasingly aggressive regulatory and criminal enforcement of anti-money laundering (AML) violations, concerns about de-risking—when financial institutions close accounts or restrict access to new clients because of high AML or counterterrorist financing (CFT) risks—have risen to the fore. Regulators and policy groups are concerned that 'wholesale' de-risking restricts financial inclusion and may violate competition laws. It goes without saying that financial institutions must

[49]Field (2016).
[50]Field (2016).
[51]Field (2016).

appropriately manage their AML risks in light of the increased enforcement and civil liability exposure. Nevertheless, in lieu of wholesale exclusion of large segments of commerce, financial institutions should develop enhanced diligence protocols during the customer account opening process and monitor account activity to manage these risks effectively. By doing so, financial institutions can ensure continued banking access to the communities these alternative money service businesses (MSBs) serve."[52]

Besides this, authorities must designate virtual worlds, very often used by remitters, subject to the anti-money laundering or anti-terrorist financing regulation in order to be able to verify user identity during registration and ensure that each virtual transaction can be traced back to identifiable senders and recipients.[53]

Although Informal Funds Transfer Systems (IFTS), as known as Hawala networks, have distinct operational characteristics—efficiency, adaptability, affordability, anonymity, cultural sensitivity, and trust through relational contracts,[54] it must follow some standard regulation. Formal remittance banking must provide access to their services in a much quicker way to encompass more relational contracts.

Here it is important to highlight the fact that "the World Bank and the Federal Government of Somalia [have been] working together to help support the flow of remittances to Somalia, to ensure they continue to reach people who depend upon them as a critical source of income. Remittances in 2015 were estimated to reach a total of US$1.4 billion in Somalia and support 23% of the GDP. Over the past two years, many banks in the United States, United Kingdom, Canada and Australia have closed the bank accounts of Somali remittance companies purportedly due to the perceived high risks of money laundering and potential links to terrorism."[55]

"The World Bank has been working alongside the Central Bank of Somalia (CBS) to implement a number of activities aimed at tackling key deficiencies in the Somali financial sector affecting remittance flows to the country. The World Bank has selected and appointed 'Abyrint AS' to act as the 'Trusted Agent' to the CBS and assist the authorities in comprehensively regulating and supervising money transfer businesses." The World Bank has also been assisting with the implementation of new regulations and guidelines for the money transfer business sector within the new regulatory regime.[56]

What is surprising in discourses on global migration is the neglect of the household as a vital institution not only in social reproduction, but also as a center for decision-making and motives for migration.[57] Remittance companies must be seen as a key social institution in local and global socioeconomic systems. Data and

---

[52]Resnick (2016).

[53]For a discussion of virtual worlds, see Landman (2009).

[54]Hariharan (2012, p. 307).

[55]World Bank (2016).

[56]World Bank (2016).

[57]Douglass (2010, p. 72).

cases must be brought together to reveal remittance companies' importance in contemporary globalization processes. Being out of compliance justifies the power to deny or revoke their licenses. Noncompliant Informal Value Transfer Systems obstruct the implementation of an effective anti-money laundering scheme because they attract legitimate transactions, making illegal transactions more difficult to identify, and do not provide adequate paper trails for law enforcement.[58]

3.1.2 NGOs and Trusts

Just as the work of beneficent entities has been important, scandals have stained some of their images and opened the door to an increase in judicial actions against their directors, increasing skepticism in proportion to news coverage of events.

Because their work is philanthropic, and they are generally motivated by altruism and compassion, charities have been immune to legal proceedings. They may be made answerable on account of internal management issues or even external problems (everything from labor suits to fraud, and even money laundering by reason of insolvency, negligence, or poor practices). A charity's entire board of directors might be held liable for some failure of accounting or diversion of funds.

Nongovernmental organizations, trusts, associations, and foundations tend to be as diverse as a country's population. People are increasingly getting involved in some kind of social or charity efforts. Donations to these social entities have been large.

Recent disclosures have tarnished the images of certain entities and brought the glare of publicity onto the conduct of some of their managers. A backlash of skepticism has brought about a proportional reaction affecting the volume of donations and volunteer work.

Because philanthropic work is normally motivated by feelings of generosity and empathy, charitable organizations often imagine themselves immune to legal proceedings. Liability could surface based on some poorly handled internal activity, or some other cause occurring outside the organization. This is why the role of the manager is so important.

By the simple fact that they operate with personal and institutional donations, charity organizations are often temples, churches, mosques, NGOs, and educational associations, and they believe that they are not required to reveal the source of their funds, nor to be examined for the large financial transactions they conduct.

The U.S. Congress has, since 1917, allowed deduction of donations to charitable, religious, educational, and other such entities organized as nonprofit NGOs. Citing a 1938 report from the House Committee on Ways and Means, Erin Thompson explains that tax revenue losses due to charitable donations are offset by

58 Watterson (2013, pp. 745, 748).

easing the financial burden, which, through the resulting benefits, promotes the general welfare.[59]

According to Andrew Cuomo, philanthropic organizations "contribute substantially to our society. They educate our children, care for the sick, preserve our literature, art and music for us and for future generations, house the homeless, protect the environment and much more."[60]

The correctness of granting large tax deductions has been the subject of frequent assessment of its effectiveness, purpose and potential for abuse. All of this has, according to Mr. Cuomo, brought about changes in the law, statutes, and regulations governing charitable deductions. Thus, a philanthropic transfer in the United States must satisfy a complex set of rules to qualify as a tax deduction. These rules are grouped, according to Mr. Cuomo,[61] into three main requirements: the transfer must be sent to a qualified addressee[62]; it must clearly state the purpose of the donation, that is, not is an exchange of goods or services[63]; and it must consist of a payment or other allowable goods.[64]

The third and last requirement brings us back to the question of payments.

In the state of New York, for instance, in order to set up a foundation or NGO, a license must be obtained to qualify for tax exemption, and returns must be filed to the State tax authorities, under penalty of being closed down, by means of Form No. 990, dated and properly signed on penalty of perjury, and containing the name and telephone number of the person who keeps books and records for the organization.[65]

The form must be filled out to include a detailed list of all of its activities and management, its revenues, overhead, and liquid assets. It must state the name and purpose of the institution; number of members; whether it has more than 25% of its liquid assets on hand; number of voting members listed within or outside of the entity; number of employees; number of volunteers; revenues from unrelated businesses and taxes paid; contributions and donations; resources invested; benefits paid by and for members; total assets and obligations; basic description of all assistance programs; whether any loans or benefits are granted to or for employees, directors, trustees or any other persons; the names, hours worked, and job descriptions of all employees and former employees (including directors, trustees and key personnel); their earnings, and their expenses (including travel or leisure).

For gross revenues of up to $100,000, no external audits are required. From $100,000 to $250,000, the information must be entered by an outside auditor (and

---

[59]Thompson (2009–2010, 241–265).

[60]Cuomo (2005).

[61]Id.

[62]Cf. I.R.C. § 170 (c) (2006).

[63]See Mcleman v. United States. 24 Cl. Ct. 109, 91-2 USTC 50, 447, 1991.

[64]In I.R.C. § 170 (e) (3) (2006).

[65]Provided they are also recognized as such in the U.S. tax code, also known as the Internal Revenue Code, Sect. 501 (c); 527; 4947 (a) (1).

documentation reviewed by that professional), who does not, however, check the truthfulness of information obtained. In other words, it is not the auditor's job to check donor transactions (to conduct the due diligence). But NGOswith gross annual revenues in excess of $250,000 are required to turn in an outside auditor's report, and that auditor must perform the due diligence.[66]

The Foundation Center, a U.S. center for information on foundations, has published some 29 standards. Brazil, meanwhile, has six unpublished standards (a true case of living in a glass house).[67]

Management and employees of nongovernmental organizations must be answerable for their management and for the protection of the goods and services that benefit us all.

A primary responsibility is to ensure proper accounting for social programs they play a role in, and for funding received from their supporters (public or otherwise). This means they must strictly comply with the law and ethical standards, be committed to the mission of the NGO they represent, protect the rights of their members and, indirectly, of those assisted, and prepare annual reports for their country's federal revenue service and regulatory authorities having jurisdiction—reports that should be available to all interested parties.

They should therefore have technical information at their fingertips to enable them to monitor and record all assets and amounts received, spent or entrusted to their care.

The website of the National Association of State Charity Officials (NASCO)[68] contains important information on recording and reporting required of NGOs. NASCO members are employees of U.S. government agencies charged with regulating NGOs and their funds.

Marion R. Fremont-Smith, who teaches Public Policy at the John F. Kennedy School of Government, produced an important comparison for Harvard University on the bookkeeping requirements for such organizations. She showed, for instance, that most U.S. states (for example, New York, California, and New Jersey) require that they have at least three directors.[69]

FATF Recommendation No. 08, in the spirit of clearly delimiting the rights and responsibilities of directors and employees of nongovernmental organizations, encourages countries to establish good policy whereby information on their activities, size, and other important characteristics such as transparency, integrity,

---

[66]State of New York—Department of Law (2015, Mar). Solicitation and collection of funds for charitable purposes. https://www.charitiesnys.com/pdfs/statute_booklet.pdf. Accessed 30 Sept 2016.

[67]According to information provided by Patricia Lobaccaro on May 16, 2012. Ms. Lobaccaro is president and CEO of Brazil Foundation, with offices at 345 7th Ave., Suite 1401, New York City.

[68]See http://www.nasconet.org/. Accessed 30 Oct 2016.

[69]In *The Search for Greater Accountability of Nonprofit Organizations. Summary Charts: State Nonprofit Corporation Act Requirements and Audit Requirements for Charitable Organizations* (document obtained on May 16, 2012, from Patrícia Lobaccaro, president and CEO of the Brazil Foundation Foundation).

openness, and best practices can be had in real time for purposes of supervision and monitoring.

It is not enough to only dimly perceive here a preoccupation with the financing of terrorism, for they could be the means of commission of any number of crimes.

In Pakistan, for example, the Central Bank has placed much stricter controls on NGOs and beneficent societies, ordering a complete review of all of their accounting before the end of 2012, on pain of making them subject to penalties. The purpose was to establish a policy and a set of rules for compliance (to strengthen due diligence) and to protect them from the risk of money laundering and terrorism financing. All of the country's financial institutions are being required to open accounts in the name of NGOs that match the documents submitted to them. In the event of an organization publicly soliciting donations or the like, accompanied by a bank account number, those financial institutions must promptly take note of and report that account in the event that the account owner of record does not match that of the publication.[70]

Similarly, two government intelligence cells were created in India to detect sources of funding used to finance terrorist activity. Analysts there believe that terrorist attacks in India are funded by neighboring countries through NGOs and nonprofits. Up until recently, they had no way of checking on how funds from abroad, purportedly intended for health and education, would actually be used.[71] In 2010, there were some two million NGOs in India, but of that number, only 71 had requested any reimbursement for taxes paid. In 2009, there were 38,600 registered with the government to receive donations from abroad. Some are suspected of being money laundering channels for the return of illegal cash received from Indian politicians or for terrorism financing, much of it qualifying as investments coming through Mauritius.[72]

NGOs, associations, and foundations lacking proper controls are recognized today as channels for money laundering for organized crime. In fact, the FATF has found that sums transferred from NGOs abroad have provided funding for the financing of terrorism on a par with counterfeiting, drug trafficking, extortion, and corruption. This has prompted India, for example, to assemble an umbrella database listing them all.[73]

Money laundering is usually carried out using a layered structure to give the appearance of legality. One such method would be to establish trust companies through which the company manages business for its clients, the beneficiary being one or more holding companies, or a series of companies in several tax havens, to

[70]Terror outfit-turned 'charity' JuD set to come under Pak Central Bank scanner (2012).

[71]Marpakwar (2011).

[72]For more on this, see Sikarwar et al. (2011).

[73]FATF (June 2014). Risk of terrorist abuse in nonprofit organisations. http://www.fatf-gafi.org/media/fatf/documents/reports/Risk-of-terrorist-abuse-in-non-profit-organisations.pdf. Accessed 28 Sept 2016; Government plans 'umbrella law' to tighten scrutiny and regulation of religious trusts and NGOs (2011, May 2). Economic Times. http://articles.economictimes.indiatimes.com/2011-05-02/news/29496119_1_religious-trusts-voluntary-sector-companies-act. Accessed 22 June 2016.

create a separation between the aforesaid holding companies and their ultimate beneficiary. Moreover, the discovery of the real beneficiary would require considerable cooperation on the part of authorities in those tax havens. Some means would have to be established to require the trust to provide its beneficiaries' names whenever requested by the authorities.

It is not even easy to establish who is in charge of the trust, for there is no obligation that that name be revealed. Hence, being its legal beneficiary is an enviable business—which may explain the rather timid recovery of illegal assets.

There are efforts underway in India to publicize the names of organizations (religious NGOs or trusts) requesting tax exemptions. One of India's wealthiest trusts collects huge sums of cash. There are a number of laws and several states seeking to monitor the activities of these entities. Yet Parul Soni (of Ernst & Young Pvt. Ltd.) believes that federal legislation will be required to achieve bookkeeping transparency and to strengthen the reporting of suspicious activity in that sector.[74] Trusts, though they may be temples, churches or mosques, nongovernmental organizations, or educational institutions registered as NGOs, must now reveal the sources of their funds and have their financial transactions closely scrutinized. This is because of new jurisprudence requirements under India's Prevention of Money Laundering Act of 2002. Indian attorney Bhusham Bahal tells us that the laundering of illegal money has been largely made possible by NGOs operated by powerful businessmen and top politicians, so that this new instrument should prove of valuable assistance to the authorities.[75]

Pakistan has also adopted strict measures to curb money laundering and terrorism financing by NGOs by putting in place a very broad know your customer policy. It requires photocopies of customer photo IDs (identification card or passport), and a copy of the assignment, if done through power of attorney. Companies must produce their charter and bylaws, and a list of directors. Similar documentation is required of individuals, along with audit documents required of clubs, associations, and nonprofit associations.[76]

The trump card in the Indian case is the requirement that sources of funds be revealed, so that know your customer policies have to be in place for donations received by the NGOs, as is already the case for financial institutions. They must also provide detailed information on investments and donations received, and anonymous donations are henceforth barred.[77]

In Canada, nongovernmental organizations are as diverse as the population. Many Canadians are involved in charity work, with estimates running to some 36%

---

[74]Government plans 'umbrella law' to tighten scrutiny and regulation of religious trusts and NGOs (2011, May 2). Economic Times. http://articles.economictimes.indiatimes.com/2011-05-02/news/29496119_1_religious-trusts-voluntary-sector-companies-act. Accessed 22 June 2016.

[75]Shah (2009).

[76]Money laundering, terror financing: SECP imposes more conditions. Business Recorder. http://aaj.tv/2009/09/money-laundering-terror-financing-secp-imposes-more-conditions/. Accessed 28 Sept 2016.

[77]Shah (2009).

of the population. Economically, the sector is a major player, inasmuch as two million people are employed within it, with another two billion hours voluntarily contributed. There are over 160,000 NGOs operating nationwide and 85% of the population makes financial contributions to Canadian social entities.[78]

Considerable customer due diligence is required. The donor's name or job title is no longer enough (photo ID is preferred). For instance, the donor's purposes and actual financial position must be known (preferably face-to-face), along with his signature or the signatures of those acting on his behalf. The source of funding must also be disclosed and supported by documentation. In the case of a donor company, a copy of the bylaws is required (in order to check the list of directors) from the civil or deed registry having jurisdiction. The true directors of the NGO must be known, again with photo ID, along with the scope of their authority, all of that backed by documentation to properly support the information provided.

Terrorists and their supporters have targeted domestic organizations, often religious organizations, which generally enjoy less governmental scrutiny and have long been considered upstanding pillars of many western societies. Part of the American government's response to this terrorist infiltration of the charitable community was to seek to ensure a regulatory climate in which donors can give to charities without fear that their donations will be misused to support terrorism. Abuses by terrorists and their private supporters have tainted the reputations of some charities, and to some extent corrupted the sanctity of charitable giving. Governments must be wise in waging its financial war on terrorism.[79]

Bibliography

Al Sayegh, H., & Torchia, A. (2016, February 23). *Bahrain to discuss bank regulations with U.S. Treasury. Reuters.* http://www.reuters.com/article/bahrain-banks-risks-idUSL8N1621YC. Accessed June 15, 2016.

Bickerton, R. (2009, December 1). *For a good cause. Canadian Underwriter.* http://www.canadianunderwriter.ca/features/for-a-good-cause/. Accessed June 23, 2016.

Candiano, L. L. (2002). Breves comentários sobre a reforma da Lei das Sociedades por Ações. *Revista Forense, 360,* 61–69.

Cappelli, S. (1996). Responsabilidade penal da pessoa jurídica em matéria ambiental: uma necessária reflexão sobre o disposto no art. 225, § 3º, da Constituição Federal. *Revista de Direito Ambiental, 1,* 100–106.

Caramante, A. (2012, June 22). *Carro da polícia civil é atingido por tiros na zona leste de SP. Folha de São Paulo.* http://noticias.bol.uol.com.br/brasil/2012/06/22/carro-da-policia-civil-e-atingido-por-tiros-na-zona-leste-de-sp.jhtm. Accessed August 2, 2016.

Chauvin, F. (1996). *La responsabilité des communes.* Paris: Dalloz.

Cintra, M. A. (2006, January 4). *O Acordo de Basiléia e os bancos públicos. Folha de São Paulo.* http://www.revistacobertura.com.br/lermais_materias.php?cd_materias=36707&friurl=:-O-Acordo-de-Basileia-e-os-bancos-publicos. Accessed September 27, 2016.

[78]For more on this, see Bickerton (2009).

[79]See Crimm (2004, pp. 1449–1450).

Code of Federal Regulations—C.F.R. § 1010.100 (ff) (2016). https://www.gpo.gov/fdsys/granule/CFR-2011-title31-vol3/CFR-2011-title31-vol3-part1010. Accessed September 10, 2016.

Coelho, F. U. (1994). *O empresário e os direitos do consumidor*. São Paulo: Saraiva.

Coelho, F. U. (2000). *Curso de direito comercial*. São Paulo: Saraiva.

Coelho, F. U., et al. (1991). *Comentários ao Código de Proteção ao Consumidor*. São Paulo: Saraiva.

Corrêa Lima, O. B. (2002). Lei das sociedades por ações: Permanência, mutações e mudança. *Revista da Faculdade de Direito da Universidade Federal de Minas Gerais, 41*, 239–252.

Correia, E. (1998). A responsabilidade jurídico-penal da empresa e dos seus órgãos (ou uma reflexão sobre a alteridade nas pessoas colectivas à luz do direito penal). Direito penal econômico e europeu: textos doutrinários. Coimbra: Coimbra Ed.

Correia, E., & Pedrazzi, C. (1990). *Direito penal das sociedades anônimas. Direito penal dos negócios: crimes do colarinho branco*. São Paulo: Associação dos Advogados de São Paulo.

Correia, E., & Pedrazzi, C. (1996). *Direito penal societário*. São Paulo: Malheiros.

Cousin, A., & Albert, J. (2002). Promoting transparency and effectively fighting international money laundering. *Journal of International Business and Law, 1*, 64–90.

Crimm, N. (2004). High alert: The government's war on the financing of terrorism and its implications for donors, domestic charitable organizations, and global philanthropy. *William and Mary Law Review, 45*, 1341–1451.

Cuomo, A. (2005, January). *Internal controls and financial accountability for not-for-profit boards. Charities Bureau*. http://www.nyc.gov/html/nonprofit/downloads/pdf/Internal%20Controls%20and%20Financial%20Accountability%20for%20Not-for-Profit%20Board%20OAG.pdf. Accessed September 27, 2016.

De Camargo Vidigal, G., & Silva Martins, I. G. (1978). *Comentários à lei das sociedades por ações (Lei 6404/76)*. São Paulo: Resenha Universitária and Instituto dos Advogados de São Paulo.

De Sanctis, F. M. (1999). *Responsabilidade penal das pessoas jurídicas*. São Paulo: Saraiva.

De Sanctis, F. M. (2003). *Punibilidade no sistema financeiro nacional*. Campinas: Millennium.

De Sanctis, F. M. (2008). *Combate à lavagem de dinheiro: Teoria e prática*. Campinas: Millennium.

De Sanctis, F. M. (2009). *Responsabilidade penal das corporações e criminalidade moderna*. São Paulo: Saraiva.

De Sanctis, F. M. (2013). *Money laundering through art. A criminal justice perspective*. Cham, Heidelberg, New York, Dordrecht, London: Springer.

De Sanctis, F. M. (2014). *Football, gambling, and money laundering. A global criminal justice perspective*. Cham, Heidelberg, New York, Dordrecht, London: Springer.

De Sanctis, F. M. (2015). *Churches, temples, and financial crimes. A judicial perspective of the abuse of faith*. Cham, Heidelberg, New York, Dordrecht, London: Springer.

Denicola, R. (2008). Access controls, rights protection, and circumvention: Interpreting the digital millennium. *Columbias Journal of Law and the Arts, 31*(2), 209–233.

Douglass, M. (2010). Globalizing the household in East Asia. *Whitehead Journal of Diplomacy & International Relations, 11*(1), 63–77.

Dow Jones Business News. (2016, July 27). *U.S. expands real-estate data targeting order. Nasdaq*. http://www.nasdaq.com/article/us-expands-realestate-data-targeting-order-20160727-01154. Accessed August 12, 2016.

Eizirik, N. (1996). *Instituições financeiras e mercado de capitais – jurisprudência* (p. 1996). Rio de Janeiro: Renovar.

FATF. (June 2014). *Risk of terrorist abuse in non-profit organisations*. http://www.fatf-gafi.org/media/fatf/documents/reports/Risk-of-terrorist-abuse-in-non-profit-organisations.pdf. Accessed September 28, 2016.

Ferrara, F. (1958). *Le persone giuridiche*. Torino: UTET.

Field, M. (2016, June 15). *Pacific hit as banks abandon remittance business. Nikkei Asian Review*. http://asia.nikkei.com/Politics-Economy/Economy/Pacific-hit-as-banks-abandon-remittance-business. Accessed July 10, 2016.

Foley, R. E. (2007, September). Bulk cash smuggling. *United States Attorneys' Bulletin, 55*(5), 41–47.

Fremont-Smith, M. R. (2007). *Summary charts: State nonprofit corporation act requirements and audit requirements for charitable organizations.* http://cpl.hks.harvard.edu/files/cpl/files/workingpaper_33.8appendices.pdf. Accessed September 28, 2016.

Galerie Furstenberg v. Coffaro, 697 F. Supp. 1282 (S.D.N.Y. 1988).

Garzón, J. C. (2008). *Mafia & co.—The criminal networks in Mexico, Brazil, and Colombia.* https://www.wilsoncenter.org/sites/default/files/mafiaandcompany_reducedsize.pdf. Accessed September 28, 2016.

Giorgi, G. (1913). *La dottrina delle persone giuridiche o corpi morali.* Firenze: Fratelli Cammelli.

Goddard, T. (2012, October 13). *How to fix a broken border: Follow the money.* Tucson Sentinel. http://www.tucsonsentinel.com/opinion/report/101312_goddard_border/how-fix-broken-border-follow-money/. Accessed September 28, 2016.

Gordon, J. E. (1995). Prosecutors who seize too much and the theories they love: Money laundering, facilitation, and forfeiture. *Duke Law Journal, 44,* 744–776.

Government plans 'umbrella law' to tighten scrutiny and regulation of religious trusts and NGOs. (2011, May 2). *Economic Times.* http://articles.economictimes.indiatimes.com/2011-05-02/news/29496119_1_religious-trusts-voluntary-sector-companies-act. Accessed June 22, 2016.

Grewal, A. (2016, June 6). Panama papers fallout will stress anti money laundering compliance. *Payments Source.* http://www.paymentssource.com/news/paythink/panama-papers-fallout-will-stress-anti-money-laundering-compliance-3024270-1.html. Accessed July 1, 2016.

Há evidências de que Lula recebeu R$ 30 mi desviados da Petrobrás, diz MPF. (2016, Mar 4). UOL. http://noticias.uol.com.br/politica/ultimas-noticias/2016/03/04/lula-e-seu-instituto-receberam-valores-expressivos-de-empreiteiras.htm. Accessed March 22, 2016.

Hamm, M. (2004). Torts—RICO—Predicate crime of extortion requires that the defendant obtain or attempt to obtain property. *Tennessee Law Review, 71,* 365–381.

Hariharan, A. (2012). Hawala's charm: What banks can learn from informal funds transfer systems. *William & Mary Business Law Review, 3*(1), 273–308.

Hidalgo, R., et al. (1994). *Entreprise et responsabilité pénale.* Paris: LGDJ.

Inter-American Dialogue. (2012, March 20). Briefing explores the factors that have influenced increases in remitting.

International Capital and Foreign Exchange Market Regulations (RMCCI). www.bcb.gov.br/?RMCCI. Accessed October 29, 2016.

International Institute for the Unification of Private Law. (1988, May 28). *UNIDRIOT convention on international factoring.* http://www.unidroit.org/instruments/factoring. Accessed October 29, 2016.

Jones Day Law Firm. (June 2016). *Supreme Court limits extraterritorial application of RICO.* http://www.jonesday.com/supreme-court-limits-extraterritorial-application-of-rico-06-22-2016/. Accessed October 24, 2016.

Landman, S. I. (2009). Funding Bin Laden's avatar: A proposal for the regulation of virtual hawalas. *William Mitchell Law Review, 35*(5), 5159–5184.

Levi, M., & Reuter, P. (2006). Money laundering. *Crime & Justice, 34*(1), 289–375.

Linn, C. J (2007, September). One-hour money laundering: Prosecuting unlicensed money transmitting businesses using section 1960. *United States Attorneys' Bulletin, 55*(5), 34–40.

Lo, B. (2016). Fatal fragments: The effect of money transmission regulation on payments innovation. *Yale Journal of Law & Technology, 18*(1), 111–147.

Lobo, J. (2002). *Curso de Direito Comercial.* Rio de Janeiro: Forense.

Macedo, F. (2015, June 20). Lava Jato apura elos de offshores com Odebrecht e Andrade Gutierrez. *Estadão.* http://politica.estadao.com.br/blogs/fausto-macedo/lava-jato-apura-elos-de-offshores-com-odebrecht-e-andrade-gutierrez/. Accessed April 1, 2016.

Marpakwar, P. (2011, December 24). State forms cells to detect source of terror funds. *The Times of India.* http://timesofindia.indiatimes.com/city/mumbai/State-forms-cells-to-detect-source-of-terror-funds/articleshow/11225140.cms. Accessed September 28, 2016.

Marqueteiro de Dilma sabia que dinheiro era de origem ilegal, diz PF. (2016, February 22). UOL. http://noticias.uol.com.br/politica/ultimas-noticias/2016/02/22/marqueteiro-de-dilma-sabia-que-dinheiro-era-de-origem-ilegal-diz-pf.htm. Accessed March 20, 2016.

Martí, S. (2012, Jan 10). Anistia poderá coibir o 'esquema Daslu'. Folha de São Paulo. http://www1.folha.uol.com.br/fsp/ilustrada/19144-anistia-podera-coibir-o-esquema-daslu.shtml. Accessed September 27, 2016.

Martins, F. (2002). *Curso de Direito Comercial*. Rio de Janeiro: Forense.

Matonis, J. (2011, May 13). Thoughts on bitcoin laundering. *The Monetary Future*. http://themonetaryfuture.blogspot.com/2011/05/thoughts-on-bitcoin-laundering.html. Accessed September 28, 2016.

Messineo, F. (2010). Máfia e crime de colarinho branco: uma nova abordagem de análise. Novas tendências da criminalidade transnacional mafiosa. São Paulo: Unesp Ed.

Money laundering, terror financing: SECP imposes more conditions. Business Recorder. http://aaj.tv/2009/09/money-laundering-terror-financing-secp-imposes-more-conditions/. Accessed September 28, 2016.

Mubangizi, J. C. (2007). "Poverty production" and human rights in the African context. *Law, Democracy & Development, 11*(1), 1–14.

Olson, E. (2012, March 29). Considering new strategies for confronting organized crime in mexico. *Wilson Center*. https://www.wilsoncenter.org/publication/considering-new-strategies-for-confronting-organized-crime-mexico. Accessed September 28, 2016.

Pariente, M., et al. (1993). *Les groupes de sociétés et la responsabilité pénale des personnes morales*. Dalloz: La responsabilité pénale des personnes morales. Paris.

Perazzi, C. (1965). O Direito Penal das Sociedades e o Direito Penal comum. Revista Brasileira de Criminologia e Direito Penal, 9.

Resnick, L. J. (2016, June 15). The regulatory pendulum: When is de-risking by financial institutions too much? *Lexology*. http://www.lexology.com/library/detail.aspx?g=72b1624b-c107-4c3e-855d-48d8fab9dea7. Accessed July 20, 2016.

Rocha, F. A. N. Galvão da. (1998, May). Responsabilidade penal da pessoa jurídica. Revista da Associação Paulista do Ministério Público, 18.

Rocha, M. A. L. (1998). *A responsabilidade penal das pessoas colectivas—novas perspectivas*. Direito penal econômico e europeu: textos doutrinários. Coimbra: Coimbra Ed.

Rothenburg, W. C. (1997). *A pessoa jurídica criminosa*. Curitiba: Ed. Juruá.

Saul, S., & Story, L. (2015, February 7). Towers of secret. Stream of foreign wealth flows to elite New York real estate. *The New York Times*. http://www.nytimes.com/2015/02/08/nyregion/stream-of-foreign-wealth-flows-to-time-warner-condos.html?module=RelatedCoverage. Accessed June 20, 2016.

Schneiderman, E. (2015, May 15). *Right from the start—responsibilities of directors and officers of not-for-profit corporations*. https://www.charitiesnys.com/pdfs/Right%20From%20the%20Start%20Final.pdf. Accessed September 27, 2016.

Sexer, I. (1996, January). Les conditions de la responsabilité pénale des personnes morales. Droit et patrimoine, [S.l.], 38–46.

Shah, P. (2009, Nov 19). Trusts, NGOs under ambit of money-laundering law. *Business Standard*. http://www.business-standard.com/article/economy-policy/trusts-ngos-under-ambit-of-money-laundering-law-109111900089_1.html. Accessed July 23, 2016.

Shecaira, Sérgio Salomão (1998, Apr). A responsabilidade das pessoas jurídicas e os delitos ambientais. Boletim do IBCCrim, 65.

Sikarwar, D. (2011, May 2). Religious trusts, non-profit organisations to face greater scrutiny. *Economic Times*. http://epaper.timesofindia.com/Repository/ml.asp?Ref=RVRNLzIwMTEvMDUvMDIjQXIwMDEwMA==&Mode=HTML&Locale=english-skin-custom. Accessed September 28, 2016.

Sikarwar, D., Padmakshan, M., & Zachariah, R. (2011, November 17). Ten means to put an end to black money issue. *Economic Times*. http://economictimes.indiatimes.com/news/economy/finance/ten-means-to-put-an-end-to-black-money-issue/articleshow/10763329.cms. Accessed September 28, 2016.

Sirvinskas, L. P. (1998, April). Questões polêmicas atinentes à responsabilidade penal da pessoa jurídica nos crimes ambientais. Revista da Associação Paulista do Ministério Público, 17.

Terror outfit-turned 'charity' JuD set to come under Pak Central Bank scanner. (2012, March 13). *Asian News International*. https://in.news.yahoo.com/terror-outfit-turned-charity-jud-set-come-under-062446259.html. Accessed September 28, 2016.

Thompson, E. (2009–2010). The relationship between tax deductions and the market for unprovenanced antiquities. *Columbia Journal of Law & the Arts, 33*(2), 241–265.

Tiedemann, K. (1982). *Delitos contra el orden económico: La reforma penal*. Madrid: Instituto Alemão.

Tiedemann, K. (1985). *Poder económico y delito (Introducción al derecho penal económico y de la empresa)*. Barcelona: Ariel.

Tiedemann, K. (1995). Responsabilidad penal de personas jurídicas y empresas en derecho comparado. *Revista Brasileira de Ciências Criminais, 11,* 21–35.

U.S. Department of Treasury. (2016, July 19). *FinCEN Guidance, Frequently asked questions regarding customer due diligence requirements for financial institutions*. https://www.fincen.gov/sites/default/files/2016-09/FAQs_for_CDD_Final_Rule_(7_15_16).pdf. Accessed September 28, 2016.

Varoto, R. L. M. (1996, January). Da responsabilidade penal dos sócios. *Repertório IOB de Jurisprudência, 2,* 30–31.

Vazamento revela ligação de políticos com offshores nas Bahamas. (2016, September 21). UOL. http://noticias.uol.com.br/ultimas-noticias/deutschewelle/2016/09/21/vazamento-revela-ligacao-de-politicos-com-offshores-nas-bahamas.htm. Accessed September 22, 2016.

Verret, J. W. (2010). Terrorism finance, business associations, and the "Incorporation Transparency Act". *Louisiana Law Review, 70*(3), 857–910.

Watterson, C. (2013). More flies with honey: Encouraging formal channel remittances to combat money laundering. *Texas Law Review, 91,* 711–748.

World Bank. (2016, June 10). *World Bank makes progress to support remittance flows to Somalia*. http://www.worldbank.org/en/news/press-release/2016/06/10/world-bank-makes-progress-to-support-remittance-flows-to-somalia. Accessed July 15, 2016.

Chapter 4
Efforts to Combat Money Laundering

The origin of money laundering as an offence can be credited to the U.S. Bank Secrecy Act of 1970 (BSA), which represents the historic starting point for efforts to detect and sanction money laundering, although the term was not yet commonly used. Michael Levi and Peter Reuter state that the "banks acquired an affirmative duty to provide information to the Department of the Treasury of transactions involving more than $10,000 in cash (Currency transaction Reports [CTRs]). In line with its 'regulatory' thrust, the BSA criminalized the failure to report, not the provision of the services to facilitate a criminal act." According to Levi and Reuter, the Money Laundering Control Act of 1986 was a component of the federal war on drugs, stimulated in part by the findings of a high-profile undercover investigation in the center of the drug trade, southern Florida. Operation Greenback found numerous instances of couriers for drug dealers carrying cash into banks in quantities just under $10,000 in order to evade the formal requirements of the BSA.[1] This strategy is called "structuring," i.e., breaking up a single transaction into two or more separate transactions, each set to a dollar amount below the threshold, for the purpose of evading the BSA's recordkeeping and reporting requirements.[2]

The United Nations Convention Against Illicit Traffic in Narcotic Drugs and Psychotropic Substances of 1988 is one of three major drug control treaties currently in force. It provides additional legal mechanisms for enforcing the 1961 Single Convention on Narcotic Drugs and the 1971 Convention on Psychotropic Substances. The Convention entered into force on November 11, 1990. Much of the treaty is devoted to fighting organized crime by mandating cooperation in tracing and seizing drug-related assets. Article 5 of the Convention requires its parties to

[1]Levi and Reuter (2006), p. 296.
[2]See also Linn (2007, Sept), p. 407.

F.M. De Sanctis, *International Money Laundering Through Real Estate and Agribusiness*, DOI 10.1007/978-3-319-52069-8_4

confiscate proceeds of drug offences. This is considered the first international document addressing money laundering.[3]

Money laundering is defined as: (1) engaging directly or indirectly in a business transaction that involves property acquired with criminal proceeds, (2) receiving, possessing, concealing, disguising, or disposing of any property derived or realized directly or indirectly from illegal activity, or (3) retaining or acquiring property knowing that the property is derived or realized, directly or indirectly, from illegal activity.

A simplistic approach defines money laundering as a crime that occurs in three successive stages—placement, layering, and integration. This can be a shortcoming if it does not consider the role of offshores and shell companies.

Regulatory and institutional frameworks should provide for the privacy and protection of whistleblowers who report suspicious transactions or suspicious activities of money laundering. Further still, possible ways in which the legal

---

[3]Article 3 of the United Nations Convention Against Illicit Traffic in Narcotic Drugs and Psychotropic Substances provides as follows:

> 1. Each Party shall adopt such measures as may be necessary to establish as criminal offences under its domestic law, when committed intentionally:
> a) i) The production, manufacture, extraction; preparation, offering, offering for sale, distribution, sale, delivery on any terms whatsoever, brokerage, dispatch, dispatch in transit, transport, importation or exportation of any narcotic drug or any psychotropic substance contrary to the provisions of the 1961 Convention, the 1961 Convention as amended or the 1971 Convention; ii) The cultivation of opium poppy, coca bush or cannabis plant for the purpose of the production of narcotic drugs contrary to the provisions of the 1961 Convention and the 1961 Convention as amended; iii) The possession or purchase of any narcotic drug or psychotropic substance for the purpose of any of the activities enumerated in i) above; iv) The manufacture, transport or distribution of equipment, materials or of substances listed in Table I and Table II, knowing that they are to be used in or for the illicit cultivation, production or manufacture of narcotic drugs or psychotropic substances; v) The organization, management or financing of any of the offences enumerated in i), ii), iii) or iv) above;
> b) i) The conversion or transfer of property, knowing that such property is derived from any offence or offences established in accordance with subparagraph a) of this paragraph, or from an act of participation in such offence or offences, for the purpose of concealing or disguising the illicit origin of the property or of assisting any person who is involved in the commission of such an offence or offences to evade the legal consequences of his actions; ii) The concealment or disguise of the true nature, source, location, disposition, movement, rights with respect to, or ownership of property, knowing that such property is derived from an offence or offences established in accordance with subparagraph a) of this paragraph or from an act of participation in such an offence or offences;
> c) Subject to its constitutional principles and the basic concepts of its legal system: i) The acquisition, possession or use of property, knowing, at the time of receipt, that such property was derived from an offence or offences established in accordance with subparagraph a) of this paragraph or from an act of participation in such offence or offences.

United Nations Convention Against Illicit Traffic in Narcotic Drugs and Psychotropic Substances (1988).

framework for fighting money laundering could be strengthened are by introducing techniques such as shifting the burden of proof from the prosecution to the accused and lowering the standard of proof from beyond all reasonable doubts to the preponderance of probability in criminal law cases of insider dealing and money laundering.[4]

There is no simple way to unmask ownership of a shell company. We saw before that exploring each of more than 200 shell companies that have owned units in the Time Warner Center, a condo building in New York, became its own journey, with its own surprise ending. There has been a large and growing range of methods for moving money across international boundaries, yet another facet of globalization.

Michael Levi and Peter Reuter state that "knowing the balance between laundering as a separate activity and as part of the offence is important in judging the likely effectiveness of the Anti-Money Laundering (AML) regime. If the same evidence that might be used to convict people of laundering could also convict them of a substantive offence, there is little marginal benefit from the existence of the offence. There could be a benefit, however, where suspicious transaction reports from institutions point the finger of suspicion or lead to greater asset recovery, or where there is court-usable evidence of their connection to the banking or concealment of the proceeds but not of their involvement in the specific offences that generated the funds. Measuring that benefit is important because the costs of the AML system, in a number of dimensions, are very substantial and are easier to see than the benefits."[5]

The fact is that money laundering has come to such prominence so rapidly and, according to Peter Alldridge, "a common tactic in the extension of criminal law is to select 'soft targets', that is, conduct to the criminalization of which few would object, and then advance the frontier of criminality incrementally from them outwards."[6] A great example is the war on drugs, under the United Nations Convention Against Illicit Traffic in Narcotic Drugs and Psychotropic Substances, signed in 1988 in New York.

In order to restrict information availability, many disguises and antidetection mechanisms have been used and mentioned in the literature, including the use of cash, and informal money transfer services among jurisdictions, the use of corporate anonymity, offshores, shell companies, attorney–client privilege, and confidentiality.

The intergovernmental standard-setting body at the Organization for Economic Co-operation and Development (OECD), the Financial Action Task Force (FATF), although not a treaty-based organization, is trying to work on norms to facilitate the cooperation among States for the global action against laundering, subjected to rigorous checks for accurate efficacy.

---

[4]Kaoma Mwenda (2006), p. 175.

[5]Levi and Reuter (2006), pp. 292–293.

[6]Alldridge (2008, Dec).

Cash payments are one of the easiest ways to not be bothered about their provenance. These payments do not fall within the regulated sector, i.e., they are out of the reach of anti-money laundering efforts. When money is invested lawfully (in legitimate business, like properties), then the real harm is the original crime, and this cannot mean that money laundering is not an additional bad crime because it permits or stimulates the continuation of the predicate crime, the overpricing of goods, and unfair business competition. So independently, it should generate severe sentences.

The simple use of lawfully acquired assets to hide illegal prior processes must be prevented due to laundering deals with capital mobility and business regulation, besides the liabilities of international companies. The traditional view of criminal jurisdiction (territorial principle, extradition, and mutual assistance[7]) is now challenged by a new era that requires efficient transnational enforcement mechanisms. That is why international intelligence gathering must be emphasized. The technological aspects of globalization bring greater exchange of information among governments.

The fact is that the conversion of criminal incomes to forms that allow the unfettered offender spending and investing has been an ongoing concern to both criminals and the State. Benefits of crime cannot weigh more positively in the utilitarian calculus of offenders than the costs associated with formal legal sanctions.[8]

According to Jean Spreutels and Caty Grijseels, although governments around the globe are grappling with the issue of how to best maximize the benefits of increasing globalization, at the same time they are trying to figure out how to minimize the potential for abuse by criminals of the financial liberalization and technological advancements that have fostered globalization. "New technologies, the removal of exchange controls and increased access to foreign financial institutions have reduced the cost of capital but also increased opportunities for tax evasion and money laundering."[9]

In money laundering prosecutions, evidence is typically based on information from the actual behavior of offenders, like seizures, house searches, statements from suspects and witnesses, and wiretappings. In terrorism, however, the primary focus of investigations is on future behavior that has to be prevented, evidenced by terrorist intentions as an outcome of concrete terrorist preparatory activities. Both crimes have been using, when organized, the international environment.[10]

Money laundering is often distanced from the original crime, and many times it is distanced far away. For that reason, it is a globalized crime and every jurisdiction

[7]Under the model of sovereignty, each country was responsible for its own criminal law and proceeds of the breach of those criminal laws were specific to the jurisdiction because they are specific to that set of criminal laws.

[8]According to Simpson and Koper (1992), the benefits of crime weigh more positively than the costs of legal sanctions, p. 368.

[9]Spreutels and Grijseels (2001), p. 12.

[10]Kleemans (2007).

should criminalize it severely regardless of where the predicate crime was committed due to the system of values that condemns this specific behavior.

Each of us, in the modern global world, must be even more vigilant and on our guard. As a globalized crime, immunity *ratione materiae* (functional immunity) cannot shield anyone from prosecution for money laundering and corruption, as well as genocide, crimes against humanity, war crimes, and torture. On the other hand, immunity *ratione personae* (personal immunity) remains, at the current stage of international law (the need of upholding state sovereignty), a defense from prosecution of heads of States, with exceptions for international tribunals, the International Criminal Court (ICC), and within the parameters of their respective mandates and jurisdictions.[11]

Working to ensure anti-Money laundering compliance by relevant sectors increases the likelihood that money laundering will be detected.

4.1 Property Confiscation

When discussing money laundering through properties, it is important to highlight that money laundering refers only to the acquirement, possession, or use of criminal assets. In legal practice, it was acknowledged that money laundering offence does not exist if the source of assets procured from the free market cannot be indicated. The law defines illicit character of the goods' origin only identifying them as goods coming from committing offences. It requires a careful assessment to determine the need for a tool that introduces the obligation of establishing the measure of confiscation, to allow for the confiscation of the equivalent value as well, so-called "extended confiscation." In this case, the confiscation extends to assets other than those for which the connection with the offence had been proved, as well as on the assets of people other than those convicted. This measure may be ordered if general conditions are met, namely, if the offender committed a previous offence.[12]

The confiscation of such resources by the State also strengthens public safety in general, by allowing for federal investment in state and federal police forces, and in education to prevent serious crime.

All of the money or assets transferred to the State will certainly result in special crime-fighting and prevention programs, as well as combined efforts on the part of the States and the federal government and its agencies, culminating in proper enforcement methods to curtail crime. The idea is to create a safe place for freedom, security, and justice. This is no small feat, for it necessarily implies a joint effort on the part of the police, prosecutors, and the courts to obtain property illegally acquired. Forfeiture, confiscation, and repatriation require cooperation. Learning from decisions made in the searching out and seizing of the proceeds of crime will

[11] Jovanovic (2009), pp. 221–222.

[12] In this sense, see Rababah (2014), pp. 244, 246–248, 250.

result in improvement of the work and training of public agents, and in the adoption of new measures to fight crime.

Despite the vast quantities of goods routinely seized and confiscated, the subject has not held the attention of scholars—unlike other issues such as the length of prison terms, the growing number of inmates, and the quality of penitentiaries and prisons.[13]

When assets are confiscated, the message that gets sent to organized crime is that financially, crime no longer pays, and is not in the best interests of its practitioners. It drives home the message that some types of behavior really are prohibited, and that to insist on engaging in them is to pay the price.

It would be better if confiscated assets could be put on exhibit, especially cultural assets, with a plaque explaining that each was confiscated by the Justice Department. Efforts to benefit artists through the dissemination of culture ought also to occupy the labor of the courts. The criminal courts from time to time encounter works of art created for public exposition in parks or city squares. These things come to light through historical studies or even disclosures by family members of the artist, sculptor, or painter.

Here, despite the enormous effort it takes to convince and garner commitments from several national and international government agencies, it is incumbent upon the judge to reconcile the interest generated by the free exposure resulting from a simple exhibition, without losing sight of the duty to preserve.

However, regarding artworks, all must be done in urging government agencies to see to the preservation of the asset, and also to direct it to a public space, even if on a provisional basis. The understanding is that the exhibit, albeit temporary, would lend an added cultural value, to allow persons of all backgrounds—even though they may use the public mass transit system—to witness works of artistic and historical value.

Confiscation differs from pecuniary penalties because of the implicit perception that the violation determines the payment. But when assets are forfeited, the amount varies in accordance with the proceeds derived from criminal behavior. The greater the proceeds from crime, the larger the confiscation. Defendants in comfortable financial circumstances ought to be subject to forfeiture of assets not trivial to them. In other words, ill-gotten goods should be taken in proportion to criminal behavior.

Pecuniary fines and confiscation are measures independent of one another, yet incorrectly distinguished by many jurists. Because they are calculated differently, they cannot be added together for purposes of establishing the penalty imposed, for that would reduce the penalty.

The system as a whole works best when confiscation is kept as one of the solutions among the several outcomes of sentencing. The clear message sent by proceeding with such measures is that unlawful behavior is in fact prohibited.

---

[13]McCaw (2011), p. 183.

In addition to criminal cases, there is also the possibility of administrative or civil confiscation. FATF Recommendation No. 04 makes it clear that no prior criminal conviction is required for the forfeiture of assets.

This is something that occurs frequently in the United States (actions *in rem*, that is, proceeding against the thing itself) whenever the property or its possession is related to criminal activity.[14] As these claims are framed, ownership or possession are considered illegal, in which case the interested party may intervene to prevent loss to the government. In such cases, it is incumbent upon the government to prove beyond a reasonable doubt that the asset is actually subject to forfeiture, inasmuch as the thing and its possessor are both somehow connected to crime.[15]

In the case of fungible goods such as cash, showing the connection between the asset and the crime is quite complicated. Thus, suppose that the government wants to show that $100,000 is revenue from drugs. The trafficker has the said $100,000 in an account, derived from that crime. If he were to spend $50,000 and has that same amount in another account, only in this case the money was legitimately earned, pursuant to the US law, that identical asset will be subject to forfeiture.[16]

In harmony with this, we have also the United Nations Conventions against Organized Crime [Article 12(a)] and against Corruption (Article 46), which operate on the idea that that the confiscation is indeed collectable, even in the event of the death of the accused or expiration of the statute of limitations.

To Catherine McCaw, civil and criminal confiscations are not mutually exclusive. Were the Government to file both actions, each on its own grounds, and lose one, this in no way precludes continuing to seek confiscation on the remaining action.[17]

The symbolism in the forfeiture of personal property is striking. People promptly perceive that the outcome is as upsetting, if not more so, when having to face, in addition to imprisonment, loss of the equivalent of the proceeds from crime.

Hence, confiscation has become a priority strategy in the fight against organized crime. However, inasmuch as criminal activity has become transnational, and criminal investments have increased incredibly outside of national boundaries, a vast network has emerged to make use of the proceeds of crime, and has taken root in loopholes or legal hurdles in the way of crime-fighting efforts.

Criminals often work off of an interpretation established in case law. This is what justifies shoring up asset forfeiture even though the assets may have been transferred to some third party who nevertheless ought to have perceived that these

---

[14]United States v. Bajakajian, 524 U.S. 321 (1998), United States v. One-Sixth Share, 326 F.Wd 36 (1st Cir. 2003).

[15]18 U.S.C. § 983 (c) (1) (3).

[16]18 U.S.C. § 984 (a) (2) provides as follows: "Except as provided in subsection (b), any identical property found in the same place or account as the property involved in the offense that is the basis for the forfeiture shall be subject to forfeiture under this section." 18 U.S.C. § 984 (b) provides: "No action pursuant to this section to forfeit property not traceable directly to the offense that is the basis for the forfeiture may be commenced more than 1 year from the date of the offense."

[17]McCaw (2011), p. 195.

were the proceeds of unlawful conduct, or had been transferred precisely to avoid confiscation (establishment of a good faith third party).[18]

No burdens should be placed on police and state's attorneys' efforts to temporarily freeze or solicit the freezing of assets liable to disappear if nothing is done, and all such measures are, to be sure, subject to consideration by the courts. Nor is any such interference warranted when the assets are located abroad.

Governments ought therefore to allow the freezing, seizure, confiscation, and repatriation of assets in order to facilitate the fight against organized crime, itself a global business, in such a manner as to force the criminals to change their ways.

FATF Recommendation No. 30 establishes the possibility of conducting freezing and seizure operations, even when commission of the predicate crime may have occurred in another jurisdiction (country). It also recommends the implementation of specialized multidisciplinary groups or task forces, thereby showing the importance of international cooperation to vitalize all necessary efforts to assist States in their mission to fight crime.

When we consider agribusiness, the confiscation must result in selling goods by the court, even though abroad, because of its nature, preventing or prohibiting the repatriation. In this case, the obtained amount from the sales can be repatriated instead of the actual cattle, swine, horses, or fish.

According to Fletcher Baldwin Jr., in examining this ongoing fight against international money laundering, there are three dimensions involved: consistent policies between national and international efforts, an efficient legal and institutional apparatus, and close cooperation between the public and private sectors.[19]

For an effective and cohesive universal policy against money laundering, participation by and commitment of all States to international cooperation is imperative.

Nowadays, there are local due diligence or good faith requirements in place as a hedge against unlawful behavior. Absent that, the buyer or the intermediate of an asset might be subject to liability for contributing to the further removal of the object from the victim (under a conscious avoidance doctrine or assumption of risk).

Due diligence means that both the buyer and the merchant must show that they have searched the official and unofficial lists of stolen items, and checked with the authorities to ensure that they do not gain possession of any item that has an illegal origin. The dealer must show that the asset was purchased in the honest belief that there was nothing suspicious or shady going on.

In other words, the burden of proof is on the third party to show legitimate possession when the government alleges that the item was transferred to him in order to dodge confiscation, or in the belief that he would deliberately act without due caution. This is how repatriation has been accomplished.

---

[18]European Commission (2012, Mar 12).

[19]Baldwin (2009, Jan), pp. 47–48.

Hence, confiscation and repatriation are two stages of legal proceedings in which the assets of criminals are forfeited on behalf of the victims, communities, or governments. Central to this procedure is the decision that a given asset was acquired as the proceeds of unlawful conduct and may therefore be confiscated.

The first stage in repatriation is the tracking and identification of goods. This normally involves coordinated efforts on the part of prosecutors and government agencies (revenue authorities, the police, and private collaborators). These efforts also require substantial expertise and skill in dealing with the financial transactions that are sometimes involved. These normally involve communication among the authorities.

4.2 International Legal Cooperation

International legal cooperation has been essential to shedding light on the activities of organized groups. It has enabled the blocking of goods and repatriation of assets that rely on companies and institutions that have their main offices in tax havens.

In the reciprocal approach to international legal cooperation, governments cooperate with one another in the absence of a treaty or international agreement, acting through mutual commitments undertaken to deal with a specific case.

The UN Convention against the Illegal Traffic in Narcotic Drugs and Psychotropic Substances (Vienna, 1988, Articles 6 and 7), Law No. 11343 dated August 23, 2006 (the Brazilian drug law, Article 65), the Extradition Treaty to which MERCOSUL Member States are parties,[20] the UN Convention against Transnational Organized Crime (Palermo, 2000, Articles 16–19), the UN Convention against Corruption (Mérida, 2003, Articles 44 and 46), the Council of Europe Convention on Laundering, Search, Seizure, and Confiscation of the Proceeds from Crime (Strasbourg, 1990, Articles 7–35), the Council of Europe Convention on Laundering, Search, Seizure and Confiscation of the Proceeds from Crime and on the Financing of Terrorism (Warsaw, 2005, Articles 15–45), Brazil's Money-Laundering Law (No. 9613, of March 3, 1998, Article 8, as amended by Law 12683 of July 9, 2012), and the Model Regulation promulgated by the Inter-American Drug Abuse Control Commission (CICAD/OAS, Article 20), all contain such provisions of mutual reciprocity.

The FATF clearly emphasizes in its Recommendations the need to reinforce international cooperation through general exchange of information relating to suspicious transactions. There is the understanding that the various standards relating to the element of intent in criminal conduct should not affect the ability or

[20]The extradition treaty specifically addresses international legal cooperation. One conclusion arrived at in Rio de Janeiro on December 10, 1998, was promulgated in Brazil through Legislative Decree No. 605 of Septembe 11, 2003, which became effective internationally on January 1, 2004, as a result of the Treaty of Asunción, creating the South American common market, MERCOSUL (signed March 26, 1991).

the will of countries to cooperate on judicial matters. The Recommendations establish: the possibility of freezing and seizure even where the antecedent crime was committed in some other jurisdiction (country), as well as the implementation of specialized multidisciplinary teams or task forces (Recommendation No. 30); international legal cooperation, pursuant to the UN Conventions of Vienna (international traffic, 1988), Palermo (transnational organized crime, 2000) and Mérida (corruption, 2003), by withdrawal of obstacles (Recommendation No. 36); direct mutual legal assistance toward a quick, constructive and effective solution (Recommendation No. 37); freezing and confiscation even where there is no prior conviction (Recommendation No. 38); extradition (Recommendation No. 39); an attitude favoring the repression of antecedent crimes, money laundering and terrorism financing (Recommendation No. 40).

International cooperation, however, requires more than just legal cooperation. It also requires administrative cooperation not contingent upon indictments. In the latter case, all communication occurs through intelligence channels. Information is exchanged by the financial intelligence units and by direct cooperation between financial intelligence units, the attorney generals' offices, and police authorities, in many countries.

As Patrícia Núñez Weber explains:[21]

> International administrative cooperation is in the strictest sense not tied to any criminal demands or occurrences, but aimed at technological improvement, exchange of information, creation and maintenance of databases, and the sharing of strategies among the agencies involved. Yet the term is also used to designate cooperation among administrative authorities quite apart from court orders.

This brings us to the possibility of direct exchanges of information through the aforementioned intelligence channels. Most of the information would originate out of legal cooperation, under the aegis of the Judicial Branch, most notably in cases that require measures such as seizure and lifting of bank or tax record secrecy, that is, whenever a court order is needed.

Brazil's basic institutions for judicial cooperation on criminal matters may be summed up as follows: extradition, transfer of convicts, certification of a foreign criminal sentence, rogatory letters, and direct assistance. These latter two are intrinsically bound up with investigations and information on criminal activity, and for this reason are given greater weight here.

International legal cooperation, generally speaking, may be viewed as active or passive depending on the relative position of each of the States involved. It is active if the requesting State formulates a petition that a measure be taken and passive when a requested State receives a request for cooperation.

It may, in addition, be direct or indirect. In the latter case, it is intrinsically related to the *prima-facie* evaluation, as in the case of rogatory letters transmitted to

[21]De Carli (2011), p. 589.

Brazil. As for the direct form, this comes about "when the Court of Examination judge is fully apprised. Here we are dealing with direct assistance."[22]

The letter rogatory is the procedural instrument through which the legal authorities in one country request of another the enforcement of an order issued by the judicial branch of the requesting State.

Brazil's Federal Constitution of October 5, 1998, provides in Article 105, Subsection I(i), that in order for a rogatory letter transmitted to Brazil to be executed, the Superior Court of Justice must conduct a *prima-facie* evaluation before issuing an *exequatur*. After this authorization is given, federal judges would then have jurisdiction to assess and pass on enforcement of the rogatory letter, as set forth in Article 109, Subsection X, of the Brazilian Constitution.

The *exequatur* is no more than the authorization given by the Superior Court of Justice to allow within Brazil the enforcement of police inquiries or procedural acts requested by the foreign legal authority.

Pursuant to Superior Court of Justice Resolution No. 09/2005, notably in its Articles 8 through 10, the *prima-facie* evaluation must be conducted with the participation of the interested parties, as follows:

> Art. 8 The interested party shall be cited to answer the request for certification of a foreign sentence within 15 days, or summoned to impugn the letter rogatory.
>
> Sole paragraph. The measure requested through the letter rogatory may be set in motion without giving the interested party a hearing whenever such advance intimation could render the international cooperation ineffective.
>
> Art. 9 In the certification of a foreign sentence and in letters rogatory, the defense is only entitled to make a statement on the authenticity of the documents, intelligence underlying the decision, and observance of the requirements of this Resolution.
>
> § 1 Whenever certification of a foreign sentence is contested, suit shall be filed for judgment by the Special Court, and a Rapporteur appointed and responsible for all other acts relating to and informing the proceedings.
>
> § 2 In the event of impugnment of letters rogatory containing judgments, proceedings may, by order of the President, be held over for judgment by the Special Court.
>
> § 3 Should respondent abscond or be incapable, a special curator shall be named and personally served notice.
>
> Art. 10 The Office of the Public Prosecutor shall have 10 days in which to examine the record in the letters rogatory and enrollment of foreign judgments, and may also impugn these.

Bear in mind that incoming rogatory letters are received in Brazil through diplomatic channels, most notably through the Ministry of External Relations, and all active rogatory letters in Brazil lack the *exequatur*.

The bureaucratic side of processing rogatory letters led to an increase in another mode of international cooperation: direct assistance. This allows us to get around the sending and procedural delays of rogatory letters, for it allows direct

[22]Cestari and Toffoli (2009), p. 24.

transmission. It has emerged as practically the most effective alternative in the fight against international crime.

Through this form of cooperation, authorities other than the judiciary may avail themselves of international requests, and the procedures are much simpler than those involving traditional rogatory letters, and even dispense with the *prima-facie* evaluation in Brazil.

This brings us back to the observations of Patrícia Núñez Weber, who assures us that:[23]

> Direct assistance is cooperation offered by national authorities and likely to satisfy the foreign request, in the performance of their legal duties as though it were a national procedure, when in fact it arises from a request by a foreign State channeled through Brazil's central authority.
>
> (…)
>
> Currently, the most widespread understanding is that direct assistance presupposes the existence of a treaty or agreement with the requesting State, or a promise of reciprocity. Our feeling is that that restriction arises from the relatively recent arrival of the institution on the international scene, compared to letters rogatory.

In direct assistance, once the request is received by the central authority and forwarded to the judiciary authorities, the judge may then examine the facts presented by the foreign nation on their merits, much as in domestic proceedings to which current procedural rules would apply. This is something that does not happen with rogatory letters.

Requests for direct assistance are generally couched in terms of international treaties or agreements. One approach is through the application of reciprocity, according to which governments may cooperate with one another in the absence of some previous treaty or international agreement, acting through mutual commitments undertaken in dealing with a specific case.

For example, José Antônio Dias Toffoli and Virgínia Charpinel Junger Cestari explain that:[24]

> Requests for direct assistance are, as a rule, couched in terms of bilateral treaties or agreements (the so-called Mutual Legal Assistance Treaties or MLATs). Absent any express understanding between the two States, assistance can still be provided based on the requester's assurance of reciprocity. This allows cooperation in many different tax, labor or pensions-related areas. Still, the treaties most frequently encountered in an international setting have to do with criminal and civil subject matter.

How to determine which acts require a granting of *exequatur* (in passive cooperation) and which require issuance of rogatory letters (for active cooperation) for their proper performance is a question that calls for a comprehensive analysis.

The Brazilian Superior Court of Justice did shed some light on how it handles cases of international legal cooperation in its Resolution No. 9/2005, specifically in

[23]De Carli (2001), pp. 593, 602.

[24]Cestari and Toffoli (2009), p. 27.

Article 7, which allows us to make out that the direct assistance mode of cooperation, where it calls for judicial consideration, should be brought to the judicial notice of the court of first instance. Specifically:

> Article 7. Letters rogatory may request decisional acts or non-decisional acts.
>
> Sole paragraph. Requests for international cooperation which do not involve prima-facie evaluation by the Superior Court of Justice shall—even if classified as letters rogatory—be forwarded or returned to the Ministry of Justice so that all necessary steps may be taken to comply with them by direct assistance.

One can infer, in this provision, that in these cases the granting of *exequatur* may be waived, allowing the central authority to take all appropriate action to provide direct assistance.

The First Panel of the Supreme Federal Court has made a declarative statement as to the need for a granting of *exequatur* by the Superior Court of Justice for acting on indictments issued by foreign judicial authorities, as follows:[25]

> Engaging in law enforcement actions within Brazilian national territory to enforce orders issued by foreign judicial authorities presupposes the transmission of a letter rogatory, for purposes of enforcement, to be passed on by the Superior Court of Justice, there being no proper way to bring about international cooperation at the cost of relegating to a lesser role a formality essential to the validity of the acts to be performed.

Afterward, the Special Court of the Superior Court of Justice was able to have its say in the matter, in Complaint No. 2645/SP, reported by Minister Teori Albino Zavascki, it having been shown that rogatory letters procedure ought only be followed for requests of a jurisdictional nature formulated by the foreign authority, and that all other solicitations ought to comply with the requirements set by international regulatory bodies.

At an opportune time, amidst allegations of usurpation of jurisdiction of the Superior Court of Justice for the granting of *exequatur* for rogatory letters, the Superior Court of Justice authorized, at the request of the Office of the Federal Prosecutor, the shipment of the hard drive confiscated from the computer in possession of a defendant to the Russian Federation's Attorney General's Office, in response to a request transmitted by the Russian Assistant Attorney General.[26]

---

[25]Supremo Tribunal Federal (2006, Dec 15), p. 95.

[26]This Superior Court of Justice decision reads as follows:

> The Office of the Federal Prosecutor in making the complaint sought to assemble an exhibit with all documents (in Russian and in English) and forward it on to the Attorney General for the Attorney General for the Russian Federation, along with corresponding official translations (folios 163-165). In the opening statement of the acknowledgment of receipt of that exhibit (folios 167/168), this Court ordered that Attachments be compiled to include all documents alluded to, and they were named as follows: 'Attachments VII and VIII.' The following was granted on an item 'c' of the decision set forth on folios 169-214, the petition likewise formulated by the Attorney General's Office for forwarding copy of the hard drives to the Office of the Attorney General of the Russian Federation, as requested by that Authority. The devices in question were at the Federal Police Intelligence Bureau in Brasilia for forensic analysis and were apprehended in May 2006 in the possession of Boris

(Footnote 26 continued)

Abramovich Berezovisk, pursuant to a search warrant, as well as a bench warrant naming the suspect, who was then taken to the Office of the Attorney General in this capital city to depose on facts being investigated in Brazil and theoretically related to the racketeering offense (Art. 288 of the Criminal Code), given the suspect's supposed association with other persons for the constant and ongoing purpose of engaging in illegal 'laundering' of money, by exploiting the partnership entered into between MSI and Sport Club Corinthians of São Paulo. At the time of the seizure, consideration was also given to the fact that the suspect had entered Brazil using the name Platon Ilyich Yelenin, and was also included in the Red Notice issued by Interpol requesting that the individual be located and arrested for extradition, even though at the time the warrant had not been through proceedings in Brazil for purposes of certification by the Supreme Federal Court (folios 932-934, 1052, 1057-1060, 1061, 1063-1064, 1065-1072, 1082-1084, 1092, 1094 and 1098 of record No. 2006.61.81.005118-0/Attachment VII, admitted in connection with the Criminal Action). The copies in question were forwarded through official communiqué No. 1040/2007-rba dated 09/28/2007 to his Excellency, Russia's Ambassador to Brazil Wladimir Turdenev, for forwarding to the Attorney General's Office in Russia (See folio 75 of the Addendum compiled pursuant to Order No. 18/2005 of this Court). The Russian Federation, like Brazil, is a signatory to the UN Convention against Corruption known as the Mérida Convention, after the Mexican city in which it was signed. It has been signed by 150 countries, 95 of which enforce it internationally, foremost among them being Argentina, Australia, Spain, the United States, China, France and the United Kingdom. The procedure adopted by this Court in response to the request formulated by the Ministry follows the recommendations set forth in that Convention, notably in the chapter relating to International Cooperation in its Articles 43, and 46, among others, and by the 2000 UN Convention at Palermo on transnational organized crime, in particular in its Articles 18, 27 and 28. And this was accomplished with no deviation from Brazil's own legal proceedings, inasmuch as it also followed the form outlined in Article 7 of Resolution No. 09 of 05/04/2005 by the President of this Respectable Court, to wit: 'Art. 7 Letters rogatory may request decisional acts or non-decisional acts. Sole paragraph. Requests for international cooperation which do not involve prima-facie evaluation by the Superior Court of Justice shall—even if classified as letters rogatory —be forwarded or returned to the Ministry of Justice so that all necessary steps may be taken to comply with them by direct assistance.' (Emphasis ours). Direct assistance, absent better options, follows from the application of the rules of procedure of the Mérida and Palermo Conventions as from the measure requested by the Office of the Federal Prosecutor, to say nothing of the policy of reciprocity which, in the absence of specific rules, underlies international relations. This is why it was unnecessary to raise the issue of the granting of exequatur as set forth in Article 105, subsection I, clause 'i' of the Federal Constitution. In fact, the Palermo Convention stipulates the duty of mutual legal assistance between the Parties when the Requesting State has reasonable grounds to suspect a transnational infraction, and hence the duty to provide all legal cooperation (Article 18, items 1 and 2), to which is added the recommendation that special investigative techniques be used, such as electronic eavesdropping (Article 20, item 1). It further provides an interchange of information to keep the State Parties apprised of trends in organized crime on their territory, of the circumstances in which it operates and of professional groups and technologies involved, and may, to that end, be shared among them (Article 28, items 1 and 2). Furthermore, and in particular, this cooperation is aimed toward detecting and tracking the proceeds of crime, transfer methods, and the dissimulating or disguising of these proceeds in the 'fight against money laundering and other financial crimes' (Article 29, item 1, 'd'). The international treaty in question, now duly integrated as the law of the land, provides a basis for the investigation, but in addition, urges the State Parties to effectively repress transnational criminal organizations. The UN Conventions against Organized Transnational Crime and against Corruption, it can actually be said, amount to an attempt by all sovereign states to eliminate groups rooted in a certain criminal milieu which systematically resorts to obstruction of justice—in addition to engaging in criminal

By the understanding set forth in the decision, the constitutional requirement contained in Article 105, subsection I, item 'i', contains no grant of exclusivity to the Superior Court of Justice to intermediate all international legal cooperation. There must be consideration of its operation in relations among the various

(Footnote 26 continued)

behavior which affronts the rule of law, and often operates by what amounts to intimidation. What we have here are global legal guidelines. There has been no news yet of forensic analysis of the hard drives, but please note that documented proof by examination was already on the record before this Court, for it was produced on account of the search warrant issued by the Brazilian Federal Justice System in May 2006 in record of proceedings under No. 2006.61.81.005118-0/Attachment VII, as we have seen, and THIS DID NOT RESULT from any request submitted by a foreign authority, so that the prima-facie evaluation was never an issue. This is simply a case of sharing legitimate evidence produced here. In the Complaint lodged before this Honorable Court, Plaintiff also holds that the official foreign documents were neither translated into Portuguese nor stamped with diplomatic or consular certification required to make them stand up in any court of law, and further postulates renewed application of Code of Criminal Procedure Articles 780 et. seq. [Jurisdictional Relations with Foreign Authorities], as previously submitted on occasion of filing for Habeas Corpus No. 2007.03.00.091069-0. No such argumentation would apply absent additional information, at the heart of a Complaint expostulating only about jurisdiction. In any case, in the aforementioned writ, in proceedings before the Second Panel of the Hon. Regional Federal Court for Region 3, the petition was not granted by the Eminent Rapporteuse for the Habeas Corpus, Her Excellency, Federal High Court Justice Cecília Mello. The foreign language document in question is accompanied by a certified translation, in full compliance with Code of Criminal Procedure Article 236. Hence no taint of irregularity or affront to the law may be ascribed to the admission of those documents, for what we have is a true copy duly forwarded by an agency of the Russian Government. This Court also understands that the provisions contained in Articles 780 et seq. of the Code of Criminal Procedure do not apply as claimed in the Complaint, for the instant case does not involve transmittal of letters rogatory. The reasons set forth in the documents comprising the record are beyond reproach, inasmuch as all provisions of the Code of Criminal Procedure which govern the matter have been fully complied with. Observe that the Claimant, in the reasons for filing the aforesaid writ acknowledged that the '... Code of Criminal Procedure contained no specific provision on admissibility of foreign documents intended as evidence in criminal proceedings...' that only being expressly required for letters rogatory (folios 952-953). The admissibility of the foreign documents is in order, in no small part for having been obtained from a foreign authority free of any imputations of illegal behavior given the absolute lack of any grounds for indicating such a thing. There is no denying that international recommendations now seek to simplify procedures and international cooperation, provided there is not, as in this case, any reason to question authenticity, and also provided there is no infringement of our national legal system. Even absent all of the above, one could still argue that the Claimant is a Russian citizen and has resided in the United Kingdom for a considerable time, circumstances that warrant the conclusion that both Counsel and Claimant ought to be familiar with the probative material. Indeed, the aforementioned Article 236 of procedural law does not even require the translation where it is patently unnecessary. Although this Court has been unable to discern any irregularity in the documentation forwarded by the Russian Authorities, it has been previously noted that if the Defense so wishes, the Defense could produce a new translation of the documents so as to clear up its misgivings. And so it did, inasmuch as it requested the translation into Portuguese of all documents contained in folios 08, 11 and 12 of Attachment No. 12, which request was met by the order issued on 11/14/2007 (folios 1392 and 1400-1414).

judiciary agencies, and, in addition, the various forms of cooperation established in international treaties.

Hence, the request for legal cooperation formulated by a foreign authority (in this case, the Office of the Attorney General for the Russian Federation, regarding the sharing of evidence during an ongoing investigation and transmitted to its Brazilian counterpart, Brazil's Office of the Attorney General), shall not be contingent upon issuance of rogatory letters by Russian judicial authorities, thereby obviating the need for an *exequatur* from the Superior Court of Justice.

For a clearer understanding, I call attention to an excerpt from the vote cast by the eminent Rapporteur, Teori Albino Zavascki:[27]

> The international system of legal cooperation clearly does not exclude cooperative measures among agents of the judiciary brought about through the use of letters rogatory, within the scope of proceedings already within the jurisdictional sphere. But in addition to these, as pointed out, mutual cooperation encompasses a host of other provisions which may even, where applicable, give rise to future criminal prosecutions. Yet insofar as their scope is restricted to prevention and investigation, they require for their performance no prior approval or judicial intermediation. There is no such requirement in Brazil's domestic law, nor is there any reason for such a requirement in the area of international law.
>
> In Brazilian law, as in most countries, the prevention and investigation of crimes, not jurisdictional by nature, is not the purview of the Judicial Branch, but rather, of police authorities or the Office of the Public Prosecutor, under the Executive Branch.
>
> Indeed, the nature of jurisdictional questions—which as a rule are submitted to formal, public, adversarial proceedings—is neither proper to nor compatible with typical police matters, such as these now under consideration, involving prevention and criminal investigation. In our system, only a few such measures require prior judicial approval, such as in the case of those requiring entry into an individual home, or wiretaps (CF, Art. 5, XI and XII).
>
> Aside from these cases, there is no reason at all—even in the case of investigations or preventive measures undertaken during international cooperation efforts—to impose jurisdictional boundaries on these activities, thereby rendering them subject to intermediation or advance prima-facie evaluation by agencies of the corresponding Judicial Branch. Because it takes account of such circumstances, the international legal cooperation system, which includes Brazil, reflects and honors the system of duties and assignments already in place in domestic law, and strictly and fully preserves all of the constitutional duties of the Judicial Branch, including those having to do with jurisdictional considerations affecting the standing of the agencies and authorities involved to take action.

Moreover, the subject of actual standing to issue a rogatory letter to Brazil was recently raised by the First Supreme Federal Court Panel in the Clarification Requests on *Habeas Corpus* Declaration No. 87.759/DF, reported by Minister Marco Aurélio, in which the Clarification Requests were honored in order to state that the Italian Attorney General's Office did indeed have standing to issue them:[28]

---

[27]Rapporteur Minister Teori Albino Zavascki (2009, Dec 16).

[28]Rapporteur Minister Marco Aurélio (2012, Mar 14).

> Once an omission was found in the judgment, faced with the treaty of cooperation on criminal matters entered into between Brazil and the Republic of Italy—as part of its national legal process—honoring the appeals for clarification would follow, albeit with no power to bring about change, it being recognized that the Italian Attorney General's office does have standing to issue rogatory letters.

Initially, at the time of the granting of *habeas corpus*, it was understood that the rogatory letter had not been issued by a judicial authority, which would have violated the provisions of Article 202, subsection I of the Code of Civil Procedure, which regulates the *indication of courts of origin*, so that nationally cooperation through letters rogatory transmitted by a foreign Attorney General's office would cease to exist.[29]. In accordance with the precedent set by the Supreme Federal Court in examining the Explanatory Restatement of Decisions, account was taken of Article 784 of the Code of Criminal Procedure, which makes provisions concerning *competent foreign authorities*, inasmuch as it allows a broader interpretation than *judicial authority* for purposes of transmitting rogatory letters to Brazil, in that it encompasses agencies clothed in judicial powers.

Legislative Decree No. 501 of March 21, 2012,[30] published in the Federal Official Gazette on March 23, 2012, made provisions regarding the procedures for

---

[29]However, in examining the appeals requesting clarification, the Rapporteur noted as follows:

> There was warning of a defect, at the beginning of the voting, in that it had not been issued by a judicial authority per se, which brought up the provisions of Article 202, subsection I of the Code of Civil Procedure. It was deemed apropos to remark on not having taken proper account of the fact that Article 784 of the Code of Criminal Procedure makes reference to letters rogatory issued not from judicial authorities, but from competent foreign authorities. Moreover, consonant with item 1 of Article 1 of the Treaty on Legal Cooperation in Criminal Matters entered into between Brazil and the Republic of Italy—promulgated through Ministerial Decree No. 862 of July 9, 1993—"each of the parties shall, on request, provide to the other party, in the form set forth in this Treaty, ample cooperation for criminal proceedings conducted by the judicial authorities of the requesting party." The reference to judicial authorities by the requesting party suggests, initially, agencies clothed in judicial appointments, as in the Brazilian system. However, in Italy, the Attorney General's office is part of the judicial system, per Articles 107, 108 and 112 under the title headed "The Courts" (Italian Constitution, Part II, Title IV). The judicial branch is organized institutionally in a linear fashion, within that same Branch, its duties involving judgment or work traditionally included in the area reserved to the Office of the Public Prosecutor. Briefly, it is a blending of functions, all of them subject to the Superior Council of the Courts. As pointed out by best doctrine, the Attorney General's Office in Italy is an agency for the administration of Justice, and includes all measures that may be taken there for purposes of criminal investigations. See "O Ministério Público na Investigação Penal Preliminar," by Marcos Kac. Hence, the Supreme Court of Justice, in Letter Rogatory No. 998/IT, through a unanimous panel decision authored by Minister Humberto Gomes de Barros, concluded: "The Attorney General's Office together with the Tribunal of Parma does have standing to request Brazilian cooperation in investigations."

[30]Legislative Decree No. 501 of March 21, 2012, provides as follows:

Art. 1 – This Decree establishes procedures for letters rogatory and both active and passive

(Footnote 30 continued)

requests for direct assistance in criminal and civil matters in the absence of any bilateral or multilateral international legal cooperation agreement, and applies only subsidiarily to this case.

Art. 2 – The following considerations apply for purposes of this Decree:

I. Request for passive direct assistance, the request for international legal cooperation which does not require a prima-facie evaluation by the Superior Court of Justice, pursuant to Art. 7, of Superior Court of Justice Resolution No. 9 of May 4, 2005; and
II. Passive letter rogatory, a request for international legal cooperation which does require a prima-facie evaluation by the Superior Court of Justice. Sole Paragraph. Definition of the request for active direct support and an active letter rogatory is in accordance with the domestic legislation of the Requested State.

Art. 3 – In all cases in which the request for passive international legal cooperation does not entail the granting of exequatur by the Superior Court of Justice, and may be handled through administrative channels, not requiring intervention by the Judicial Branch, the Ministry of Justice shall, together with the competent administrative authorities, see to its granting.

Art. 4 – The Ministry of External Relations shall forward to the Ministry of Justice all requests for passive international legal cooperation, on criminal and civil matters, transmitted through diplomatic channels.

Art. 5 – In the absence of bilateral or multilateral international legal cooperation agreements, the Ministry of Justice shall forward to the Ministry of External Relations all active requests for international legal cooperation on criminal and civil matters, to be handled through diplomatic channels.

Art. 6 – The Ministry of Justice shall:

I. Provide attachments and opinions to and coordinate the granting of requests for international legal cooperation in criminal and civil matters, by forwarding these to the competent judicial or administrative authority;
II. Issue and publish understandings on international legal cooperation within the scope of its powers.

Art. 7 – Letters rogatory must include:

I. Identification of the requesting and requested courts;
II. The address of the requesting judge;
III. A detailed description of the measure requested;
IV. The purpose to be achieved by the requested measure;
V. Complete name and address of the person to be cited, notified, served a summons or questioned in the jurisdiction of the requested court, and, if possible, full particulars, specifying the mother's name, date of birth, place of birth and passport number;
VI. Closure, with the judge's signature; and
VII. Any other information which might be of use to the requested court for purposes of facilitating compliance with the letter rogatory. § 1 – Should a requested measure consist of interrogation of the party or questioning of a witness, it is recommended, under penalty of inability to comply with the measure, that the letters rogatory further include: a) The text of the questions to be asked by the requested court; b) Setting up a hearing, beginning with the transmittal of the letter rogatory to the Ministry of Justice, with a lead time of at least: (i) Ninety (90) days, for criminal matters; and (ii) One hundred eighty (180) days, for civil

(Footnote 30 continued)

matters. § 2 – In the event of civil cooperation, letters rogatory must also include, where appropriate, the full name and address of the person responsible, at the addressee end, for payment of court costs and procedural fees arising from performance of the letter rogatory in the requested country, except for those taken from actions: I. Handled under the auspices of free justice; II. For the sending of foodstuffs abroad, for countries bound by the New York Convention, promulgated in Brazil by Ministerial Decree No. 56826 of September 2, 1965, pursuant to Article 26 of Law No. 5478 of July 25, 1968; III. Coming under the jurisdiction of child and adolescent courts, pursuant to Law No. 8069 of June 13, 1990.

Art. 8 – Letters rogatory must be accompanied by the following documents:

I. Initial petition, criminal information or complaint, depending on the nature of the matter;
II. Background documents;
III. Court order for its transmittal;
IV. Original copy of the official or certified translation of the letter rogatory and all accompanying documents;
V. Two original copies of the letter rogatory, of the translation and all accompanying documents; and
VI. Other documents or exhibits considered indispensable by the requesting court, in accordance with the nature of the action. Sole paragraph. Where the purpose of the letter rogatory is forensic examination of a document, it is recommended that the original be sent to the requested court, the copy remaining in the record of the requesting court, otherwise the measure may not achieve fruition.

Art. 9 – All petitions for direct assistance must include:

I. Indication of provision contained in an international bilateral or multilateral legal cooperation agreement or reciprocity agreement;
II. Indication of the requesting authority;
III. Indication of Central Authorities in both requesting and requested States;
IV. Summary containing the number(s) of proceedings or lawsuits in their requesting State, to serve as the basis for the request for cooperation;
V. Complete and accurate particulars on all persons to whom the request makes reference (name, last name, nationality, birthplace, address, birth date and, wherever possible, mother's name, profession and passport number);
VI. A clear, objective, concise and complete narrative couched in the actual verbiage of the request for international legal cooperation, of the events which gave rise to it, to include: a) Place and date; b) Causal nexus between the ongoing proceedings, all those involved, and measures solicited in the request for assistance; and c) All documentation attached to the request.
VII. References to and full transcripts of all applicable laws and regulations, especially, on criminal matters, criminal laws;
VIII. Detailed description of the assistance requested, indicating: a) In cases of tracing or freezing of bank accounts, the account number, the name of the bank, the bank location and the endpoints of the desired timeframe, along with specific instructions as to how the documents to be obtained shall be forwarded (physical or electronic media); b) In cases requiring notice, citation or summonses, full particulars on the person to be served notice, cited or issued a summons, and the corresponding address; c) In cases of interrogations and questioning, the list of questions to be asked.
IX. Description of the purpose of the request for international legal cooperation;

handling rogatory letters and requests for direct assistance, this after the Chief Department of Justice (Ministry of Justice) and Chief State Department (Ministry of External Relations) modernized their rules for handling requests for international cooperation, always to make the procedure move faster. This Decree established that whenever the request can be granted administratively, that is, with no intervention from the Judiciary, action on the part of the Superior Court of Justice may be dispensed with, and the Ministry of Justice shall see to the performance by the competent administrative authorities, as set forth in Article 3.

The institution of Central Authority came about to speed up and facilitate cooperation between countries. As the name itself suggests, the primary role of the Central Authority is to function as a centralizing agency, the focus of all cooperation—requests and investigations alike—whether coming from abroad or transmitted from Brazil. All rogatory letters and requests for legal assistance, whatever their purpose, shall be handled through the intermediation of central authorities.

In Brazil, as in most countries, the Central Authority lies in the Executive Branch,[31] given that it typically represents the State in international relations. The Central Authority is an idea espoused in Hague Conventions and international conventions on public international law, arising out of the need to have an agency in each country to regulate the administrative procedures for International Legal Cooperation.

Its creation was imperative given the increase in volume and complexity of mechanisms for international cooperation. It imparts uniformity of performance, standardizes all procedures, and provides the necessary specialization for handling such matters, avoiding duplication and waste in the requests.

There are countless advantages to the institution of a single Central Authority: specialization, speed, efficiency, publicity, and affordability of proceedings. It is

(Footnote 30 continued)

X. Any other information which might prove useful to the requested authority, for purposes of facilitating the granting of the request for international legal cooperation;
XI. Other information solicited by the requested State; and XII. Signature of the requesting authority, location and date.

Art. 10 – This Decree revokes Foreign Office/Justice Ministry (MRE/MJ) Interministerial Order No. 26 of August 14, 1990, and the MRE/MJ Interministerial Order of September 16, 2003, published in the Federal Official Gazette on September 19, 2003.

Art. 11 – This Order shall take effect as of the date of its publication.

[31]According to Goal No. 02 of 2004 from the National Strategy for the Fight Against Money Laundering Report (ENCLA), now the National Strategy for the Fight Against Corruption and Money Laundering (ENCCLA), requests for active international cooperation from the Judicial Branch or the Office of the Public Prosecutor and federal and state police authorities, regarding authorization for direct cooperation on operations (which require an international reciprocity agreement), all go through the Ministry of Justice Asset Recovery and International Legal Cooperation Council Department (DRCI) (Art. 13, IV, of Decree No. 4991 of February 18, 2004).

argued that placing Central Authority in the Executive Branch will also ensure neutrality, transparency and due process, inasmuch as Executive Branch agencies are subject to oversight by the Office of the Public Prosecutor, their acts subject to review by the Judicial Branch.[32]

It is important to mention that the Central Authority is by no means a *sine qua non* for making international cooperation feasible. Cooperation may occur directly between the competent authorities. However, the institution of a Central Authority brings these authorities closer together to eliminate obstacles in the way of rapid realization of shared national interests. Indeed, there is no point to demanding the establishment of a Central Authority unless it is committed to achieving efficiency, simplification, and necessary speed of information and action.

4.3 Asset Repatriation

Legal assistance has allowed the freezing and repatriation of assets, but often requires an affidavit—an internally consistent sworn statement—to enable such measures as freezing assets or bank accounts.[33]

Freezing and seizure operations require a hard sell. It is not enough to simply attach a court order. At times one has to turn over convincing documents to establish a link between assets or a bank account and illegal behavior. It also helps if the goods in question are the proceeds from criminal activity abroad or at least flow (by action or omission) from corrupt practices.

Consider the impact on U.S. asset forfeiture legislation of the case in which Brazil filed for freezing of assets belonging to a Brazilian defendant and for keeping those assets in the United States. At issue was whether, based on 28 U.S.C. § 2467

[32]The great challenge at this point is to further popularize the benefits of adopting a single Central Authority for all International Legal Cooperation issues and broaden the horizon of this institution. With the assistance of the policies of Brazil's Justice Ministry, through the National Anti-Money Laundering Qualification and Training Plan (PNLD), the idea is being spread that, even in the absence of an agreement, it is possible to have requests for active or passive cooperation routed through the Central Authority.

[33]A bill is being submitted in Brazil (No. 1982, dated September 16, 2003), by national Congressman Eduardo Valverde, to regulate International Legal Assistance on Criminal Matters, irrespective of the transmittal of rogatory letters. It would provide for temporary administrative freezing of proceeds of crime undergoing laundering. It also establishes a Council on International Legal Assistance, empowered to formulate directives, and serving as a permanent clearinghouse for information among the various government agencies it represents (the Federal Courts, Office of the Federal Prosecutor, Ministry of External Relations, Office of the Attorney General, Brazil's Federal Revenue Secretariat, the Central Bank, the Council for Financial Activities Control (COAF), the Federal Police Department, and the Office of the Comptroller General), all offering guidance to Brazilian authorities needing to secure international cooperation.

(d)(3) (Enforcement of Foreign Judgment),[34] foreign assets may be frozen only after a foreign court has definitively ruled in favor of forfeiture, or if it may be done before any final decision on confiscation has been rendered. The United States Court of Appeals for the District of Columbia Circuit, on review of two lower court decisions from March and April 2009, decided that a final decision by Brazil regarding confiscation was required according to its interpretation of 28 U.S.C. § 2467(d)(3).[35] Following this decision, the U.S. Department of Justice requested and obtained from Congress a resolution of the problem because, if upheld and

[34]28 U.S.C. § 2467(d) provides as follows:

(d) Entry and Enforcement of Judgment.

(1) In general.— The district court shall enter such orders as may be necessary to enforce the judgment on behalf of the foreign nation unless the court finds that—

(A) the judgment was rendered under a system that provides tribunals or procedures incompatible with the requirements of due process of law;

(B) the foreign court lacked personal jurisdiction over the defendant;

(C) the foreign court lacked jurisdiction over the subject matter;

(D) the foreign nation did not take steps, in accordance with the principles of due process, to give notice of the proceedings to a person with an interest in the property of the proceedings in sufficient time to enable him or her to defend; or

(E) the judgment was obtained by fraud.

(2)Process.— Process to enforce a judgment under this section shall be in accordance with rule 69(a) of the Federal Rules of Civil Procedure.

(3) Preservation of property.—

(A) Restraining orders.— (i) In general.— To preserve the availability of property subject to civil or criminal forfeiture under foreign law, the Government may apply for, and the court may issue, a restraining order at any time before or after the initiation of forfeiture proceedings by a foreign nation. (ii) Procedures.— (I) In general.— A restraining order under this subparagraph shall be issued in a manner consistent with subparagraphs (A), (C), and (E) of paragraph (1) and the procedural due process protections for a restraining order under section 983(j) of title 18. (II) Application.— For purposes of applying such section 983(j)— (aa) references in such section 983(j) to civil forfeiture or the filing of a complaint shall be deemed to refer to the applicable foreign criminal or forfeiture proceedings; and (bb) the reference in paragraph (1)(B)(i) of such section 983(j) to the United States shall be deemed to refer to the foreign nation.

(B) Evidence.— The court, in issuing a restraining order under subparagraph (A)— (i) may rely on information set forth in an affidavit describing the nature of the proceeding or investigation underway in the foreign country, and setting forth a reasonable basis to believe that the property to be restrained will be named in a judgment of forfeiture at the conclusion of such proceeding; or (ii) may register and enforce a restraining order that has been issued by a court of competent jurisdiction in the foreign country and certified by the Attorney General pursuant to subsection (b)(2).

(C) Limit on grounds for objection.— No person may object to a restraining order under subparagraph (A) on any ground that is the subject of parallel litigation involving the same property that is pending in a foreign court.

[35]United States v. Opportunity Fund and Tiger Eye Investments, Ltd., 613 F.3d 1122 (D.C. Cir. 2012).

followed, the decision would have compromised international cooperation efforts with other countries.

The disposal of confiscated assets is provided in the 1988 UN Vienna Convention against Illicit Traffic in Narcotic Drugs (Article 5, item 5, clause "b") and in the Convention at Palermo on Transnational Organized Crime (Article 30, item 2, clause "c"), and can stimulate cooperation among authorities in different countries.

By the principle of specialization, applicable to relations among States and, therefore, to international legal cooperation efforts, no information or documents obtained through legal assistance may be used with regard to crimes for which International Cooperation is excluded on account of jurisdiction being regarded as an attribute of the State, on which we cite the example of Switzerland, with regard to exchange quota violations.[36]

Insistence on dual criminality, that is, the existence of criminal behavior in both of the jurisdictions involved in the request for legal assistance on criminal matters is, in principle, a common requirement in cooperation cases—with the proviso that the two criminal categories need not be exactly the same, but only similar. Indeed, the UN Convention on Corruption signed at Mérida makes it clear that "in matters of international cooperation, whenever dual criminality is considered a requirement, it shall be deemed fulfilled irrespective of whether the laws of the requested State Party place the offence within the same category of offence or denominate the offence by the same terminology as the requesting State Party, if the conduct underlying the offence for which assistance is sought is a criminal offence under the laws of both State Parties" (Article 43).

The rule cannot, however, be interpreted as an absolute. The FATF advocates international legal cooperation, pursuant to the UN Conventions of Vienna (international traffic, 1988), Palermo (transnational organized crime, 2000), and Mérida (corruption, 2003), by withdrawal of obstacles (Recommendation No. 36) and direct mutual assistance toward a quick, constructive, and effective solution (Recommendation No. 37).

Yet not even the FATF gives the rule the proper crucial weight with regard to money laundering. Failure to honor the principle of dual criminality, which is no novelty in international public law, may prove devastating in future requests for cooperation, in specific cases, and completely bar new freezes or obtaining of evidence, among other diplomatic difficulties.

Brazil's Money Laundering Law (Law No. 9613/1998, as amended by Law 12683/2012) does contain provisions on assets located abroad:

---

[36]Pursuant to ENCLA 2005 Target No. 40, the Justice Ministry's Asset Recovery and International Legal Cooperation Council Department agreed to share information on the need to keep within limitations on the use of documents obtained through International Legal Cooperation, and reaffirmed the principle of specialization at the international level.

Art. 8. The judge shall determine, given the existence of an international treaty or convention and by request of the competent foreign authority, measures to secure assets, securities or amounts proceeding from crimes described in Article 1, and committed abroad.

§ 1. All provisions contained in this article shall apply, irrespective of any treaty or international convention, whenever the government of the country whose authorities make the request promise reciprocity to Brazil.

§ 2. Absent a treaty or convention, all goods, securities or amounts subject to security measures at the request of the competent foreign authority—or the proceeds from their alienation—shall be divided equally between the requesting States and Brazil, following proper provisions for injured or good-faith third parties.

With specific regard to the division of goods, as observed above, the UN Convention signed at Mérida (corruption) made no provisions; however; there was an understanding that there ought to be full restitution of assets to the injured-party-State in view of the legal assets affected (Articles 51–59).

Finally, with regard to seizure or freezing of assets, there are no obstacles in the way of their international application once the universal rule of reciprocity is in effect, and it is still possible to divide up the goods confiscated or seized, and consequently repatriate them, once the decision awarding forfeiture to the government becomes final.

It is extremely difficult to obtain repatriation of assets based only on an appealable decision, even if reciprocity is invoked.

The authorities of requested States usually wish to be informed regarding: (1) Evidence that all owners, agents, curators or others involved with the articles in question are aware of issuance of the order that they be seized, and of its content, including a list of works; (2) Evidence to show that the Brazilian seizure order was signed prior to the legal sale or transfer of the articles abroad; (3) Proof of direct association between the artwork and fraud detected in Brazil which would demonstrate that its acquisition does indeed flow from criminal behavior; (4) Unavailability of the assets precisely because such a procedure is public knowledge and one might therefore infer that the interested parties had knowledge of the illegal events involving large holdings; and (5) Listing of all legal events (seizure orders, forfeitures, decisions that have become final) relating to the accused, including all corresponding dates.

At the first Judicial Roundtable Meeting between federal judges from Brazil and the United States, attended by several judges from Colombia and Mexico,[37] in Washington, DC, October 27–31, 2011, initial conclusions were drawn that the more evidence, the easier the seizure and sequestering, and that where drug trafficking is concerned, it is easier to secure the granting of the request because the laws are not as difficult to understand. The purpose of this unprecedented encounter was to establish a framework of judicial decisions to render international legal cooperation feasible as quickly as possible.

[37]Two judges per country, along with U.S. federal prosecutors, attended the meeting organized by the U.S. Department of Justice.

With regard to the content of judicial decisions, Brazil made the following proposals:

I. Request for Legal Assistance (direct assistance)

1. Regarding Assets, Securities or Cash:

- Identification;
- Location or request to identify the location, or notification through some national information network for purposes of future repatriation;
- Causal connection (between asset and criminal or suspected criminal behavior) or relevant information (illegal enrichment).

Record of a JUDICIAL DECISION (not necessarily final), but for REPATRIATION, A FINAL DECISION (that has become final, that is, unappealable), excepting only such crimes as corruption and the like (UN Convention, Mérida, Art. 57) or a special interest case, such as artworks.

2. Bank Secrecy:

- Identification of account holders;
- Name, address, and branch location;
- Description of requested documents (signature cards, transfers, statements);
- Dates or timeframe (delimited);
- Causal connection (between asset and criminal or suspected criminal behavior) or relevant information (illegal enrichment).

II. Legal basis for its grounding (for ease of understanding and to verify dual criminal liability):

- A clear, objective and complete narrative.

III. Literal transcription of all provisions to be able to verify a similar crime in the requested State.

The document summing up the importance of Judicial Round Table Meeting reads as follows:

JUSTIFICATION FOR LEGAL DIALOGUE AIMED AT ESTABLISHING CASE LAW PRECEDENT

WHEREAS there is a need to facilitate International Cooperation;

AND WHEREAS the fight against organized crime must not be defeated by lack of understanding regarding the various international legal systems;

AND WHEREAS explanation of domestic legal systems has converged on the stripping away of assets from criminal organizations from small conceptual changes;

AND WHEREAS standardization of judicial decisions to facilitate cooperation among all countries involved in the fight against organized crime is important;

AND WHEREAS there is a need for States to unite behind the seizure, confiscation and repatriation of goods, securities and money,

BE IT RESOLVED THAT WE ESTABLISH THE FOLLOWING TO ENSURE BETTER UNDERSTANDING TOWARD PROPER INTERNATIONAL COOPERATION WITH NEEDED STANDARDIZATION OF JUDICIAL DECISIONS:

1. The fight against crime is independent of the place where the crime was committed, and confiscation is indispensable;
2. Cooperation through Letters Rogatory is not recommended because it is slow and bureaucratic, and because analysis in the requested country is limited to checks on public policy and affronts to sovereignty;
3. Cooperation by Direct Assistance is a response to be followed by States because it is faster, based on mutual trust and conveys to the requested State a proper analysis of the requests;
4. The simplified Mutual Legal Assistance Treaty (MLAT) approach is recommended, and must be objectively clear;
5. Central authorities have placed no obstacles in the way of direct contact between magistrates or competent authorities and channels of communication must be opened up to ease unnecessary bureaucratic burdens (Article 18.13 of the UN Convention against Organized Crime at Palermo does not prohibit such understandings);
6. The regular legal systems of countries involved must be respected (requesting and requested States), and it is no bar to cooperation if the request originated with or was addressed to the police, the Office of the Public Prosecutor, or the courts;
7. If Extradition is refused, on grounds of citizenship, then the persons believed to be involved ought to be promptly submitted to authorities in their own country (Art. 16.10, Palermo). However, if extradition is accepted, it is recommended that the sentence be served out in the requested State (Art. 16.11, Palermo), otherwise, require serving the sentence or part of it in the requesting State (Art. 16.12, Palermo);
8. Possibility of joint prosecution or transfer of criminal proceedings (Art. 21, Palermo) for final disposal of assets and joint measures (cooperative debriefings with effects in both countries) and to achieve better administration of Justice;
9. International Cooperation ought not to be blocked while the whereabouts of an asset are unknown. The requested State should try all available measures for tracing or seizure for future confiscation or repatriation;
10. As a condition for restitution to the interested party, the requested State should provide proof of the legality of the asset, security or pecuniary amount whenever the requesting State requires seizure with an eye to confiscation or repatriation, but which request was mooted by legal decisions setting aside the merits as to its legal origin;
11. Invocation of absence of dual criminality cannot justify failure to cite or subpoena defendants, victims, witnesses or affected third parties once criminal proceedings have been initiated in the requesting State;

12. Information gained for criminal proceedings may be used in other such proceedings if the requested State so authorizes, even if retroactively;
13. Assets, securities, or pecuniary amounts shall be restituted for indemnification of victims or to be turned over to the United Nations Fund for technical assistance among countries or even for reimbursement of the State. A division might be arrived that to deduct only expenses, except for such crimes as corruption and the like, and also with regard to cultural goods, which should be so disposed of as to give priority to public access;
14. Reimbursement of States lies outside the reach of the statute of limitations, which does not nullify International Cooperation;
15. What does negate International Cooperation is invocation of a need for a court order for a mere citation, subpoena, or copies, and it is incumbent upon States to simplify their legal system to make Direct Assistance workable;
16. Defense witnesses ought to be heard in the country filing charges or, otherwise, by teleconference from embassies or consulates, with International Cooperation not being invoked except where the evidence is accepted by the prosecution;
17. International Cooperation does not require the attachment of proof, but rather, a presentation of arguments leading to the decision to see that measures be taken abroad;
18. No specific Mutual Legal Assistance Treaty is required for each asset, security or pecuniary amount if the requesting State attaches to its request a list of assets and gives grounds.

Bibliography

Alldridge, P. (2008). Money laundering and globalization. *Journal of Law and Society, 35*(4), 437–463.

Baldwin, F. (2009, Jan). Art theft perfecting the art of money laundering. Unpublished article sent to the U.S. Library of Congress.

Cestari, V. C. J., & Toffoli, J. A. D. (2009). Mecanismos de cooperação jurídica internacional no Brasil. Manual de cooperação jurídica internacional e recuperação de ativos—Matéria civil. Brasília: Ministério da Justiça.

De Carli, C. V. (2011). *Lavagem de dinheiro: prevenção e controle penal*. Porto Alegre: Verbo Jurídico.

European Commission. (2012, Mar 12). Confiscation and asset recovery: Better tools to fight crime. http://europa.eu/rapid/press-release_MEMO-12-179_en.htm?locale=en. Accessed September 28, 2016.

Jovanovic, I. (2009). Immunity of heads of state for international crimes: Deflating dictators' lifebelt? *Annals of the Faculty of Law of Belgrade*, pp. 202–224.

Kleemans, E. R. (2007). Organized crime, transit crime, and racketeering. *Crime and Justice, 35,* 163–215.

Levi, M., & Reuter, P. (2006). Money laundering. *Crime and Justice, 34*(1), 289–375.

Linn, C. J. (2007, Sept). One-hour money laundering: Prosecuting unlicensed money transmitting businesses using section1960. *United States Attorneys' Bulletin, 55*(5), p. 407.

Linn, C. J. (2010). Redefining the bank secrecy act: Currency reporting and the crime of structuring. *Santa Clara Law Review, 50,* 407–513.

Lutescu, D., & Bucur, C. (2008). Money laundering—An International phenomenon. *Agora International Journal of Juridical Sciences, 2*(1), 154–158.

McCaw, C. (2011). Asset forfeiture as a form of punishment: A case for integrating asset forfeiture into criminal sentencing. *American Journal of Criminal Law, 38*(2), 181–220.

Mwenda, K. K. (2006). Can insider trading predicate the offence of money laundering? *Journal of Business and Securities Law, 6,* 127–175.

Rababah, M. A. (2014). The measure of extended confiscation and money laundering. Law Annals Titu Maiorescu University, pp. 237–252.

Rapporteur Minister Marco Aurélio. (2012, Mar 14). First Panel. HC 87759 ED. Unanimous Panel Ruling DJe-053. Decided on December 13, 2011.

Rapporteur Minister Teori Albino Zavascki. (2009, Dec 16). Rcl. 2.645/SP. Special Court. Decided on November 18, 2009.

Simpson, S. S., & Koper, C. S. (1992). Deterring corporate crime. *Criminology, 30*(3), 347–376.

Spreutels, J., & Grijseels, C. (2001). Interaction between money laundering and tax evasion: Belgian and international measures in the fight against money laundering. *EC Tax Review, 10* (1), 2–12.

Supremo Tribunal Federal. (2006, Dec 15). Habeas Corpus No. 85.588/RJ, Rapporteur: Minister Marco Aurélio. First Panel. Daily Judicial Gazette.

United Nations Convention Against Illicit Traffic in Narcotic Drugs and Psychotropic Substances. (1988). https://www.unodc.org/pdf/convention_1988_en.pdf. Accessed January 24, 2017.

United States v. Bajakajian. (1998). 524 U.S. 321.

United States v. One-Sixth Share. (2003). 326 F.Wd 36 (1st Cir. 2003).

United States v. Opportunity Fund and Tiger Eye Investments. (2012). Ltd., 613 F.3d 1122 (D.C. Cir. 2012).

Chapter 5
Conclusions

The pursuit of assets of fleeing dictators, politicians, and businessmen must be a recurring phenomenon. The increasing frequency with which the assets are sought emphasizes the need for the legal system to develop the adequate means to handle such litigation.

According to Adam C. Robitaille, "Whereas in ancient times stolen wealth was recycled in the community, today wealth has great mobility, and is often transferred to distant countries. Thus, what was once a problem limited to politically unstable areas is now a problem for all countries, especially those attracting investment."[1]

This book shed light on the less glamorous side to real estate in which ownership of homes is obscured through variations on family names listed on deeds and through shell companies, and it is very difficult to penetrate who is the beneficial owner of these shell companies.[2] As revealed through the Nguema Obiang cases and the ownership of properties in the Time Warner Center, foreigners who have owned properties in the United States have been the subject of government inquiries, either personally or as heads of companies.

Federal banking guidelines are clear: "Banks should take all reasonable steps to ensure that they do not knowingly or unwittingly assist in hiding or moving the proceeds of corruption." This means screening customers to determine whether they are "politically exposed people"—foreign officials and their relatives and associates—and filing a suspicious activity report if the customers transfer unusually large amounts of money.

The regulation of financial law, especially financial criminal law and here we are generally referring to the idea of the war on money laundering, is justified by the simple idea that market rules alone cannot provide all of the aspirations emerging within the context of the course of business practices—oftentimes through dangerous, ethical gray areas.

---

[1]Robitaille (1984).
[2]Saul and Story (2015).

F.M. De Sanctis, *International Money Laundering Through Real Estate and Agribusiness*, DOI 10.1007/978-3-319-52069-8_5

There is a need to fill loopholes that ordinary criminal law (protecting property from forgery and counterfeiting) has largely been insufficient to properly suppress given the increase in financial crime arising out of the exponential increase in international crime. Steps must be taken to improve the legal system and adopt measures to close legal and institutional loopholes through which crime perpetuates itself—and this is in addition to rethinking the application or pecuniary sentences or curtailment of rights.

It is a tricky analysis, easily swung toward the trivialization of human rights, and the serious danger of their being seen as so irrelevant that any conclusion weighing them in on either side is self-disqualifying. Criminal Law for enemies, as advanced by Günther Jakobs, or Criminal Law for enemies as a "third speed," as advanced by Silva Sánchez,[3] would serve to preserve not only the law but also people's confidence in the system of criminal laws, so that the purpose of the penalty is to reaffirm the rule of law.

There is a regulatory and functional concept of culpability (reproachability), without ontological foundation, and based on general positive prevention.[4] Hazards facing the foundations of a punitive system are acquiescence in a criminal law system based on potentialities (preemption of punishability), on future events rather than actual occurrences, on the imposition of disproportionate and harsh penalties and nonobjectivity of procedural guarantees. This is Criminal Law divorced from context, only to meet the expectations of general prevention: a dangerous instrumentality, violative of human dignity.[5]

The idea here is neither to defend this theory, nor to nullify Criminal Law through the practical impossibility of its enforcement. Even worse would be to perpetuate the general impression that this branch of law penalizes poor criminals while catering to the wealthy. That would be frustrating, unjust, evil, and in its consequences a danger to democracy and to belief in democracy.

Hence, a clear and systematic ordering of existing rules on money laundering, especially laundering made possible through properties, so as to block off any possibility of criminal behavior, must be defended. Here then it would make sense to put every effort into effective crime fighting not restricted to setting up regulations for the sector, but also aiming at the improvement of payment methods and a clearer notion of the kind of work done by NGOs, offshores companies, and beneficial owners.

The study of this problem does not stop at an analysis of conduct held to be criminal, but rather, addresses the need to tailor the preventive system to social

---

[3]Jakobs and Meliá (2005).

[4]"Autonomy (the subject's capacity to abide by law) is held to be a functioning capacity where its outcome is functional, and absent that there must be another way of resolving the conflict." Roxin (2006).

[5]We would have violations of human dignity, and the subject would come to be used by the State to further its preventive convenience. Roxin, Claus. Reflexões sobre a construção sistemática do direito penal. RBCCrim 82/35.

realities. Simply bringing awareness to a sizable fraction of those involved has not sufficed to contain those who would defy the law.

To give substance to its purpose, the quest for truth and all that it implies would be a compatible systemic reaction. This is the existential minimum, for truth is a value intrinsic to the judicial function, one that does not apply solely to the parts, subject as they are to the imperfections of humanity: laziness, selfishness, dereliction, and disdain.

On a par with seeking a proper judicial decision we have, most notably, prevention as carried out by society to keep serious events from coming to the courtroom, or delaying too long in arriving there due to the dereliction that accompanies a preventive system that does not work.

Thus, rethinking the role of actor (intermediates) of properties' deals, to get them to adapt to the situation we face is in order, and to do likewise with regard to the way suspicious payments are made, the hazards of which have hardly been assessed.

States, the police, prosecutors, judges, and government agencies are all essential to efforts toward international cooperation and repatriation of goods. As pointed out by José Paulo Baltazar Júnior, "failure to act on the part of a legislator is practically the same, in effect, as counterproductive interference."[6] Thus, the things the law is there to protect by positive action by the State must be protected, and the means to do so effectively must be accepted. This is to say that we must adopt clearly-defined government standards to perform existing protective duties (prohibition of insufficiency).

Hence, the fight against money laundering requires concerted action that is not restricted to the regions affected by the criminal behavior. One task requiring systematic protection from governments is protection of the integrity of international financial systems.

It is not just the concern of immediate participants in the property world, but primarily is of public authorities, including police, government agencies, prosecutors, and even judges. Thus, everyone, including Governments, must contribute to profound and broad concerted action. This means cooperation at the national and international levels.

Many people went to the United States and left behind their properties, which are to this day the subject of claims for restitution in U.S. courts. Facts such as these accurately exemplify much of our recent history, in which we came to learn of investments by criminals in different sectors for purposes of money laundering, and possibly even the financing of terrorism.

It is important to mention that the number of shell companies identified by the Panama Papers as of June 2016 is 214,000. These shell companies have hundreds of thousands of people behind them, including political figures, business moguls, and celebrities.

---

[6] Baltazar (2010, pp. 53–54).

In the wake of all these discoveries, it was an important improvement to discipline the figure of beneficial owners or final beneficiaries due to the need to gear up due diligence and monitor transactions and payments. Certainly, there is increasingly greater international and political interest around shell companies and their role in anti-money laundering and tax avoidance activity.

The Panama Papers has affected correspondent banking and third party entity identification, with possible transaction monitoring. The issue raises glaring gaps in anti-money regulations and possible implications for global banks. As banks mitigate risk and keep in line with existing compliance requirements, forensic accountants will find themselves quite busy and recruited by financial institutions. There will be more stringent guidelines to follow and more stringent Know Your Customer procedures. Banks have to flag and or block transactions directly associated with Mossack Fonseca (a prolific generator of offshore shell companies and questionable accounting advisory services) to comply with Know Your Client and internal processes. Regulators will alter their expectations in relation to customers, who must be reclassified and subject to Know Your Customer (KYC), Customer Due Diligence (CDD), Politically Exposed Persons (PEPs), and Transaction Monitoring (TM) processes and evaluations. In the wake of the Panama Papers, significant revisions and updates will be necessary for any clients identified. The cost of declaring "innocent" will be expensive and individuals and firms may take a significant hit on their reputations.

Financial service providers like remittance companies have shown that they were hesitant to embrace anti-money laundering legislation, being recognized as playing a proactive role.

The FATF has cautioned that de-risking may unintentionally "drive financial transactions underground, which creates financial exclusion and reduces transparency, thereby increasing money laundering and terrorist financing risks." As urged by the U.K. Financial Conduct Authority (FCA), financial institutions should take a proportionate approach, not a "blanket approach," to their AML/CFT compliance responsibilities. In a recent speech discussing this issue, the Deputy Director of FinCEN, Jamal El-Hindi, called for federal and state cooperation in creating transparency in the industry to combat the wholesale de-risking of MSBs, "especially considering the potential economic impact of money transmission to developing countries and MSBs to financial inclusion generally." Regulators in the United Kingdom and the United States have recently issued reports concerning the potential for excessive de-risking policies by financial institutions that will have the unintended effect of pushing money laundering and terrorist financing further underground.[7]

Policy makers should strive to induce voluntary compliance by making the regulatory scheme simpler and by making the formal channels more competitive by reducing the burdens of regulatory compliance through a single, national regulator.[8]

[7]Resnick (2016).

[8]Watterson (2013, p. 748).

The concept of money laundering through properties covers a complex international activity involving placement, layering, shell companies, wire transfers, and unfamiliarity. Everything we have seen emphasizes the complexity, sophistication, international element, and glamour of laundering. We have seen several ways in which property purchases are made with money from crime but are dealt with in such a way to conceal the criminal origins been acquired otherwise than by crime (i.e., the use of cash and informal money transfer systems, money transfer between jurisdictions, and the use of corporate anonymity through attorney-client privilege and banking confidentiality to restrict availability of information).

The FATF expects a substantial and compelling justification for the global action against laundering, and for actions to be subject to rigorous checks as to their efficacy. As launderers are continuously looking for new routes, there is an overwhelming preponderance of Suspicious Activity Reports. The dummy shell companies often have as partners companies established in tax havens or offshore financial markets (like Panama).

The regulation now is challenged again by existing criminal creative activity. It is important to construct a universal framework to deal with international capital movements. If banks, financial services, and others are regulated, then money will go into real property (like we saw in some international cities like New York), or jewels, fine art, antiques, and other areas that must be covered by anti-money laundering regulations.

Secrecy and confidentiality cannot have different treatment according differences between jurisdictions. Otherwise, rational actors in possession of property that might trigger anti-money laundering reporting requirements will try to place it in jurisdictions where it is likely to escape attention.

The same must be said in domestic approaches. The introduction of a law like the *Incorporation Transparency and Law Enforcement Assistance Act*, according to Carolyn B. Maloney, follows a groundbreaking initiative, halting with the common practice of using U.S.-based shell corporations to launder money linked to criminal enterprises. Telling us who the real owner is, or take your business elsewhere must be the message.[9]

The idea is to create a law which should gather beneficial ownership information from companies that thus far have been able to escape oversight and thwart law enforcement.

It is important to empower a governmental enforcement body, like the Treasury Department, to issue regulations requiring corporations and limited liability companies formed in a state that does not already require basic disclosure, to file information about their beneficial ownership with Treasury as a backup by name,

[9]Reps. Maloney, King and Senator Whitehouse introduce bills to stop anonymous money laundering operations by requiring disclosure of shell corporation beneficial owners, Carolyn B. Maloney Press Release https://maloney.house.gov/media-center/press-releases/reps-maloney-king-and-senator-whitehouse-introduce-bills-to-stop, published on Feb. 3, 2016, accessed on Nov. 5, 2016.

current address, and nonexpired passport or state-issued driver's license. Also with identification of any affiliated legal entity that will exercise control over the incorporated entity; and consistent updating of lists of beneficial owners no later than 60 days after any change in ownership.

A quick response is mandatory, especially with respect to international cooperation, to make enforcement consistent.

The high-end real estate market has become less and less transparent—and more alluring for those abroad with assets they wish to keep anonymous—even as the United States pushes other nations to help stanch the flow of American money leaving the country to avoid taxes. Yet for all the concerns of law enforcement officials that shell companies can hide illicit gains, regulatory efforts to require more openness from these companies have failed.

The international movement to control money laundering forces to put in place more stringent monitoring of financial movements than had ever hitherto been the case. If it is easy for capital to be moved within jurisdictions, then the anti-money laundering regime must prevent those movements by at least making them less easy, where the money is "dirty," and so to diminish the advantage of committing the original crime, then a redirection of the money to a different haven. In a globalized world, money can be sent anywhere at the touch of a keyboard and at little cost. That is why some jurisdictions must be forced to give up laxity, absence, or weakness of formal enforcement rules.[10]

There is no desire to halt economic growth with necessary anti-money laundering measures. It is important to enhance the role of the financial market to effectively mobilize and distribute economic resources to achieve efficiency and equality. To reach these goals, it is relevant to improve it with the following issues: (1) the development of a disclosure system to facilitate the issuance of financial transactions and protect investors[11]; (2) the refinement of the accounting system to enable effective auditing, which will secure the credibility of financial information gathered from corporations, offshore companies, and trusts; (3) the enactment of effective regulation on fraud and crime; (4) the addition of regulations on mergers and acquisitions to maximize the positive functions while minimizing the negative aspects of such corporate restructuring; (5) the provision of effective mediation of the prosecutorial system, allowing and stimulating active whistleblower procedures to expedite judicial decisions; and finally, (7) stiffer punishments for violations.[12]

If Foreign Direct Investment depends on the interrelation of several factors, including few restrictions in terms of investments, equal treatment regardless of the country of origin, the existence of a relatively sound company law or commercial code, transparent customs, tariff procedures, and the adoption of an understandable

[10]Alldridge (2008).

[11]Such laws must not become an obstacle to the development of the industry, being compatible with international practices.

[12]In some similar outcomes about the securities market, see Hong (Hong 1996, p. 196).

and perceived as fair code,[13] I would add healthy business practices guaranteed by regulators based on a clean environment rules.

Financial records can provide a critical link between an offence and an accused. It may prove motive, intent, or facts underlying the charged offence.[14] The intensity of regulation would impose a great burden on societies that place considerable value on the free flow of commerce and on individual and commercial privacy.[15] It seems that truly comprehensive regulation, covering all the methods by which the origins of criminal incomes could be hidden or by which funds could be conveyed to terrorists is too ambitious, but it is necessary.

Although some investors have largely been happy with the *status quo* and the easy access to investment in tax havens and agribusiness, if these typologies are allowed to remain, the shift in the financial paradigm, from centralized and regulated to decentralized and unregulated, would allow for the furtherance of some of the most dangerous criminal activity.

Legislators and jurists might be able to defend reasonable but meaningful restrictions or constraints on capital movements without fear of punishing some activities that have been attractive due to the current few controls of them.

According to John C. Mubangizi, "human rights therefore are those rights which one possesses by virtue of being a human being and one need not possess any other qualification to enjoy human rights other than the fact that one is a human being. Form his definition a link between poverty, poverty production and human rights can clearly be discerned. This is because just as with human rights which are unique to human beings, poverty is a condition that afflicts only human beings. Poverty is the outcome of human creation and also of uncaring international community."[16]

The simple use of lawfully acquired assets to hide illegal prior processes must be prevented due to laundering deals with capital mobility and business regulation, besides the liabilities of international companies. The traditional view of criminal jurisdiction (territorial principle, extradition, and mutual assistance[17]) is now challenged since this new era requires efficient transnational enforcement mechanisms. That is why international intelligence gathering must be emphasized. The technological aspects of globalization bring greater exchange of information among governments. Each of us, in the modern global world, must be even more vigilant and on our guard.

The most subtle ways of making the owner and the possessor of a direct foreign investment uncomfortable is to compel them to comply with the international laws

[13]See Hunter et al. (2003, p. 871).

[14]MacDonald (2012, p. 20).

[15]Levi and Reuter (2006, p. 368).

[16]Mubangizi (2007, p. 2).

[17]Under the model of sovereignty, each country was responsible for its own criminal law and proceeds of the breach of those criminal laws were specific to the jurisdiction because they are specific to that set of criminal laws.

under stringent penalty of expropriation. The international community must be mindful of the impacts of excessive regulation and remove its intrusive and burdensome regulation, but when it is necessary, add real transparency by requiring detailed disclosures in the review processes of international transactions. It is clear that self-regulation that was introduced in the belief that it offered distinct advantages over government sovereign regulation failed to provide any credible deterrence against business misconduct. Here, there is no space for symbolic victories sanctioning less powerful nations. If some countries are allowed not to identify beneficial owners, but the Offshore Group of Banking Supervisors and smaller economies are required to identify them on pain of economic sanctions, the claimed effectiveness cannot be justified. The new mode of regulation of international criminal activity cannot constitute a false dawn or an important set of globalized phenomena restricted to poorer countries.

Working to ensure anti-money laundering compliance by relevant sectors increases the likelihood that money laundering will be detected.

The subject is one of constant concern, for much is said about the need to improve the sector. As national borders have opened and trade barriers have fallen, transnational crime has grown to unprecedented levels. The current situation, better revealed by the so-called Panama Papers, is a combination of a lack of real interest on cooperation in the investigation, prosecution, and extradition. This is particularly true throughout capital movements where the nexus between money laundering, corruption, financial crimes, false documents, identities, and business records has found fertile ground among governments that profit from the use the proceeds of international criminal enterprise to maintain ill-gotten wealth. The two typologies of money laundering is under examination in this book, real estate and agribusiness, are enabled by "investments" through offshore companies and wire transfers. There is effort to establish international mechanisms to combat it. Whether the efforts have been successful or unsuccessful, and whether multilateral instruments are a formidable tool in the war against international organized crime or merely toothless tigers, are still open questions.

If these typologies continue to be treated as they are today, the shift in the financial paradigm from centralized and regulated to decentralized and unregulated would allow for the furtherance of some of the most dangerous criminal activity. The proceeds of crime contributed to and spent on certain activities possess many of the traits that can explain the respect of their regulation and their review by unveiling the property characteristics behind capital movements.

Furthermore, with the study done on these sectors, the preferred method of payment was at least brought into focus. This is important in any business environment, and could make things easier for money launderers.

The concern has emerged in several debates, but still in a timid or incipient form. The real work ahead is to get all government agencies to put some teeth into the prevention and punishment of money laundering.

Bibliography

Alldridge, P. (2008, December). Money laundering and globalization. *Journal of Law & Society, 35*(4), 437–463.
Baltazar, J. P., Jr. (2010). *Crime organizado e proibição de insuficiência*. Porto Alegre: Livraria do Advogado.
dos Anjos, L. (2016, June 2). PF prende 2 pessoas com armas em operação contra lavagem de dinheiro. G1. http://g1.globo.com/mato-grosso/noticia/2016/06/pf-prende-2-pessoas-com-armas-em-operacao-contra-lavagem-de-dinheiro.html. Accessed July 15, 2016.
Goddard, T. (2012, October 13). How to fix a broken border: Follow the money. Tucson Sentinel. http://www.tucsonsentinel.com/opinion/report/101312_goddard_border/how-fix-broken-border-follow-money/. Accessed September 28, 2016.
Hong, I.-K. (1996). Securities laws in Korea and regulations on foreign investment. *Columbia Journal of Asian Law, 10*(1), 157–197.
Hunter, R. J., Shapiro, R. E., & Ryan, L. V. (2003). Legal considerations in foreign direct investment. *Oklahoma City University Law Review, 28,* 851–873.
Jakobs, G., & Meliá, M. C. (2005). *Direito penal do inimigo. Noções e críticas* (pp. 66–69). Porto Alegre: Livraria do Advogado.
Kaoma Mwenda, K. (2006). Can insider trading predicate the offence of money laundering? *Journal of Business & Securities Law, 6,* 127–175.
Kobor, E. (2007, September). Money Laundering Trends. *United States Attorneys' Bulletin, 55*(5), 14–20.
Levi, M., & Reuter, P. (2006). Money laundering. *Crime & Justice, 34*(1), 289–375.
MacDonald, M. S. A. (2012, February). Follow the money: Obtaining and using financial information in military criminal investigations and prosecutions. *The Army Lawyer*, 12–24.
Marpakwar, P. (2011, December 24). State forms cells to detect source of terror funds. The Times of India. http://timesofindia.indiatimes.com/city/mumbai/State-forms-cells-to-detect-source-of-terror-funds/articleshow/11225140.cms. Accessed September 28, 2016.
Mubangizi, J. C. (2007). "Poverty production" and human rights in the African context. *Law, Democracy & Development, 11*(1), 1–14.
Olson, E. (2012, March 29). Considering new strategies for confronting organized crime in mexico. Wilson Center. https://www.wilsoncenter.org/publication/considering-new-strategies-for-confronting-organized-crime-mexico. Accessed September 28, 2016.
Resnick, L. J. (2016, June 15). The regulatory pendulum: When is de-risking by financial institutions too much? Lexology. http://www.lexology.com/library/detail.aspx?g=72b1624b-c107-4c3e-855d-48d8fab9dea7. Accessed July 20, 2016.
Robitaille, A. C. (1984). The Marcos cases: A consideration of the act of state doctrine and the pursuit of the assets of deposed dictators. *Boston College Third World Law Journal, 9*(1), 81–115.
Roxin, C. (2006). *Derecho penal – Parte general – Fundamentos. La estructura de la teoria del delito* (p. 806). Madrid: Civitas.
Saul, S., & Story, L. (2015, February 7). Towers of secret. Stream of foreign wealth flows to elite New York real estate. The New York Times. http://www.nytimes.com/2015/02/08/nyregion/stream-of-foreign-wealth-flows-to-time-warner-condos.html?module=RelatedCoverage. Accessed June 20, 2016.
Sikarwar, D., Padmakshan, M., & Zachariah, R. (2011, November 17). Ten means to put an end to black money issue. Economic Times. http://economictimes.indiatimes.com/news/economy/finance/ten-means-to-put-an-end-to-black-money-issue/articleshow/10763329.cms. Accessed September 28, 2016.

Theodoro Júnior, H. (2009). *Direitos do consumidor: A busca de um ponto de equilíbrio entre as garantias do Código de Defesa do Consumidor e os princípios gerais do direito civil e do direito processual civil*. Rio de Janeiro: Forense.

Watterson, C. (2013). More flies with honey: Encouraging formal channel remittances to combat money laundering. *Texas Law Review, 91*, 711–748.

Chapter 6
Proposals to Improve the War Against Money Laundering Through Real Estate and Agribusiness

Several international and national initiatives have been put forth in the war against money laundering and terrorism financing. International treaties and recommendations from multilateral organizations have sought to improve the global system of enforcement to curb financial crime.

There has been no word of advancements in effective enforcement, however, in the two sectors under study: real estate and agribusiness. Within these two sectors, financial criminals have discovered an extraordinary array of techniques to put a legal face on the criminal proceeds. An immediate rereading of all mechanisms of prevention and enforcement is necessary, with specific attention given to these two areas.

This chapter sets forth specific proposals to improve the war against money laundering through real estate and agribusiness. The proposals are not intended to be the final word, but rather the beginning of a new debate over prevention and enforcement techniques.

6.1 An International Perspective

The international legal framework must be challenged to curb international crime, especially money laundering, by developing international norms for all countries, financial institutions, and other affected persons. According to Herbert V. Morais, "the challenges faced by governments, financial institutions, corporations, and law enforcement officials in fighting international crime are quite formidable. They need to be addressed in a systematic and coherent way if the war against international crime is to be won. It is everybody's business. It is particularly interesting to note that the evolution of the norms toward fighting international crime has increasingly incorporated the active involvement of the private sector such as financial institutions, nonfinancial businesses and professions, nonprofit organizations and

F.M. De Sanctis, *International Money Laundering Through Real Estate and Agribusiness*, DOI 10.1007/978-3-319-52069-8_6

"gatekeepers" that can be misused for the laundering of criminal proceeds or the financing of crime such as terrorism."[1]

6.1.1 Financial Action Task Force (FATF)

The FATF has expressed particular concern regarding real estate agents, nonprofit organizations, trusts, and beneficial owners,[2] but has not spoken a single word about agribusiness despite the significant number of cases involving money laundering through agribusiness. The FATF should designate rural activity as a "Designated Non-Financial Business and Profession."[3] To prevent property owners

---

[1]Morais (2005, pp. 643–644).

[2]See FATF Recommendation Nos. 8 (recommending that countries review the adequacy of laws and regulations that relate to NPOSs), 10 (recommending that financial institutions be prohibited from keeping anonymous accounts or accounts in obviously fictitious names and that financial institutions be required to undertake customer due diligence measures), 12 (recommending that financial institutions be required to perform heightened due diligence for accounts related to politically exposed persons), 14 (recommending that countries take measures to ensure that providers of money or value transfer services (MVTS) are licensed or registered and subject to effective systems for monitoring and ensuring compliance), 16 (recommending that countries require financial institutions to include accurate originator and beneficiary information), 22 (concerning "designated non-financial businesses and professions—DNFBPs), 24 and 25 (concerning transparency and adequate, accurate, and timely information on the beneficial ownership of legal persons and legal arrangements), and 36, 37, and 38 (concerning international cooperation, including mutual legal assistance for freezing and confiscation). FATF (2016 June). The FATF Recommendations. http://www.fatf-gafi.org/publications/fatfrecommendations/documents/fatf-recommendations.html. Accessed 3 Aug 2016.

[3]FATF Recommendation No. 22 provides that the due diligence and record-keeping requirements should apply to DNFBPs in the following situations: "(a) Casinos—when customers engage in financial transactions equal to or above the applicable designated threshold. (b) Real estate agents —when they are involved in transactions for their client concerning the buying and selling of real estate. (c) Dealers in precious metals and dealers in precious stones—when they engage in any cash transaction with a customer equal to or above the applicable designated threshold. (d) Lawyers, notaries, other independent legal professionals and accountants—when they prepare for or carry out transactions for their client concerning the following activities: buying and selling of real estate; managing of client money, securities or other assets; management of bank, savings or securities accounts; organisation of contributions for the creation, operation or management of companies; creation, operation or management of legal persons or arrangements, and buying and selling of business entities. (e) Trust and company service providers—when they prepare for or carry out transactions for a client concerning the following activities: acting as a formation agent of legal persons; acting as (or arranging for another person to act as) a director or secretary of a company, a partner of a partnership, or a similar position in relation to other legal persons; providing a registered office, business address or accommodation, correspondence or administrative address for a company, a partnership or any other legal person or arrangement; acting as (or arranging for another person to act as) a trustee of an express trust or performing the equivalent function for another form of legal arrangement; acting as (or arranging for another person to act as) a nominee shareholder for another person." FATF Recommendation No. 23 provides that the requirements set out in Recommendations 18–21 apply to all DNFBPs, subject to the following

from placing their property in jurisdictions without anti-money laundering reporting requirements, secrecy and confidentiality privileges should be uniform among jurisdictions.

Proposal 01. Include agribusiness in the Suspicious Transaction Reporting Recommendation for nonfinancial companies and professions alongside casinos, real estate brokers, dealers in precious metals or gemstones, attorneys, notaries, and accountants.

6.1.2 Tax Havens, Offshore Accounts, and Trusts

The advantage of offshore accounts is that they enable the free movement of capital, which is only taxed in negotiations taking place in-country, with exemptions for transfers to other offshore or nonresident accounts, corporate income taxes, and income tax withholding on payments made to nonresidents. Arnaldo Sampaio de Moraes Godoy has apropos observations on these, especially concerning Barbados, Panama, the Bahamas, and Vanuatu.[4] Moreover, there are treaties to avoid double taxation and which allow governments to establish unilateral measures domestically (such as, for instance, exemptions for fiscal credits at a reduced proportional rate and deduction of taxes paid abroad from domestic taxable income), which is why they are referred to as tax havens.

The Organization for Economic Cooperation and Development (OECD) published the ninth edition of the Model Tax Convention on Income and on Capital in 2014. The convention has thirty-one articles distributed over seven sections and is aimed at eliminating obstacles relating to double taxation. It provides, for example, that dividends paid by a company having its home office in one State Party to someone living in another State Party to the Convention will be taxed by the latter, and their remuneration taxed by the State in which the services are rendered.[5]

(Footnote 3 continued)

qualifications: "(a) Lawyers, notaries, other independent legal professionals and accountants should be required to report suspicious transactions when, on behalf of or for a client, they engage in a financial transaction in relation to the activities described in paragraph (d) of Recommendation 22. Countries are strongly encouraged to extend the reporting requirement to the rest of the professional activities of accountants, including auditing. (b) Dealers in precious metals and dealers in precious stones should be required to report suspicious transactions when they engage in any cash transaction with a customer equal to or above the applicable designated threshold. (c) Trust and company service providers should be required to report suspicious transactions for a client when, on behalf of or for a client, they engage in a transaction in relation to the activities referred to in paragraph (e) of Recommendation 22." FATF (2016 June). The FATF Recommendations. http://www.fatf-gafi.org/publications/fatfrecommendations/documents/fatf-recommendations.html. Accessed 3 Aug 2016.

[4]de Moraes Godoy (2005, pp. 83–84).

[5]Organization for Economic Cooperation and Development (2015).

Although offshore accounts facilitate the circulation of goods, services, and capital, they are also an effective instrument for evading taxes with considerable legitimacy. They lend themselves to legal uses, of arguable utility, but also to illegal practices. There are considerable advantages to be had using them as conduits, especially by those interested in laundering ill-gotten money, on account of defective or nonexistent government control, but also because they make it easy to generate false trails. Offshore bank accounts make it possible to disguise their real controllers because ownership (according to the legislation in the countries in which they are located) is evidenced by bearer paper, and partners or officers are simply proxies, often proxies for hundreds of companies of the same pattern. All of this amounts to creating a veil for the actual owners to hide behind. Their paper cannot be traded on the domestic market nor cashed in without considerable expense and questions about possible complicity in money laundering directed at anyone who converts it.

Loan agreements are often written so as to lay hold of funds from offshore accounts without exposing them to tax liability. There are transparency requirements for beneficiaries of companies, with countries required to obtain reliable real-time information (FATF Recommendation No. 24), including information on trusts, settlors, and trustees or beneficiaries (Recommendation No. 25), which would preclude anonymous accounts. This is why the customer and actual beneficiary must be identified (i.e., know-your-customer duties, often called Customer Due Diligence). There must also be a requirement to collect enough information about the institution to which service is rendered so that the trustee who administers the assets is accountable for submitting suspicious transaction reports. The FATF takes a clear stand against the invocation of banking secrecy or professional privilege as a means of obstructing its recommendations (Recommendation No. 9).

Proposal 02. Tax havens must comply with all provisions of the FATF Recommendations and provide information to the proper international authorities. Noncompliance should be punished. Tax havens must place ethical and legal considerations above financial considerations and require disclosure of the identities of account owners (beneficial or ultimate beneficial owners) and controllers. Indeed, the controllers merit special attention, and their very existence ought to be looked into to check whether they might be providing services to criminal enterprises. The hurdles in the way of their suppression are closely related to the Janus-faced discourse of many States that rely on tax havens to conduct nontransparent transactions purportedly having connections to "reasons of State" or for the management of assets belonging to their political elite. The most subtle way of making the owner and the possessor of a direct foreign investment uncomfortable is to compel them to comply with the international laws under stringent penalty of expropriation. The international community must be mindful of the impacts of excessive, intrusive, and burdensome regulation, but such regulation is often necessary for real transparency including detailed disclosures in the review processes of international transactions. It is clear that self-regulation—introduced under the belief that it offered distinct advantages over government sovereign regulation—failed to provide any credible deterrence against business misconduct. Here there is no space for symbolic victories sanctioning less powerful nations. If some countries are allowed not to identify beneficial owners, but the Offshore Group of Banking Supervisors and smaller economies are required to identify them on pain of economic sanctions, the claimed effectiveness cannot be justified. The new mode of regulation of international criminal activity cannot constitute a false dawn or an important set of globalized phenomena restricted to poorer countries.

6.1.3 International Legal Cooperation and Repatriation

The new era of globalization challenges the traditional view of criminal jurisdiction (territorial principle, extradition, and mutual assistance) and demands efficient transnational enforcement mechanisms. The technological aspects of globalization bring greater exchange of information among governments and allow for effective international intelligence gathering. In this respect, improving international cooperation to provide repatriation of assets and to lend substance to the administration of justice, which ought to be considered universal, through the following measures and national policies is essential.

As the FATF has already established, freezing and seizure of laundered assets is necessary even if the antecedent crime occurred in another jurisdiction (country). Specialized multidisciplinary teams, task forces if you will, must also be deployed (Recommendation No. 30). The FATF also recommends international legal cooperation, pursuant to the UN Conventions of Vienna (international traffic, 1988), Palermo (transnational organized crime, 2000), and Mérida (corruption, 2003), by withdrawing obstacles (Recommendation No. 37) and providing direct mutual assistance to achieve a quick, constructive, and effective resolution (Recommendation No. 38). The fight against organized crime must not be defeated by a lack of understanding regarding the various international legal systems.

Proposal 03. Cooperation through rogatory letters is not recommended because it is slow and bureaucratic, and because analysis in the requested country is limited to checks on public policy and affronts to sovereignty.
Proposal 04. Prioritize cooperation by direct assistance because it is faster, is based on mutual trust, and conveys to the requested State a proper analysis of the requests.
Proposal 05. Give preference to the simplified and standard Mutual Legal Assistance Treaty (MLAT) format. Specific, separate MLATs are not required for each asset, security, or pecuniary amount if the requesting State attaches to its request a list of assets and gives grounds.
Proposal 06. Central authorities have facilitated matters because they removed obstacles in the way of direct contact between magistrates or competent authorities. Channels of communication must be opened to ease unnecessary bureaucratic burdens.

Proposal 07. Respect the legal systems of the requesting and requested countries. Cooperation should not be halted on the basis that the request originated with or was addressed to the police, the Office of the Public Prosecutor, or the courts.
Proposal 08. If extradition is refused on the grounds of citizenship, then the person believed to be involved ought to be promptly submitted to authorities in their own country (Article 16.10, Palermo). If extradition is accepted, it is recommended that the sentence be served out in the requested State (Article 16.11, Palermo), otherwise, the sentence or part of it should be served in the requesting State (Article 16.12, Palermo).
Proposal 09. Consider the possibility of joint prosecution or transfer of criminal proceedings (Article 21, Palermo) for final disposal of assets and joint measures (cooperative debriefings with effects in both countries) to achieve better administration of justice.
Proposal 10. International cooperation ought not to be blocked while the whereabouts of an asset are unknown. The requested State should try all available means for tracing and seizing for future confiscation or repatriation.
Proposal 11. As a condition for restitution to the interested party, the requested State should provide proof of the legality of the asset, security, or pecuniary amount whenever the requesting State requires seizure with an eye to confiscation or repatriation but the request was mooted by legal decisions setting aside the merits as to its legal origin.
Proposal 12. Invocation of the absence of dual criminality cannot justify failure to cite or subpoena defendants, victims, witnesses, or affected third parties once criminal proceedings have been initiated in the requesting State.
Proposal 13. Information gained for criminal proceedings may be used in other proceedings if the requested State so authorizes, even if retroactively.
Proposal 14. Assets, securities, and pecuniary amounts shall be restituted for indemnification of victims or turned over to the United Nations Fund for technical assistance among countries—or even for reimbursement of the State. A division might be arrived at to deduct only expenses, except for such crimes as corruption and the like, and also with regard to cultural goods, which should be so disposed of as to give priority to public access.
Proposal 15. Reimbursement of States lies outside the reach of the statute of limitations, which does not affect international cooperation.
Proposal 16. Invocation of a need for a court order for a mere citation, subpoena, or copies negates international cooperation. It is incumbent upon States to simplify their legal systems to make direct assistance workable.
Proposal 17. Allow defense witnesses to be heard in the country filing charges or by teleconference from embassies or consulates. Avoid invoking procedures of international cooperation unless evidence is being withheld.
Proposal 18. International cooperation does not require the attachment of proof, but rather, a presentation of arguments leading to the decision to see that measures be taken abroad.

6.2 A National Perspective

6.2.1 Freezing, Seizing, Confiscating, and Repatriating Assets

The hazards of globalization may be minimized if our notions of law draw authority from social and philosophical—as opposed to just economic—considerations. Criminal organizations must be curbed by denying them what gives them their mobility and power, continuous and unprecedented illegal wealth. The degradation afoot in the world today, which regards economics as the standard of value, can never so bind our numbers together as to gloss over such indispensable critical thinking. Social movements and individuals must assume a stance for ethical values to compel obedience to basic rules of coexistence. Standing these rules at defiance by parallel paths amounts to the real breakdown of rights both *de facto* and *de jure*.

There is a duty to perform Customer Due Diligence for all financial and nonfinancial activity, whether with natural or artificial persons, to ban anonymous accounts or those bearing fictitious names, and to require identification of their beneficial owners, with records to be kept for at least five years (FATF Recommendation Nos. 10 and 11). There are, at times, requirements to make suspicious transaction reports on nonfinancial companies engaged in domestic or international cash transfer services, obliging them to record the amounts transferred, form of payment, transaction date, purpose of the wire transfer, name, individual or corporate taxpayer ID, where applicable, of both sender and receiver and addresses for both.[6] These requirements give a false impression that any money laundering occurring sector could actually be detected.

There is also a need to make dealers in real estate and agribusiness liable to these rules, inasmuch as they may have knowledge or probable knowledge (willful blindness doctrine) of criminal behavior. Limiting the scope of forfeiture to assets involved in transactions in which the possessor intends to launder money would protect the innocent without unduly burdening prosecutors. It is the ideal. Under the intent-based standard, people would be protected from having heavy costs imposed on the basis of only probable cause, and wrongdoers would not be automatically deprived of the right to own property.[7]

Proposal 19. Allow administrative freezing and seizure to be accomplished quickly, thereby preventing the disappearance of the assets and thwarting acts of terrorism.

Proposal 20. Allow confiscation of assets when the assets were transferred to an outside party that was aware that the assets were illegal or that they were transferred solely to avoid confiscation.

---

[6]See, for example, the Resolution by the Brazilian Financial Intelligence Unit, the Council for Financial Activities Control, Resolution No. 10 of November 19, 2001.

[7]Gordon (1995, pp. 775–776).

Proposal 21. Allow confiscation of illegal assets when a conviction cannot be obtained due to death, statutory limitations, or immunity. Adopt civil actions to terminate ownership.
Proposal 22. Even after a decision has become final, allow further financial investigations to enforce prior confiscation orders covering all criminal proceeds.
Proposal 23. Once criminal proceedings are initiated, the statute of limitations ought to stop running, for there is no reason to count government inertia or lack of interest in criminal prosecution.

6.2.2 Regulatory Agencies

Proposal 24. Establish a regulatory agency if the FIU cannot provide proper oversight or access financial and administrative information in a timely manner, thus fully complying with FATF Recommendation Nos. 26, 27, 29, and 31. Supply the agency with the human and material resources necessary to inspect for fraudulent sales or acquisitions, forged documents, financing of nonexistent objects, loans taken out in the name of third parties or trustees, and the involvement of offshore accounts to disguise the true identity of a buyer or seller.
Proposal 25. Empower the regulatory agency to demand secure records with profound and specific evaluations of clients (photo identification and proof of domicile), of their assets, and of similar institutions for constant review (because many entities stop everything when they believe that companies similar to their own are not enforcing compliance).
Proposal 26. Compare records with the contents of market and agricultural databases to determine whether the underwriters demanded complete documentation before extending coverage. Whenever a third party is involved, check whether guarantees are accepted without proper appraisal. Some offshore corporations are organized solely to put up guarantees.

6.2.3 Payments, Remittances, and Financial Institutions

Cash sales of properties are one of the easiest ways to avoid questions about the provenance of funds because there are few documents and regulations that trigger scrutiny other than public documents identifying property owners. When criminal proceeds are invested lawfully (in legitimate business, like properties), then the real harm is the original crime. But this does not mean that money laundering is not an additional crime because it permits and fuels the continuation of the predicate crime, the overpricing of goods, and unfair business competition. Accordingly, money laundering should independently generate severe sentences. Financial service providers and remittance companies have shown that they are hesitant to embrace anti-money laundering legislation.

Proposal 27. All cash payments for the purchase of vehicles, boats, airplanes, real property, and agricultural products in excess of US$10,000 should be banned.
Proposal 28. Payments by third parties should be illegal so as to preclude their use for purposes of masking real ownership of the goods and resources, with the potential for tax fraud that this entails.
Proposal 29. Ban all wire transfer payments that do not allow money to be tracked. There is always a separation between the nonfinancial remittance company and the financial institution receiving the investor's money whenever these come from individuals or companies unrelated to the negotiations (cash deals negotiated by factoring companies or companies having home offices in tax havens). Currency brokers or hawala systems are often resorted to, as are wire transfers from and to secret banks or banks in tax havens—often by people having no connection whatsoever to the institution receiving the resources. These people are either not account holders, or are unconnected with the account holder receiving the wire transfer, or are transferring an amount that is actually the sum of many small deposits. Allowing this sort of practice amounts to having no preventive measures whatsoever. In wire transfers, detailed information should be obtained on the sender as well as the beneficiary, with monitoring made possible, and there should be an option to prohibit transactions by certain people pursuant to UN Security Council Resolutions 1269 of 1999 and 1373 of 2001, for the prevention and suppression of terrorism and its financing. (FATF Recommendation No. 16). Suspicious operations on the part of designated nonfinancial businesses and professions such as casinos, real estate offices, dealers in precious metals or stones, attorneys, notaries, and accountants must be reported, and internal controls and protection of whistleblowers from civil or criminal liability must be required (FATF Recommendation No. 22, in combination with Nos. 18 through 21). There should be transparency requirements for beneficiaries of companies, with countries also required to timely obtain sufficient information (FATF Recommendation No. 24), including information on trusts, settlors, and trustees or beneficiaries (Recommendation No. 25).
Proposal 30. Tighten controls on remittance companies, so as to have real knowledge of situations which might allow clandestine wires or wires not subject to suspicious operation reporting requirements (poor or borderline tracking by authorities). One example would be requiring a declaration by the bank accredited by the Central Bank to handle the conversion whenever called upon by the government to appear for settlement of the currency exchange operation.
Proposal 31. Subject virtual worlds, which are very often used by remitters, to anti-money laundering anti-terrorist financing regulation in order to be able to verify user identity during registration and ensure that each virtual transaction can be traced back to identifiable senders and recipients.[8]

[8]For a discussion of virtual worlds, see Landman (2009).

Proposal 32. Although Informal Funds Transfer Systems (IFTS), also known as hawala networks, have distinct operational characteristics—efficiency, adaptability, affordability, anonymity, cultural sensitivity, and trust through relational contracts, they must follow the same standard regulations that formal remittance bankers follow.[9]
Proposal 33. Regardless of the potential difficulties, formal banking institutions should learn lessons from IFTS in their attempt to provide greater access to financial services for the poor and underserved in developing and post-conflict regions. Banks should flag and or block transactions directly associated with Mossack Fonseca (a prolific generator of offshore shell companies and questionable accounting advisory services) to enforce Know Your Client standards and internal processes.
Proposal 34. Require covered financial institutions to establish and maintain written procedures that are reasonably designed to identify and verify the beneficial owners of legal entity customers. These procedures must enable the institution to identify the beneficial owners of each customer at the time a new account is opened unless the customer is otherwise excluded or the account is exempted. Also, the procedures must establish risk-based practices for verifying the identity of each beneficial owner to the extent reasonable and practicable. The procedures must contain the elements required for verifying the identity of customers that are individuals under applicable customer identification program requirements. In short, covered financial institutions are now required to obtain, verify, and record the identities of the beneficial owners of legal entity customers.

6.2.4 *Offshore Accounts and Trusts*

As launderers are continuously looking for new routes, there is an overwhelming preponderance of Suspicious Activity Reports. Dummy or shell companies often partner with companies established in tax havens or offshore financial markets like Panama. The international regulatory framework is again challenged by creative criminal activity and must be adjusted to respond more effectively to international capital movements. If banks, financial services, and others are regulated, then laundered money will go into real property (like we saw in New York City), jewels, fine art, rural activity, and antiques. Thus, all of these areas must be covered by anti-money laundering regulations. Obtaining information has been hampered considerably by a lack of channels of communication with the competent authorities —to say nothing of timely notice—in the conduct of international legal cooperation.

Proposal 35. Full particulars absolutely must be obtained on all actual investors, even if they belong to companies chartered abroad, provided they do business and

[9]Hariharan (2012).

are represented in the country. A simple listing of proxies or stockholders is not enough. Complete identification must also be required of partners and administrators concealed within offshore accounts or trusts domiciled in tax havens. A listing of all partners and administrators ought to be required for being listed or removed from the tax rolls.

6.2.5 NPOs and Foundations

There ought to be a complete record by type of business and types of NPOs. NPOs should be required to keep records on all transactions entered into both within the country and abroad. This would comply with FATF Recommendation No. 08, in the spirit of clearly delimiting the rights and responsibilities of directors and employees of NPOs. It would encourage countries to establish good policy whereby information on their activities, size, and other important characteristics such as transparency, integrity, openness, and best practices can be indicated in real time for purposes of supervision and monitoring (FATF Recommendation No. 8). Organizations have even been used for the financing of terrorism.[10] Some governments have initiated policies to curb the practice, most notably in Pakistan.[11]

Proposal 36. Licensing should be required for operation under tax exempt status, and continuation of this status ought to be contingent upon regular reporting to revenue authorities of all relevant information, in an official document duly dated and signed under penalty of perjury, listing the name and telephone number of the person in charge of the books and records of the organization or foundation.

Proposal 37. The organization's books and records ought to include a detailed list of its activities and management, all revenue and expenses, and liquid assets, to include: the name and purpose of the institution; number of members; whether they have on hand more than 25% of their liquid assets; number of voting members listed within and outside of the organization; number of employees; number of volunteers; unrelated business revenue and amount paid in taxes; contributions and donations; resources invested; benefits paid to and for members; total assets and liabilities; basic description of all assistance programs; whether any loans or benefits were granted to employees, directors, a trustee or any other person; name, number of hours worked, and job description of all employees and former employees (including directors, trustees and key personnel); earnings had by these individuals; expenses claimed (including travel and entertainment); and names and particulars of all donors.

[10] See, for example, Marpakwar (2011).

[11] Terror outfit-turned 'charity' JuD set to come under Pak Central Bank scanner (2012).

Proposal 38. An external audit should be required above a given gross revenue ceiling (more than $100,000, for example), as the state of New York so capably provides.[12]

Proposal 39. Organizations should include in their bylaws requirements for distribution of financial reports and outside audit reports for all directors and management personnel (president, manager, and financial department), for easy review.

Proposal 40. NPOs, associations, and foundations should allow universal access to their bank account transactions, records, and reporting requirements.

Proposal 41. In the case of a temple, church, mosque, educational institution or trust, even if registered as an NPO, association, or foundation, all sources of funding must be provided in sufficient detail.

Proposal 42. There should be a bar on receiving cash donations, or at least a cap above a certain amount (say, $3000), which would, above that amount, restrict donations to banking instruments.

Proposal 43. Review accounts of all such entities to reinforce due diligence and check whether they actually perform the purposes for which organized. Allow the opening of accounts only in their own names and in accordance with the documentation submitted.

Proposal 44. If announcements are made that a given account will be receiving donations or something similar, banking institutions must monitor this to check on the beneficiary of wire transfers made from that account, and promptly make out a suspicious activity report to the Financial Intelligence Unit if the published account is different from the account owned by the NPO or foundation.

Proposal 45. Check that all donations and contributions received for specific purposes are being properly recorded and faithfully accounted for.

Proposal 46. Provide clear procedures for board membership to ensure diversity among the members.

Proposal 47. See to it that all board members act in good faith to avoid any conflict of interest between the entity, its purposes, and themselves.

Proposal 48. Secure independent and exempt financial evaluations.

6.2.6 Money Laundering Laws: Reports, Rural Activity, and Lawyers

The communications system for reporting suspicious transactions is the key to effective suppression of money laundering. It turns up a number of shady deals. Many others go unnoticed when there is no cooperation from those whose legal duty it is to report transactions. The failure of one of the methods of control held to be essential in the fight against money laundering, namely, reportability, can give

[12]State of New York—Department of Law (2015).

rise to misleading statistics. Moreover, making one liable to criminal charges for incorrect notices of suspicious transactions is aimed at protecting privacy and image, on the one hand, and the effectiveness of early investigations on the other, for the danger is that future freezes on accounts and other confidential security measures might be rendered inoperative. The FATF expects a substantial and compelling global action against money laundering and for actions to be subject to rigorous checks as to their efficacy. Since launderers are continuously looking for new routes, inadequate controls are particularly vulnerable. It is important to increase the liabilities of international companies knowing that the location of the predicate offence is a matter of little significance. If banks and financial services are well-regulated, money goes into real property and agribusiness, with the help of professionals, like accountants and lawyers.

Directive (EU) 2015/849 of the European Parliament and of the Council of May 20, 2015 on the prevention of the use of the financial system for the purposes of money laundering or terrorist financing (amending Regulation EU No 648/2012 of the European Parliament and of the Council includes Directive 2005/60/CE of the European Parliament and of the Council) is the fourth directive to address the threat of money laundering. Council Directive 91/308/EEC defined money laundering in terms of drugs offences and imposed obligations solely on the financial sector. Directive 2001/97/EC of the European Parliament and of the Council extended the scope of Directive 91/308/EEC both in terms of the crimes covered and in terms of the range of professions and activities covered. In June 2003, the FATF revised its Recommendations to cover terrorist financing, and provided more detailed requirements in relation to customer identification and verification, the situations where a higher risk of money laundering and terrorist financing may justify enhanced measures and also the situations where a reduced risk may justify less rigorous controls. The present Directive encourages States to require corporate and legal entities to obtain accurate information about the beneficial owner (Article 30), and includes professionals, like auditors, accounting experts, notaries, and independent legal professionals, (Articles 2 and 3), compelling them to report suspicious activities (Article 33). The exemption provided for the Directive applies to information they receive from one of their clients or obtain on one of their customers, when assessing the legal position of their client or performing their task of defending or representing that client in legal proceedings or concerning such proceedings, including in the framework of advice on instituting or avoiding proceedings, whether such information is received or obtained before, during, or after this procedure (Article 34.2).[13]

It is important to get full information about the beneficial owner, as it is stated by the Brazilian Internal Revenue Service (Normative Instruction No. 1634 of May 6, 2016), compelling foreign legal persons when they make their inscription to the National Register of Legal Entities to invest in Brazil to provide complete information about beneficial owners under penalty of suspension of the registration. Managers of foreign

[13]Directive (UE) (2016).

legal persons are not considered beneficial owners, and their names must be mentioned on the Qualification of Members and Administrators (QSA).[14]

When lawyers are pushed to report suspicious activity the legislation is protecting their jobs, the right of defense, and the confidentiality of a relationship between the professional and client before the courts. Heloisa Estellita stated that when there is no regulatory obligation to report suspicious transactions, the bar provides a disservice.[15]

Proposal 49. Defining money laundering as a simple crime that occurs in three successive stages—placement, layering, and integration—can be a shortcoming because it does not consider the role of offshore and shell companies.
Proposal 50. An institutional framework should provide for the privacy and protection of whistleblowers who report suspicious transactions or suspicious activities of money laundering, considering the introduction of techniques such as shifting the burden of proof from the prosecution to the accused and lowering the standard of proof from beyond all reasonable doubt to the preponderance of probability in criminal law cases of insider dealing and money laundering.
Proposal 51. The law should clearly include rural activity in businesses and sectors required to conduct enhanced monitoring and reporting.
Proposal 52. Lawyers must have clear legal obligations to report suspicious activity. Each of us, in the modern global world, must be even more vigilant and on our guard.
Proposal 53. Failure to report, delays in reporting, incomplete or false reporting, making public the required reporting, and structuring transactions or operations to circumvent reporting requirements should render the perpetrators liable to criminal prosecution.
Proposal 54. Money laundering permits and stimulates the continuation of the predicate crime, the overpricing of goods, and unfair business competition. The commission of a money laundering offence should independently generate severe sentences.
Proposal 55. States must require people forming companies to reveal the names of the owners and show identification of owners and their intermediates.

6.2.7 Law Enforcement Agencies and Financial Intelligence Units (FIUs)

The FATF recommends that all countries identify, evaluate, and understand the hazards they face because of money laundering and the financing of terrorism, and

[14]See Articles 8(6) and 19 of Instrução Normativa RFB no. 1634 (2016).

[15]de Vasconcellos (2016). For a fascinating personal account of a lawyer who spent seven years in U.S. prison for laundering his clients' drug money globally, see Aguilar (2004).

that they take coordinated action to mitigate it (Recommendation No. 1). This would provide for cooperation and national coordination of prevention and enforcement policies, with proper actions and Financial Intelligence Units (FIUs) (Recommendation No. 2). The FATC also requires Customer Due Diligence (CDD), whether for companies or individuals, a ban on anonymous accounts or those bearing fictitious names, and identification requirements for their beneficial owners (Recommendation No. 10). Records must to be kept for at least five years (Recommendation No. 11). States should define and identify Politically Exposed Persons, that is, persons more readily able to launder money, such as politicians and their relatives (in prominent positions). These things require closer monitoring, and enlargement of their definition (2012 revision) to include both nationals and foreigners, and even international organizations (Recommendation No. 12). Suspicious operations on the part of designated nonfinancial businesses and professions (DNFBPs) such as casinos, real estate offices, dealers in precious metals or stones, and even attorneys, notaries, and accountants must be reported. Internal controls must be established along with protection for whistleblowers from civil or criminal liability (Recommendation No. 22, in combination with Nos. 18 through 21). Moreover, transparency ought to be required of the beneficiaries of companies, and countries should obtain sufficient information in real time (Recommendation No. 24), including information about trusts, settlors, and trustees or beneficiaries (Recommendation No. 25). FIUs need to have timely access, direct or indirect, to financial and administrative information in the hands of law enforcement authorities in order to fully perform their functions. This includes analysis of suspicious activity reports (Recommendations Nos. 26, 27, 29, and 31). Proper regulation of casinos is recommended, with effective supervision and rules to prevent money laundering (Recommendation No. 28).

It was a mistake to not publish recommendations similar to these for rural activity. But this does not mean that FIUs cannot proceed thus, as indeed the Brazilian units saw fit to do, even with no reports due to a lack of an acknowledged regulator government body. On the other hand, the breach of trust violates the consumer rights arising from an improper procedure. It compromises fair competition in the market. Good faith or loyalty contracts should be a rule of conduct submitting to administrative penalty in order to prevent fraudulent business practices. The misconduct is not acceptable:[16]

Proposal 56. Establish regulations, irrespective of any obligation arising in law, as to the requirement of suspicious activity reports by individuals or companies that sell, import, export, or intermediate a sale—whether on a permanent or temporary basis, in a principal or accessory role, and cumulatively or otherwise, to prevent the laundering of money through rural activity, with rules clear enough to include swine, horses, cattle, and fish. In the absence of a regulatory agency, oversight shall be performed by the FIUs, so that no one may be induced to believe that money laundering through the mentioned sector is less risky than through other industries.

[16]Theodoro Júnior (2009, p. 25).

Proposal 57. Regulators must alter their expectations in relation to customers, who must be reclassified and subjected to their Know Your Customer (KYC), Customer Due Diligence (CDD), Politically Exposed Persons (PEPs), and Transaction Monitoring (TM) processes and evaluations.

Proposal 58. Require suspicious activity reports on the part of deed Registries or by agencies in charge of regulating real estate brokers, or by insurance companies, most notably when cash payments or attempted cash payments occur, or payments are made through overseas accounts. There are frequent reports of politicians acquiring real estate and paying for it entirely or in large part in cash, which has caused unprecedented inflation in the real estate market. Gathering beneficial ownership information from companies that thus far have been able to escape oversight and thwart law enforcement, approving an authorizing law if necessary. It is important to empower a governmental enforcement body to issue regulations requiring corporations and limited liability companies formed in a state that does not already require basic disclosure, to file information about their beneficial ownership with Treasury as a backup by name, current address, and nonexpired passport or state-issued driver's license. Also with identification of any affiliated legal entity that will exercise control over the incorporated entity; and consistent updating of lists of beneficial owners no later than 60 days after any change in ownership.

Proposal 59. Require punishment of the offence of business practices that violate the good faith or the loyalty contract which are protected by consumers' rights. They are supervised by, in Brazil, the National Consumer Protection System, and in the United States at the federal level, by the Federal Trade Commission and the U.S. Department of Justice.

6.2.8 Investigating and Prosecuting Tax Fraud

The advisability of granting tax deductions ought to take account of a complex set of rules and also requires some professional training on the part of agents.

Proposal 60. Tax deductions should be allowed only if the donation is something other than an exchange of goods or services and the beneficiary has been previously registered and qualified. Hence, a license should be required to be tax-exempt.

Proposal 61. Even if a license is granted, it must be required of the entities so benefited, with relevant information entered—under penalty of being closed down—on a form for that purpose, dated and properly signed on penalty of perjury, and containing the name and telephone number of the person who keeps books and records for the organization.

Proposal 62. Check that all donations and contributions received for specific purposes are being properly recorded and faithfully accounted for.

Proposal 63. Require distribution of financial reports and outside auditor reports for all directors and management personnel (president, manager, and financial department) for easy review.

Proposal 64. Require an understanding of all internal controls of the organization or foundation, its purposes, a check on whether there are documented updates of policies and activities, changes in its structure, procedures, and programs.
Proposal 65. Check the precise role of each manager (president, administrator, director) and verify compliance with the obligation to follow bylaws.
Proposal 66. Check for clear procedures for board membership to ensure diversity among the members, and observe whether this is being strictly complied with.
Proposal 67. Check for any conflict of interest between the organization and its purposes and members, so as to ensure that all involved are committed to working toward the public interest.
Proposal 68. Check unusual loans, loans outside of where the organization normally operates, deliberately vague documentation, and financing of unconvincing or unlikely social works backed by invoices for nothing verifiable (talks, consultation, services, etc.).

6.2.9 Real Estate Brokers and Joint Owners

Real estate brokers are invariably an intermediate in the case of high-end properties, which are handled differently than ordinary personal property. Being less and less transparent and permitting the real owner to remain anonymous, the high-end real estate market, especially with the use of shell companies, must be submitted to obligations to avoid money laundering and tax fraud. Regulatory efforts should be made to make these companies more open, considering these luxury real estates are being organized as co-ops, in which residents are joint owners of the buildings.

Proposal 71. Real estate brokers and insurance companies must conduct customer due diligence. Anonymous accounts should be banned both for companies and individuals. Make identification requirements, with records kept for at least five years. Closely monitor accounts associated with politically exposed persons, that is, people in prominent positions, such as politicians, their relatives, and wealthy business people from countries known to be entrenched with corruption, because they are more readily able to launder money. This brings us to the establishment of a compliance position or department responsible for preventing the artificial inflation of property appraisals, forged documents, unconvincing or nonexistent identification, negotiations made in the name of outside parties or trustees, and the involvement of offshore accounts to conceal the true identity of the buyer or seller.
Proposal 72. Extend the concept of the "know your customer" banking rule to the identities of people behind limited liability companies and other shell companies that open bank accounts.
Proposal 73. Be aware that invoking discretionary options and confidentiality does not work with enforcement authorities or in courts of law.
Proposal 74. Compare records from underwriters' databases because insurance companies are often themselves offshore corporations organized only to put up

guarantees. If the insurance company does exist but is in the name of some third party in a tax haven, that company might in the future claim not to have been a party to the contract.

Proposal 75. Cancel negotiations with or donations from businesses that cannot provide enough financial justification to make it possible to verify the investor's financial strength.

Proposal 76. Refuse payments in cash, in prepaid access cards, through electronic transfers, and through other methods that are untraceable and usually are the result of some sort of tax evasion or illegal act.

Proposal 77. Refuse payments on behalf of outside parties or trustees. Refuse payments that involve offshore accounts that mask the true identity of the buyer. The use of third parties may be a device for concealing the actual owner of the asset or resources, and possibly for tax fraud. Hence, payments should be accepted only by the buyer who appears on the invoice.

Proposal 78. Cancel sales if there is any suspicion of money laundering or that the funds arose from terrorism financing. Notify the competent authorities irrespective of whether there is a specific regulation requiring Suspicious Activity Reports.

Proposal 79. Provide information to federal revenue authorities and to the Financial Intelligence Unit, including detailed records on clients (name, address, identity, profession, fingerprints, profits or losses, deals made), under penalty for noncooperation.

Proposal 80. Require all personnel to participate in training on the prevention of money laundering and terrorism financing. Reward managers who properly enforce all compliance obligations.

Bibliography

Aguilar, H. J. (2004). Confessions of a money launderer: A personal perspective. *4 Asper Review of International Business & Trade Law*, *4*, 45–61.

Alldridge, P. (2008, December). Money laundering and globalization. *Journal of Law & Society*, *35*(4), 437–463.

Bradford, W. (2015). "Because that's where the money is": A theory of corporate legal compliance. *Journal of Business Entrepreneurship & the Law, 8*(2), 337–465.

de Moraes Godoy, A. S. (2005). *Direito tributário comparado e tratados internacionais fiscais*. Porto Alegre: Sergio Antonio Fabris.

de Vasconcellos, M. (2016, July 24). OAB precisa dizer ao advogado como reportar operações suspeitas de lavagem. *Consultor Jurídico*. http://www.conjur.com.br/2016-jul-24/entrevista-heloisa-estellita-advogada-professora-fgv. Accessed September 28, 2016.

Directive (UE). (2016). *2015/849 of the European Parliament and of the Council of 20 May 2015*. http://eur-lex.europa.eu/legal-content/EN/TXT/?uri=celex%3A32015L0849. Accessed January 24, 2017.

FATF. (2016, June). *The FATF Recommendations*. http://www.fatf-gafi.org/publications/fatfrecommendations/documents/fatf-recommendations.html. Accessed August 3, 2016.

Goddard, T. (2012, October 13). How to fix a broken border: Follow the money. *Tucson Sentinel.* http://www.tucsonsentinel.com/opinion/report/101312_goddard_border/how-fix-broken-border-follow-money/. Accessed September 28, 2016.

Gordon, J. E. (1995). Prosecutors who seize too much and the theories they love: Money laundering, facilitation, and forfeiture. *Duke Law Journal, 44,* 744–776.

Hariharan, A. (2012). Hawala's charm: What banks can learn from informal funds transfer systems. *William & Mary Business Law Review, 3*(1), 273–308.

Instrução Normativa RFB no. 1634. (2016, May 6). http://normas.receita.fazenda.gov.br/sijut2consulta/link.action?idAto=73658. Accessed August 5, 2016.

Jakobs, G., & Meliá, M. C. (2005). *Direito penal do inimigo. Noções e críticas.* Porto Alegre: Livraria do Advogado.

Kobor, E. (2007, September). Money laundering trends. *United States Attorneys' Bulletin, 55*(5), 14–20.

Landman, S. I. (2009). Funding Bin Laden's avatar: A proposal for the regulation of virtual hawalas. *William Mitchell Law Review, 35*(5), 5159–5184.

Marpakwar, P. (2011, December 24). State forms cells to detect source of terror funds. *The Times of India.* http://timesofindia.indiatimes.com/city/mumbai/State-forms-cells-to-detect-source-of-terror-funds/articleshow/11225140.cms. Accessed September 28, 2016.

Morais, H. V. (2005). Fighting international crime and its financing: The importance of following a coherent global strategy based on the rule of law. *Villanova Law Review, 50*(3), 583–644.

Mwenda, K. K. (2006). Can insider trading predicate the offence of money laundering? *Journal of Business & Securities Law, 6,* 127–175.

Olson, E. (2012, March 29). *Considering new strategies for confronting organized crime in Mexico.* Wilson Center. https://www.wilsoncenter.org/publication/considering-new-strategies-for-confronting-organized-crime-mexico. Accessed September 28, 2016.

Organization for Economic Cooperation and Development. (2015, October 30). *Model Tax Convention on Income and on Capital 2014.* http://www.oecd.org/ctp/treaties/model-tax-convention-on-income-and-on-capital-2015-full-version-9789264239081-en.htm. Accessed September 30, 2016.

Resnick, L. J. (2016, June 15). The regulatory pendulum: When is de-risking by financial institutions too much? *Lexology.* http://www.lexology.com/library/detail.aspx?g=72b1624b-c107–4c3e-855d-48d8fab9dea7. Accessed July 20, 2016.

Roxin, C. (2006). *Derecho penal—Parte general—Fundamentos. La estructura de la teoria del delito.* Madrid: Civitas.

State of New York—Department of Law. (2015, March). *Solicitation and collection of funds for charitable purposes.* https://www.charitiesnys.com/pdfs/statute_booklet.pdf. Accessed September 30, 2016.

Terror outfit-turned 'charity' JuD set to come under Pak Central Bank scanner. (2012, March 13). Asian News International. https://in.news.yahoo.com/terror-outfit-turned-charity-jud-set-come-under-062446259.html. Accessed September 28, 2016.

Theodoro Júnior, H. (2009). Direitos do consumidor: A busca de um ponto de equilíbrio entre as garantias do Código de Defesa do Consumidor e os princípios gerais do direito civil e do direito processual civil. Rio de Janeiro: Forense.

U.S. Department of Treasury. (2016, July 19). *FinCEN Guidance, Frequently asked questions regarding customer due diligence requirements for financial institutions.* https://www.fincen.gov/sites/default/files/2016-09/FAQs_for_CDD_Final_Rule_(7_15_16).pdf. Accessed September 28, 2016.

Index

F.M. De Sanctis, *International Money Laundering Through Real Estate and Agribusiness*, DOI 10.1007/978-3-319-52069-8

MIX
Papier aus verantwortungsvollen Quellen
Paper from responsible sources
FSC® C105338

If you have any concerns about our products,
you can contact us on
ProductSafety@springernature.com

In case Publisher is established outside the EU,
the EU authorized representative is:
Springer Nature Customer Service Center GmbH
Europaplatz 3, 69115 Heidelberg, Germany

Printed by Libri Plureos GmbH
in Hamburg, Germany